# BUILDING SKILLS IN

# high-risk families

# Also from the Boys Town Press

*Books*

The Well-Managed Classroom
Teaching Social Skills to Youth
Effective Skills for Child-Care Workers
The Ongoing Journey: Awakening Spiritual Life in At-Risk Youth
Working with Aggressive Youth
Caring for Youth in Shelters
Helping Teens Unmask Sexual Con Games
Common Sense Parenting
The SAY Books: Group Therapy for Sexually Abused Youth
I Think of My Homelessness
Letters from the Front
Boys Town:  A Photographic History


*Videos*

Helping Your Child Succeed
Teaching Responsible Behavior
Videos for Parents Series
Sign With Me:  A Family Sign Language Curriculum
Read With Me: Sharing the Joy of Storytelling with Your Deaf Toddler


For a free Boys Town Press catalog, call 1-800-282-6657.

BUILDING SKILLS IN

# high-risk families

## Strategies for the Home-Based Practitioner

By
Jane L. Peterson, M.H.D.
Paula E. Kohrt, M.Ed.
Linda M. Shadoin, M.S.W.
Karen J. Authier, M.S.W.

**BOYS TOWN PRESS**

**BOYS TOWN , NEBRASKA**

# Building Skills in High-Risk Families

Published by The Boys Town Press
Father Flanagan's Boys' Home
Boys Town, Nebraska 68010

Copyright © 1995 by Father Flanagan's Boys' Home

---

## Publisher's Cataloging in Publication
*(Prepared by Quality Books Inc.)*

Building Skills in High-Risk Families: strategies for the home-based practitioner / by Jane L. Peterson... [et al.]. p.cm.
Includes bibliographical references and index.
ISBN 0-938510-73-8

    1. Family services. 2. Child welfare. 3. Problem families – Services for. 4. Father Flanagan's Boys' Home. I. Peterson, Jane L. II. Father Flanagan's Boys' Home.

HV699.B69 1995        362.82'8
                              QBI95 – 20320

# Acknowledgments

This manual would not have been possible without the commitment and ongoing efforts of many people. Father Val Peter inspired us all with his vision to "change the way America takes care of its children." From the beginning, the Iowa Department of Human Services was open and willing to work with us throughout our program development. The first Family Consultants — Craig Ferguson, Jayne Ferguson, and Nancy Johnson-Meester — must be thanked for their dedication as they put in countless hours developing, testing, and refining the Model. We also want to thank Dr. Kathy Lenerz for providing the research and database that allowed us to evaluate the effectiveness of the program.

In writing this manual, the contributions of many helped to formulate and critique our ideas so that we could produce a readable product that truly reflected the essence of our program. We are grateful to Drs. David Coughlin and Dan Daly for supporting our efforts and providing suggestions, and to Mary Anna Barbee, Amy Elofson, Nancy Kenney, Julie Nickolisen, Clarence R. Reed, and Cindy Tierney for their comments and technical assistance in reading and refining drafts of this manuscript. Terry Hyland, our editor, deserves a special mention for the guidance, assistance, and patience he provided us throughout every draft and redraft we presented him.

And for the many families, Family Consultants, Coordinators, and Site Directors who have contributed the most by holding us accountable for producing a Model that is replicable and works for keeping families together, we are grateful.

## Book Credits

| | |
|---|---|
| *Editing* | Terry L. Hyland |
| *Cover and Page Design* | Rick Schuster |
| *Page Composition* | Michael Bourg |
| *Cover Photographs* | Inga Vesik |

# A Word to Our Readers

This manual for the in-home worker is the first publication produced that comprehensively describes the Boys Town Family Preservation Model. Our intention is to provide practitioners with a full explanation of how the Model works in a systematic fashion. Although reading this manual will help the reader understand the premises, techniques, and design upon which the Model is founded and applied, it will not enable the reader to replicate the Model.

For those interested in replicating the Boys Town Family Preservation program, we would encourage you to contact our Family Preservation Services office. We can provide additional information about and training in the essential consultation, administration, and evaluation components of the Model.

For more information about the Boys Town Family Preservation program, call **(402) 498-3327** or write to:

**Boys Town Family Preservation Services**
**Family-Based Programs**
**Boys Town, NE 68010**

# Table of Contents

# Introduction

In order to understand your role as a Family Consultant in the Boys Town Family Preservation Program, it is important to know the history of this intervention and how it became part of Boys Town's mission. This introduction provides information about the concept of family preservation and its origins, and the history of Boys Town and its Family Preservation Services program.

It also is important to note here that while this manual was written primarily to supplement the intensive training Boys Town provides for its Family Consultants, the Family Preservation program can be adapted by other agencies that work with families in crisis. Boys Town believes that by making its programs available to other organizations, more families can receive the help they need.

For agencies that are interested in adapting this intervention treatment, Boys Town can provide the training and additional materials that are necessary to develop an effective program.

## History of Family Preservation

Like many human service and child welfare programs, family preservation has a history based in social and political trends. In

1962, Henry Kempe wrote an article on the "battered child syndrome." This triggered a national movement to protect children from abuse and neglect. At the time, out-of-home placement was seen as the best way to protect children. By the late 1970s and early 1980s, however, there were half a million children in foster care and concern developed about the treatment of children in out-of-home care.

Concerns about the foster care system began surfacing as early as the 1960s. McGowan (1990) cited criticism by several child welfare experts in the early 1960s regarding the placement process within the child welfare system. These experts studied children who grew up entirely in foster care, foster children who had been through multiple placements, and the emotional disturbances that affected foster children. Their criticisms included: 1) children were removed from homes more frequently than necessary and often by default, due to lack of alternatives; 2) children from minority, poor, and single parents were greatly overrepresented in foster care; 3) children were often placed in unstable and unnecessarily restrictive settings; and 4) little effort was made to keep biological parents involved, or to facilitate reunification of children and parents.

By the late 1970s, others were writing about the negative effects of foster care. Most articles focused on "foster care drift," and long-term foster care placements. At the same time, the media started reporting "horror stories" of abuse in foster care settings. Simultaneously, the psychological literature drew attention to attachment theory — the importance of a child's attachment to his/her mother or primary caretaker. Goldstein, Freud, and Solnit (1973) wrote about "psy-

chological parents" — the importance of having someone to perform a parent's role and function for each child. In addition, a parallel trend in the mental health and juvenile justice arenas emphasized the importance of placement in the least-restrictive environment.

Four trends involving child care emerged: 1) the recognition of abuse and neglect; 2) concerns about the inappropriate use of foster care; 3) emphasis on importance of children's attachment/connection with parents; and 4) least-restrictive environment philosophy.

This led some states to focus on permanency planning, which was mandated by the federal government as part of the Adoption Assistance and Child Welfare Act of 1980 (PL 96-272). This federal policy mandated the following: a written case plan to prevent drift in foster care; periodic case reviews of continuing care for placement and appropriateness of placement; procedural safeguards for child and parents when parental rights are challenged; creation of an inventory and information system to track children in foster care; and the development of state services designed to reunify children with their families and prevent unnecessary placement of children.

The goals of PL 96-272 were to prevent out-of-home placement when possible and to provide permanent homes for children through reunification or adoption when placement was necessary. States get federal reimbursement only when "reasonable efforts" are made to prevent placement of a child in foster care. The states must show that active efforts have been made to provide remedial services and that these efforts have been unsuccessful before a child may be removed from home. This keeps with the belief that foster care should be reserved for children who can be protected in no other way.

In this atmosphere, an emergence of family preservation programs virtually blossomed across the United States. **Homebuilders**, developed in 1974 in Tacoma, Washington, was one of the first intensive family preservation programs that set a precedent for how families could be served. This program, co-founded by psychologists Jill Kinney and David Haapala, was based on a crisis intervention model for families whose children were about to be placed outside the home. It followed the premise that families that are in crisis are most motivated to change. Program design called for short-term, intensive intervention with small caseloads for counselors. These ideas were revolutionary in the child and family service system. All across the nation, other agencies were developing in-home family preservation services that focused on preventing placement of children by providing services to the entire family. Boys Town was one of the organizations that recognized the need for changing the way services were offered to families, and hence the Family Preservation Services program was born.

## History of Boys Town

In 1917, Father Edward J. Flanagan founded a home in Omaha, Nebraska, for abused, abandoned, and homeless boys. The priest believed that by providing love, care, and hope for these boys, he could put them on the path to being responsible, productive citizens.

In 1921, Father Flanagan bought a farm near Omaha and moved his "family" of boys there. Boys Town became a haven for boys who had no one to care for them or about them. As more and more boys found a home at Boys Town, its fame and reputation became known worldwide. Father Flanagan died in 1948, but his dream and mission of caring for troubled youth lived on, and Boys Town continued to grow.

By the late 1960s, America was in the throes of a great social upheaval. Kids began to come to Boys Town with problems spawned by the times — drug and alcohol addiction, suicide attempts, sexual and physical abuse, and emotional abuse.

Boys Town saw the need for new ways to help these young people, and began searching for more effective treatment methods to meet the increasingly complex problems. Adapting work done at the University of Kansas on treatment methods, Boys Town expanded the program, and developed it far beyond what it had been.

Family-style homes, where youth live with married couples called Family-Teachers, replaced the dormitories of the past. Boys Town began teaching youth how to solve their problems. The youth also learned the social skills they would need to succeed after they left. Amid this change, one thing remained constant — the love for children that was Father Flanagan's hallmark.

Boys Town continued to expand. In 1979, girls were accepted for the first time. In 1988, Boys Town underwent another transformation. Even though our boys and girls were benefiting from their treatment, there wasn't enough room for everyone who needed help. And after treatment, some youth were returning home to dysfunctional families. To meet the challenge, Boys Town developed four Family-Based Services Programs: Family

Preservation Services, Emergency Shelter Care, Treatment Foster Family Services, and Common Sense Parenting. At the same time, a national expansion effort established Boys Town USA sites in metropolitan areas across the country.

Today, Boys Town provides direct care and assistance for thousands of troubled youth and families all over the country. By 1996, Boys Town expects to be offering its services in 17 major metropolitan areas.

## Boys Town Family Preservation Services

In the spring of 1989, Boys Town began serving families in southwest Iowa through its new Family Preservation program. The methods developed to work with families in crisis were based on the proven technology implemented in the Boys Town residential program. Like all Boys Town programs, Family Preservation Services strives to provide and ensure quality care through comprehensive staff training, consultation, and evaluation.

To meet the needs of more families, Boys Town has continued to expand the Family Preservation program. So far, it has been replicated at five other sites nationwide: Central Florida in November 1990; Rhode Island in February 1991; central Nebraska in July 1991; Southern California in August 1991; and Southern Florida in October 1991.

We've helped many families but there are still many more who need help and healing. We cannot reach every family; that's why we also want to share our knowledge and technology with others. We want to help agencies and individuals deliver quality services to families using the proven methods of our program.

## Purpose of This Manual

This manual is designed to complement the training our Consultants receive before they begin working with families. It includes a detailed, comprehensive description and explanation of the program's components, strategies for working with troubled families, and other aspects of the services Consultants provide.

Our hope is that you will gain an understanding of the values and technologies that make Boys Town Family Preservation Services unique and effective in bringing about lasting change to troubled families. We believe our Model of Family Preservation offers a sound and proven strategy for working with families to prevent unnecessary out-of-home placements.

This manual is divided into three sections. In the first section, we present the foundational principles from which the Boys Town Family Preservation program was developed. This section provides an overview of the program, and discusses important fundamentals such as cultural and family values, community resources, child abuse and neglect, assessment, and building relationships. In the second section of the manual, we introduce the specific intervention techniques that make Boys Town's program effective. We describe the components of each technique and explain how the techniques are best used in the intervention. How to identify and capitalize on the many opportunities to teach by employing these techniques also is discussed.

In the final section, we present Boys Town's uniquely structured Model of Family Preservation. All of the elements that are discussed in the first two sections are brought together in the final two chapters in the description of the skill-based, competency-driven Boys Town Model. The success of the Model is attributed to using a systematic method for building on a family's strengths to bring about change. These chapters outline the specific steps for identifying and building on the family's strengths, and offer an easy-to-follow intervention process called Phases. This guides the family preservation worker in how best to help families gain competency in the skills they need to stay together.

This manual provides many examples and exercises to enhance your understanding of the Boys Town Model. We encourage you to read through each chapter, complete the exercises, and consult the cited additional readings to best comprehend the whole program.

In writing this manual, we recognize that some of the terms we use are similar to terms used by others in the field; some of those terms, however, may have a unique meaning for their use in our program. For example, the term "strength" is very specifically defined in our program and is considered a critical component to the intervention process. When terms differ from their more common usage, we have tried to thoroughly define and distinguish them to avoid confusion.

There are two terms we consistently refer to throughout this manual that we would like to clarify here. First, the word "family" is used to refer to the primary client group that will be receiving services. "Family" has a broad and general meaning in this text. Family can include those persons related by blood or marriage as well as those related by circumstances in which the members consider themselves a familial unit. This would include foster parents and children, extended relatives,

adoptive persons, and nonmarital partnerships. Our perspective is that those members who form the unit define family membership for themselves.

Second, the term "Family Consultant," or simply "Consultant," is used to refer to the family preservation worker who is directly providing the services to the family. The title of Family Consultant was carefully chosen for its use in the Boys Town Family Preservation program. We wanted to give the family preservation worker a title that best fit the role the worker fulfills in the intervention process. Like the word implies, consultation is a way of viewing the worker/family relationship as an equal partnership that is formed to work through problems and improve family functioning. Our Family Consultants do just that: establish partnerships, respect a family's expertise, and advise, support, and assist. Although many of our Family Consultants are qualified as professional counselors, therapists, and social workers, we wanted to emphasize to other agencies the importance we place on being engaged in a professional, consultative role with the families we serve.

We believe the title of Family Consultant conveys much more about our relationship with families and how we approach the intervention than terms such as "therapist" or "practitioner." Family Consultants assist a family in resolving its problems in a way that promotes empowerment and autonomy.

Whether your program is interested in replicating the Boys Town Family Preservation program or simply wants to learn more about the Boys Town approach to family preservation, we would like to highlight some of the guiding principles we see as critical to any family preservation effort:

**1. To prevent out-of-home placement for children while working in their best interest.** Family Preservation Services will afford the Consultant many opportunities to assist and advocate for families so that the children are not removed from their home. However, preservation of the family must always be weighed against the safety of the children. Keeping children safe is always considered the top priority. Family preservation is a secondary goal to the child's ultimate safety. Not all families can or should be preserved.

**2. To provide individualized treatment.** Every family is unique and has specific needs and strengths. Each deserves the full respect and complete efforts of the Consultant to help the family members make the changes that will allow them to remain together. The Consultant must strive to tailor the intervention to the family's needs and be available to assist the family as much and for as long as is "reasonably" possible.

**3. To be systematic.** Trained Consultants use a systematic method that helps the family sort through chaos and crisis in order to prioritize issues and reduce risk factors that threaten the family's unity. The intervention approach needs to be theoretically sound, solution-oriented, and responsive to constant evaluation. Methods used should be effective and efficient in producing lasting change. This change can and should be measurable.

We believe the Boys Town Family Preservation program adheres to these principles. In the first chapter, we will discuss the values and components of our Model that put these principles into operation.

During your training and work, you will no doubt get a sense of the incredible responsibility and influence your efforts can have on helping families. We hope that you will find the tasks to be ever challenging, and the outcomes to be highly rewarding.

Boys Town's mission is to change the way America takes care of its children. One way to do that is to teach families the skills they need to solve problems, to survive crises, and to maintain a stable, safe home environment for children. We welcome your commitment to achieving these goals with us.

# Foundations To Family Preservation

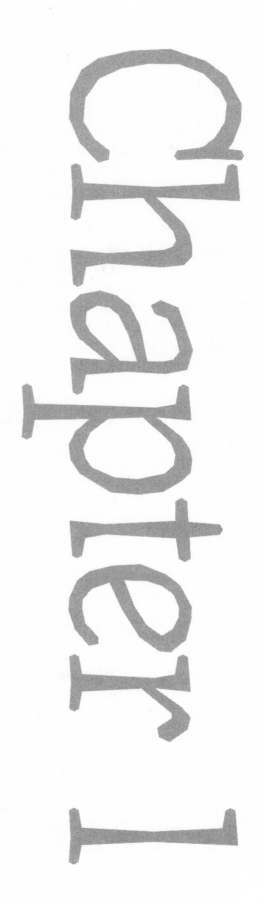

# Overview of Boys Town's Family Preservation Model

Over the last 15 to 20 years, experts in the fields of child development, psychology and pediatrics, education, research, social work, and counseling have been challenged and frustrated by their lack of success in addressing special treatment needs of multirisk/multicrisis families. Part of this frustration stems from the fact that a number of agencies, each with its own methods and ideas, usually are involved in the treatment of such families. Evidence of this can be seen at a case conference on a multirisk family, which often is attended by representatives from the half-dozen community agencies that are working with the family. Each participant will have a file that is several inches thick, with entries sometimes going back several generations (Greenspan, 1987).

Out of frustration and failure in using traditional approaches to treat some families came radical program experiments that took services into the family home, focused on the total family, and scuttled the tradition of the 50-minute therapy hour (Berg, 1991; Kagan & Schlosberg, 1989). Many of the program experiments introduced new ideas for how to think about serving families and studied the techniques that seemed to be most effective in working with multirisk/multicrisis families. Several of these ideas and techniques have been adapted and incorporated into the Boys Town Family Preservation program. We will highlight some of these, and then provide an overview of the hallmarks and basic structure of the Boys Town Model that make it unique.

## In-Home Models Established

Many models for delivering services to the family in the home have been established. In his research, Greenspan (1987) sought to identify the ideal combination of clinical techniques and service delivery models that would be needed to reverse maladaptive patterns. The collaborative elements he chose for his model of comprehensive intervention services included: services responding to concrete survival needs such as food, housing, and basic medical care; a planned effort to meet the family's and child's need for an ongoing, trusting human relationship; specific clinical techniques and services that focus on the many lines of a child's development; a special support structure; innovative outreach to the family; and ongoing training and supervision of program staff.

Berg's (1991) approach contends that the best way to provide services to a child is to strengthen and empower the family as a unit. By involving the family as a partner in the decision-making and goal-setting process, and by recognizing, respecting, and using the family's existing strengths and resources, you can enhance the family members' sense of competency and control over their own lives.

A third approach, the Homebuilders Model, draws from four theoretical bases: person-centered theory, crisis theory, cognitive-behavioral theory, and the ecological perspective. This combination of theories has created the concepts and techniques which make up the Homebuilders Model. These include: seeing clients as "colleagues"; actively involving clients in goal-setting and case-planning; working with the family rather than the individual; teaching necessary skills to prevent placement; small caseload size and time-limited intervention; intake criteria; assisting clients in regaining a precrisis level of functioning and moving beyond it; favoring functional, behaviorally specific assessments; the need for observable and measurable therapeutic outcomes; the regular use of concrete services; and encouraging assessment and intervention at multiple levels of the environment (Morgan, Fisher, Anderson, & Kinney, 1990).

## Boys Town's Family Preservation Model

The Boys Town Model derives much of its approach to bringing about change in a family from cognitive-behavioral theory. We understand that principles of classical and operant conditioning can be applied to an assortment of problem behaviors. In addition, we believe that what people think or believe about events contributes to their behavior. The major assumption here is that behaviors are learned. Therefore, behaviors that may be problematic and no longer functional can be unlearned and new, more functional behaviors can be learned in their place. In this theoretical base, Family Consultants can serve as teachers, coaches, partners, and catalysts in the change process.

Client motivation is a key ingredient in this action-oriented method of treatment. A supportive and trusting therapeutic relationship is necessary, but not sufficient, for change. Consultants strive for concrete, behavioral descriptions of problems and goals. Assessments must be behaviorally specific and practical. Outcomes need to be observable and measurable. Concepts and procedures are explicitly described, empirically tested, and continually revised.

Building on our own and others' research, the Boys Town Family Preservation Model combines all of the following elements:

- **Short Term** (six to eight weeks)
- **Intensive** (up to 20 hours in the home each week; only two families per Consultant)
- **In-Home** (treatment provided in the family's natural environment)
- **Individualized** (flexible schedule; treatment focuses on the family's specific strengths and needs)
- **Skill-Based** (teach skills that work to resolve many problems)
- **Crisis-Oriented** (no waiting lists; available to family 24 hours a day)
- **Competency-Based** (length of intervention determined by family's achieved level of competency in using skills that keep family safe)
- **Strength-Oriented** (intervention builds on behavioral strength of family members)
- **Family and Consultant as partners** (relationship emphasized between family and Consultant; treatment based on family's expertise)

Boys Town believes that in order for parents and children to begin behavior change it is important that professionals are available to strengthen already-used techniques. Many problem behaviors are a result of families never having learned the importance of consistently applying already-stable strengths across a broad spectrum of social situations and settings such as at home, in school, on the job, etc. (Father Flanagan's Boys' Home, 1990). Implementation levels can be dramatically increased with ongoing, in-the-home support. Without such support, performance often deteriorates. Individuals often forget certain basic skills and concepts. As a result, they may begin to rely on superstitious or sporadic treatment methods (Father Flanagan's Boys' Home, 1990).

## The Family Consultant's Role

The Boys Town Family Preservation program emphasizes skill-building. In order to build skills in the family the Consultant needs to engage in ongoing assessment of the family's strengths and agendas. During intervention, Boys Town's Consultants continually assess a family's strengths and use those strengths to begin building skills.

The Consultant remains with the family until the goals of the family, Consultant, and caseworker are met. The family members should be able to demonstrate competency in the necessary skills so that they can remain together. This type of intensity requires the Consultant to work diligently on developing a relationship with all members of the family. To do this he or she must:

- **Be available to the family 24 hours a day, seven days a week.**
- **Focus on the family's issues.**

- **Be the family's advocate.**
- **Be empathetic to the family's issues.**
- **Take part in the family's daily activities.**
- **Schedule visits at the family's convenience and during potentially troublesome times for the family.**
- **Treat family members as partners.**

Building on the family's existing strengths is a crucial component of this program. It is easier for the family to repeat successful behavior patterns than it is to try to stop or change existing symptomatic or problematic behavior. Getting family members to repeat success is easier than trying to teach them totally new and foreign skills (Berg, 1991). This emphasis on strengths provides a respectful sense of accomplishment and enhances the family members' sense of competency and control over their own lives.

For example, a family's agenda might involve having difficulty with a child who runs away, doesn't attend school, and is verbally aggressive. The parents are observed yelling and screaming at the child, grounding the child for a month, and finally throwing up their hands and leaving the house. In our program, we would identify the strengths in these behaviors: The parents tell the child what he or she did wrong, use consequences, and walk away when angry. The parents may not be using any of these actions perfectly or purposely but they are using them. These are the actions, viewed as strengths, that will be further developed and refined.

This emphasis on a family's strengths, values, and priorities aids the Consultant in individualizing treatment and maintaining a **family's** focus throughout the intervention.

Your ability to understand the historical, environmental, and current perspective of each family will determine the rate of progress within each family.

The family members are viewed as the experts on their own interactions and relationships. The parents usually have lifelong insight into their children's behaviors. The children know best their parents' typical responses and activities. As a Consultant, you must understand the family members' expertise and work within that context in order to elicit change within the home (Patterson, 1971). You also must remember that no family is perfect and that no matter how dramatic the situation appears, every family has strengths that can be built on to assist it in its crisis and any other crisis that may arise.

When working with a family, you should view every situation as an opportunity to teach. Whether you are helping a parent do laundry, playing cards with the children, taking a family member to the doctor, or observing the family in crisis, each situation provides you with an opportunity to assess firsthand the family's strengths and values, and possible roadblocks to solving future crises.

## Phases: A Road Map for Treatment

The beliefs that have been discussed have guided Boys Town in developing a unique model of structured treatment that prohibits Consultants from focusing on a family's problems and requires them to focus on individual strengths. The structure for treatment identifies key steps in the treatment process and provides guidelines for moving from one step to the next.

In the past, service agencies have defined families in terms of their problems, or families have been alienated from "helping" agencies and professionals who seem critical. When this happens, the families also may begin to define themselves in terms of their problems. Boys Town's structured Model of intervention defines families and their progress in terms of their strengths. This emphasis encourages development of skills that can be generalized, thereby empowering families to prevent the occurrence of problems. The intent of this Model is to provide a new perspective and framework for helping families and to provide Consultants with guidelines for individualizing and focusing treatment for families.

In her book, *Family Based Services: A Solution Focused Approach* (1991), Insoo Kim Berg describes the cases of some families that have so many problems and issues that even a seasoned worker could get overwhelmed and feel lost about where to begin. Kagan and Schlosberg (1989) also write that the family worker who is working with chaotic families tends to feel overwhelmed and is easily caught adrift in the current of chaotic and disorderly sessions. At the end of such sessions, Family Consultants often say they can recall only a succession of events with little coherence or meaning. Interventions appear pointless and work with the family appears doomed to repetitive crises. These are the kind of traps that dot the path of Consultants working with multiproblem families. The Boys Town Model is designed to provide a map so that such traps can be avoided.

This Model is represented in two distinct levels of treatment, beginning with teaching and ending with empowerment. Within these two levels of treatment, there are six Phases, or progressions, for the Consultant to follow in order to remain focused and strength-oriented. An overview of these Phases is presented here. They will be discussed in depth later.

## Overview of Phases

Phases I and II concentrate on developing and building on a parent's or child's existing strength. This strength, which is identified within the family's agenda, helps the Consultant tie the family's goals in with his or her goals and those of the referral agency.

By concentrating on this first strength and basing assignments on what the parents or children are doing correctly, a Consultant can quickly establish rapport and the family can experience success. The family members will feel successful for several reasons: 1) This outcome is based on something **they** were already doing, not something the Consultant suggested; 2) The intervention stays within the family's agenda (their perspective of what needs to be fixed); and 3) Typically, family members will quickly see improvement by building on a strength.

Phases III and IV are used to either fully develop the first skill or concept, or to identify a second necessary concept. When fully developing the first skill, the Consultant enhances the family's strength to the point where the family members experience satisfaction with their desired goals or outcomes.

Teaching additional skills to the family members is a judgment call. It is easier for the family to maintain existing skills than to learn new skills. If additional skills are needed to prevent placement of the children outside the home, these skills should be taught in Phases III and IV.

It is important for the Consultant and family to first successfully stabilize the skills taught in Phase I and II and apply them consistently. The family should also see the benefit of adapting its strengths. Then Phases III and IV can provide the opportunity to teach an additional skill or concept if it is necessary to keep the children in the home.

For example, let's look at how you would work with a family that has been referred to Family Preservation Services for child neglect. During Phase I, you determined that the parents provide food and clothing for their children but do not fix or schedule meals, or monitor what the children wear or whether they bathe. They do, however, tell them to eat, dress, and bathe. The means to meet the children's basic needs are present and the parents verbalize instructions to bathe, dress, and eat. These have been identified as family strengths. In Phases I and II, you may decide that you can build on the parents' strengths of identifying basic needs and verbalizing instructions in order to prevent neglect. You can teach them the behaviors and skills they need in order to meet the children's basic needs consistently. You might teach them how to follow through with verbal instructions and to monitor what the children wear, and when they bathe and eat. Later, you may decide to use Phases III and IV to further enhance the parents' skills by teaching additional skills such as budgeting, housekeeping, or establishing routines.

The primary focus in Phases I, II, III, and IV is to strengthen or build sufficient skills within the family so that the children are no longer in danger of being placed outside the home. Concentrating on one or two skills or concepts enables the Consultant and the family to remain clear and focused.

Phases V and VI focus on the family's ability to solve future crises, generalization of stabilized skills, and promoting self-awareness of the family's accomplishments. By building the family's confidence, the Consultant prepares the family for the conclusion of intervention and teaches the family members to reflect on their ability to work together as a family. By this point, the child in the home is no longer at risk of outside placement and the intensity of visits decreases dramatically so that the family members have opportunities to use their enhanced skills without outside influences. The Consultant remains available only to ensure that the family has the necessary confidence to face and resolve new situations that may arise.

As you will discover during your examination of this book and the Boys Town Model, our basic premises are rooted in the belief that families have the basic building blocks to "fix" their own problems; we simply provide the tools to aid them in this endeavor.

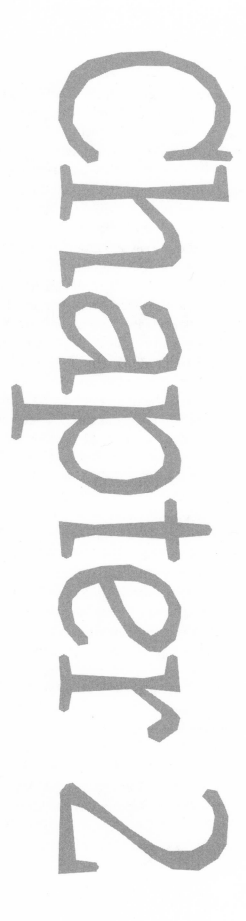

# Cultural and Family Differences

When you hear the term "cultural differences," perhaps you think of ethnic festivals with colorful native costumes, elaborate folk dances, and samples of delicious but unfamiliar food. Or maybe you're reminded of some distant place where people practice strange customs and speak in an exotic language.

"Culture" is a difficult term to define, but we will use Longres's (1991) definition that culture is "a set of group-based norms and values exhibited in the attitudes, beliefs, and behavioral inclinations of individual group members" (p. 41). Cultural differences would be defined as differences in group-based norms and values that would lead to a variety of different attitudes, beliefs, and behavioral inclinations exhibited by individuals.

Every family is influenced by its culture and these influences shape the family's attitudes, beliefs and behaviors. The extent to which the family is influenced by its culture does vary. Every family is unique in its set of beliefs, values, traditions, rituals, preferences, and rules, and just how different those are from your own also will vary. We define a family's particular set of beliefs, values, traditions, and behaviors as "family differences." Family differences are influenced by a variety of factors such as culture, ethnicity, geographics, race, upbringing, nationality, and religion.

Have you ever spent a holiday with another family that was not related to you? Did it feel uncomfortable to celebrate that holiday with traditions that were different from your own? Have you ever traveled to a city or country you'd never visited? Did you question the purpose of some of the laws, customs, or norms that you observed? Differences between individuals and groups of people permeate our society. However, the impact of these differences is often minimized, misunderstood, and even ignored. When differences are not acknowledged and understood by the Family Consultant, the results can be devastating. Family differences will profoundly affect your role as a Consultant, whether you acknowledge them or not. We believe it is important to understand family differences by learning what factors make families different and how those differences play into the therapeutic process.

The philosophy of Boys Town's Family Preservation program is for the Consultant to work within cultural and family differences. We believe that all families have a right to be who they are. Our goal in this chapter is to help you understand cultural and family differences and the role they play within a family so that you can develop a culturally sensitive and competent approach in your interventions.

How do you become a culturally competent professional? The best way is by carefully observing, actively listening, participating in family activities, and asking lots of questions. Investigate the family's answers by asking more questions. The information you obtain is vital. Why? Because in the Boys Town Family Preservation program, Family Consultants provide help in a family's home, within that family's environment, traditions, beliefs, values, and rules. Culture is a key element in any family, and nothing will shut down your work faster than being insensitive to a family's deeply felt values.

When a Consultant and a client family get together, they bring their own values, beliefs, and traditions with them. This means both will have different perceptions of why troubles exist and different ideas about what to do about them. This often results in miscommunication and failure of services (Longres, 1991).

So what can we do? The first step is to understand your own values and beliefs. As a Consultant, you need to realize that the way you live, which is influenced by your cultural background, how you were brought up, your values, and so on, is only one way of living. You must believe that people live in other ways, not necessarily better or worse, only different (Kadushin, 1983). By examining various family traditions and values, you can better understand your own. Identifying your values will enable you to recognize your clients' values as separate from your own and work within them.

Acknowledging and working within a family's preferences will help you in several important ways. First, you can tailor your teaching to fit within the family's values. For example, if adult family members believe the children should call you "Sir" or "Ma'am" or "Miss" or "Mister," then ask the children to use those titles when they speak to you. If a family communicates very directly and dislikes vague language, then be direct in your sessions. If the family believes you should always direct questions to the male first, then to other family members, then do so. Your communication with the family members will be clear and they will sense that you are "tuned into" their style.

Suppose you are working with parents who believe in continually hugging and kissing their children, even after the children misbehave. You can work within that practice, but also can teach the value of hugging and kissing the children to reward appropriate behavior. The parents will appreciate the fact that you did not eliminate a family value and the caseworker will be pleased that the parents have learned a new, appropriate way to manage their children.

Another way that respecting a family's differences can help you is that each family member will be more at ease. As a result, you can teach them new skills more quickly, since they will be less likely to resist your suggestions. (See Example 1.)

Respecting family differences also can help you build better relationships with family members. As they see you work within their preferences and traditions, they realize that you aren't out to change their value systems and traditions, and they fear you less, trust you more, and sense your acceptance of them as people. In turn, a family will be more open to your suggestions.

## Origins of Differences

Family differences originate both in the past and in the present. Childhood experiences and patterns of behavior we develop as children form the basis for these differences. In the present, many influences — lifestyles, the places where we live, our choices in raising our own children, and the large or small number of people we live among — create differ-

## Example 1

*You are working with a 27-year-old single mother and her four children. They live with the maternal grandparents and one adult uncle. Thirteen cats, three dogs, and various small animals also live in the house. The house is small, so the two boys sleep with the uncle and mom and the two girls sleep on the living room floor. As the family's Consultant, you have seen no evidence that the safety of the children is being threatened, but you are unhappy with the sleeping arrangements and the number of animals present in a home with limited funds.*

*If you begin your relationship by imposing your values and telling the mom that she has to get her own place, get rid of most of the animals, and get the children their own rooms, she prob-*

*ably will stop listening immediately and it will take valuable time to repair your relationship with her. However, if you begin with the family's concerns and goals, and identify the family members' strengths within their traditions, culture, and values, they will be more willing to work with you.*

*In this instance, if you have identified the grandparents as an integral part of the family who actively contribute to keeping the family going on a daily basis, then insisting that the mother move would be devastating to all family members and would unnecessarily interfere with the family's value system. You will want to look for solutions that do not contradict or interfere with the family's values.*

ences in families. Together, these influences shape a family's beliefs, self-image, and view of the world. Some basic factors that can influence family differences are:

1. **Environment**
2. **Family of origin**
3. **Religion**
4. **Ethnicity**

All of these factors and more also can affect and be affected by the culture to which a family member belongs and identifies with. As these factors affect the cultural norms on a more general level, the family norms will be affected as well.

**1. Environment.** Where a family lives greatly influences its lifestyle. Does the family you will work with live in a large metropolitan area, an average-size city, or a small town or rural area? Each of these settings varies in its type and quality of housing, population density, cost of living, availability of resources, amount of crime, number of homeless people, and number of recreational areas. In some large cities where housing costs are high, you may find several generations of a family living together. In a farming community, you may find that children miss a great deal of school to help their family harvest the crop. In areas with few resources, you may find families that have difficulty meeting their medical or financial needs. (See Example 2.)

Another aspect of how environment affects the family is the home itself. Does the home have every state-of-the-art gadget but no food? Is the home dirty and unsafe or just cluttered? Do the holes in the walls, the mice in the attic, and the mattresses on the floor endanger the children or simply offend your sensibilities? Are there a lot of valuable collectibles displayed so that it's hard to walk around without bumping into something? Do people share bedrooms, or does everyone

## Example 2

*A child in a family you are working with has to play inside the house every day. You would need to find out what environmental factors might make this necessary — a busy highway nearby, gang activity in the neighborhood, or a secluded woody area near the house that is home to large animals.*

*In another situation, a family has been referred for neglecting the children's basic needs: an 18-month-old is given only milk and the oldest child is sent to school without a coat and in shoes that are two sizes too small. Again, you will assess the possible environmental factors and determine whether the resources needed to get appropriate food and clothing for the children are available to the family.*

*What if a family is referred for medical neglect of a 16-year-old child who has severe asthma and allergies? The medical report indicates that the home has molds, that multiple animals live there, and that cigarette smoke from people who live in the home could threaten the child's life. When you enter the home, you need to assess environmental factors such as the family's smoking habits, cleanliness, and care of the animals. Which of the environmental factors present are true health risks to the youth?*

have his or her own room? Assessing a family's environmental situation before beginning an intervention helps you determine with the family what changes can be made in the home and what parts of the environment will need to change. But you must make your assessment fairly, remembering not to impose your own values if the home conditions do not endanger the family.

How we relate to the family in all these situations is vital to accomplishing our goal of keeping families together. You must remember that there are many environmental factors that can influence a family's decisions and actions. If these actions or decisions are not harmful to the children in the home or do not place them at risk of being removed, you should respect and conform to them while working with the family.

**2. Family of origin.** Parents in every family have rules, values, and traditions that originated in their upbringing and the rules, values, and traditions of their parents. In other words, how a person was treated by his or her parents while growing up often has a great impact on how that person treats his or her own children. Your job as a Consultant is to observe and assess each family member's parenting values and work within their existing systems.

Parents in the families you will work with may have similar or very different styles of rearing children. More subtly, they may have different attitudes about key child-rearing issues, including sex and sex roles, discipline, competition and achievement, autonomy and dependence in personal problem-solving, the definition of success and failure, and desirable lifestyles. Attitudes toward all of these issues may be different for different families (Kadushin, 1983). For example, one family may have several of the following traits: authoritative, nurturing, uncommunicative, disciplined, warm, comfortable with praising their children, watchful, safety-conscious, inattentive, controlling, or unconcerned with the children's cleanliness.

Different combinations of parenting styles can bring about positive results in children. Helping parents understand each other's styles can reduce friction in the family and help them be a better team.

To illustrate how different styles exist in families, Exercise 1 (next page) asks you to look at this concept from the perspective of your own family when you were a child.

How are the rules of these three individuals in your own family different? How are they similar? This exercise also can be done with other rules such as negotiating, doing chores, or free time.

**3. Religion.** Religion can be culturally, ethnically, or individually defined. Religious beliefs can strongly influence the family's value system and can be the source of many family differences. Families could adhere to a number of religious rituals and events to which you must be sensitive. Some pray at certain times of the day, some dress in a particular manner, and some decorate their homes in accordance with religious practice. For example, some religions do not allow medical intervention for children, only prayer and religious healing. Members of these religious groups might refuse to use health providers unless a family member can convince them to do so.

## Exercise 1: Family Rules

On a separate piece of paper, list three rules your mother had regarding eating/manners.

1.

2.

3.

List three rules your father had regarding eating/manners.

1.

2.

3.

List three rules one of your grandparents had regarding eating/manners.

1.

2.

3.

**4. Ethnicity.** Differences in this area can come from many cultural sources — nationality, region, and race. Some cultures believe that several generations of a family should live together in the same household — parents, children, grandparents, aunts, uncles, and cousins. In some cultures it may be unaccept-able to work on or discuss family problems with the children unless the parents are present. Some ethnic groups have a strong group affiliation and interpret life events in racial terms, especially if someone who is not part of their culture is involved. In some cultures, eye contact is avoided when an individual is being corrected, and walking away from a confrontation is a sign of weakness. Some ethnic groups generally have learned to distrust the government. Others believe that society's "weak" members — women and children — have few or no rights.

In the United States, there are regional differences. In the South, people generally take their time formulating ideas and speak slower. In the North, people often are direct and speak faster. Some regions have a large number of migrant workers; others have populations that are less transitory. In the rural areas of the Midwest, many jobs and occupations are related to agriculture; in metropolitan areas, industry and service-related occupations are dominant.

Some people believe in keeping a family together no matter what. The parents of an aggressive teenager who engages in many violent and potentially dangerous behaviors may not seek help if they think the child may be removed from the family. The pressure of "keeping the family together at all costs" sometimes conflicts with the desire to solve family problems. Just admitting to an outsider that a problem exists may go against a family's beliefs that are founded within its culture.

What if you are working with a family that is in the United States illegally, and the mother has been diagnosed with tuberculosis? The family refuses to get medical attention for the mother because it could result in deportation of the entire family. To this family, being deported would be worse than the death of the mother.

In these examples, you have to remember that you are in a partnership with the families you work with and that therapy is taking place in their homes, not in your home or office. Therefore, you must treat family members as the experts on their homes, families, and children, and respect them for the decisions they make.

Because there are so many different influences within cultures and variations among families, we don't believe families can or should be stereotyped. To do so would be detrimental to the family you are working with and to the work you do as a Consultant. Although any family can be described in terms of its cultural or ethnic characteristics or the characteristics of a group it is associated with, that family is, at the same time, uniquely dissimilar from every other family of that group (Kadushin, 1983). This is why it is so important to use the techniques of active listening and assessment to identify the family's ethnic influences before beginning an intervention. (See Exercise 2.)

## Contrasts in Family Differences

Now that we've looked at a sampling of factors that can influence a family's differences, let's look at several areas in which these differences are generally contrasted in every day family life.

To varying degrees in each family, you will encounter family differences in the following areas:

### Exercise 2: How Are You Different?

On a separate piece of paper, list something about yourself for each of the four difference factors we discussed in this section (environment, family of origin, religion, and ethnicity).

1.

2.

3.

4.

Now list something about your partner or a friend for each of the four areas.

1.

2.

3.

4.

How do these differences affect your relationship with your partner or friend? Consider how these differences in values and beliefs might affect your work with a family who has very different values than the ones you have listed.

1. **Parenting styles or tolerances.**
2. **How families relax and spend free time.**
3. **Educational and vocational choices.**
4. **Holiday celebrations and rituals.**
5. **Food preferences.**

**1. Parenting styles or tolerances.** Every family develops its own parenting styles and tolerances. In fact, no two individuals have identical parenting styles or tolerances, whether they're in the same family or not. Some parents have a low tolerance for children getting dirty and may insist that their children be neat and tidy at all times. If their children get dirty while playing, these parents insist on washing them immediately. In other families, children may spend most of their time outdoors, helping with outside chores or playing with pets. The parents of these children may ask them to wash only at mealtime and before bedtime, or not at all.

Another area in which tolerances differ is in how closely parents monitor their children's behavior and whereabouts. Some parents allow their children to roam the neighborhood all day in search of playmates. Other parents teach their children to ask permission to leave the yard and to tell them where they will be playing. In some homes, a youth may be telling siblings and the parents when to be home, and giving them permission to leave.

Discipline is another area in which beliefs and values influence parental practice. Some parents use spanking; others never use physical punishment. Still others may wash out their children's mouths with soap, ground them from playing away from home, or send them to bed without supper. In some families, the older children have as much freedom and

authority as the parents to set their own rules and discipline siblings.

The parents are not always the primary or sole disciplinarians. Extended relatives or community members may play a large role in setting the tolerances for the children's behaviors and discipline the children accordingly.

Parents also develop different types of structure for children. In some homes, children must follow a set schedule of waking up, eating, going to school, playing, and bedtime. In other families, these activities may never happen at the same time two days running. A parent's tolerances or comfort level with scheduling has a tremendous impact upon how a home is run.

These are just a few examples of the different types of parenting styles and tolerances you may encounter when working with families. In many cases, these styles and tolerances will be different from your own. But that doesn't mean they are wrong. They're just different and should be respected as such.

Many family traditions and values regarding raising children have been handed down through generations and are well established. A family's choice of discipline or tolerances may have been learned from past generations and should be respected. That's why you may hear parents say, "My parents raised me that way and I turned out pretty good." Or parents may reject the parenting style of their parents, saying, "My parents made me do that and punished me for every little mistake. I'll never do that to my kids."

While it is important to respect and be responsive to different parenting styles, the safety and best interests of children and other family members must come first. Try to identify and understand the beliefs and values that are influencing a family's parenting style and acquire information through listening and asking questions to determine whether the parents' tolerance levels are safe for the children. If so, respect the parents' values regarding their home, their children, and their family, and work within these values.

**2. How families relax and spend free time.** Families relax and spend free time in different ways. These can include involvement in church group activities, outdoor recreation, social clubs or bars, and various hobbies and pastimes. One family's relaxation time may revolve around a country club and traveling, while another's may be spent at bingo halls and flea markets. Some pastimes are more active than others. For example, a family might prefer to play sports rather than watch them on television. One family may enjoy a wide social network, while another spends most of its social time with relatives.

The level of involvement in family activities also may vary for individual family members. While being together or doing something is a priority for one family, the members of another family may be so actively involved in outside interests that they spend little time together. As children mature, traditions for family time may change dramatically. Adolescents often prefer to spend more time with their friends than with their families.

While working in the home, be prepared to participate in family activities. These may include hiking, boating, hanging out at the local mall, or attending auctions, garage sales, carnivals, rodeos, or the zoo. It could even be something as simple as playing cards. Participation in family activities provides an insight into family dynamics. You could easily miss this insight, which can provide valuable information for your intervention, if you don't participate in family activities.

**3. Educational and vocational choices.** Education choices often are influenced by how much value a family places on education. Families that place a high value on education stress the importance of school attendance, achieving good grades, selecting challenging subjects, earning a high school diploma, and going on to college or trade school. When parents don't stress the importance of school, or when parents, their children, and the school have conflicting values, the children often have problems in school (i.e. truancy, failing grades, illiteracy, suspension, and dropping out).

Many families view education as the measure of a child's independence, competence, and interpersonal skills. However, each family measures these skills by different criteria and may value them differently, depending on whether they are relevant or irrelevant to the child and his or her environment (Gibbs & Huang, 1990). Parents in one family may just want their daughter to behave so she can quit school at 16 instead of getting kicked out; in another family, the parents may want to place their son outside the home because he isn't attending school and they feel that placement will assure him of an education. In other families, school is the main priority for children, and the parents feel that lack of achievement is a personal reflection on them as parents.

Family differences also may be evident in the vocations and socioeconomic status of the family. In some situations, parents even model their occupational choices. Many occupations, such as farming, mining, or practicing medicine or law, tend to be passed on this way from generation to generation. In some families, members will work two or three jobs so that they can eventually buy their own business. In many family businesses, every family member is expected to work to make the business successful.

And just as some vocations are passed on, researchers have noted a similar tendency for some families that are dependent on welfare to pass on this dependency, creating a cycle that is difficult to break. A low-income lifestyle — "the culture of poverty" — is, of course, a convenient fiction, much as the middle-income lifestyle is. It would be difficult to find any middle-income or low-income family that exactly mirrors the lifestyle patterns detailed in a sociology textbook. Still, there is sufficient empirical material to suggest that low-income families do have beliefs, attitudes, and patterns of behavior that are distinguishable from their middle-income counterparts (Kadushin, 1983). According to Kadushin, characteristics of low-income families that are most likely to affect a Consultant and his or her work include: less concern with scheduling; responding to a problem only when it causes maximum discomfort; having definite, immediate goals; wanting to alleviate discomfort immediately rather than working toward long-range objectives; more concern with consequences of behavior than with explanations of cause; more concern with day-to-day survival and with threats to physical survival than with difficulties in personal relations.

So whether you work with a low-, middle-, or upper-income family, you need to remember that a family's value system often is influenced by and reflected in its economic status and vocational preferences. (See Example 3.)

## Example 3

*You are working with a family in which the aunt and uncle have good blue-collar jobs. They did not graduate from high school and they are not encouraging their niece, whom they adopted, to go to college. The niece excels in school and talks about being a social worker, psychologist, or teacher. The aunt and uncle, however, reject her ideas about these careers and are proud of the simple fact that she will be the first in the family to graduate from high school. They believe that blue-collar work is honest hard work, and that having their niece attend college so she can enter a profession would be a waste of time and money.*

*What values might be influencing the niece's career choices? They may be values she developed through association with peers, teachers, social workers, therapists, church members, etc. The values of her aunt and uncle and past generations of the family also may be affecting her choices. As a Consultant, you need to recognize that all of these influences come into play here and respect the decision of the family.*

**4. Holiday celebrations and rituals.** Family differences can be clearly seen in a family's holiday celebrations and rituals. The family's culture influences not only whether a holiday or ritual is celebrated but also how it is celebrated. For example, families observe Christmas in various ways. Some celebrate the holiday privately with immediate family members; others choose to include friends, neighbors, and extended family members in a holi-

24

day celebration. There are families that prefer little or no celebrating and instead do volunteer work on that day. Some families consider Christmas a significant holy day while others see no religious significance at all.

The way families celebrate national holidays and family birthdays also reveals their traditions. Does a family enjoy a fireworks show or parades and speeches on the Fourth of July? Does a family celebrate New Year's together, or is it a holiday celebrated only by adults? Do the family members observe national holidays or specific ethnic traditions of their native land? Are family members' birthdays celebrated with big parties or are they pretty much ignored?

It is important for Consultants to know which holidays, if any, are important to the family. Do parents exchange gifts for their wedding anniversary? Is Easter a major holiday? Or Martin Luther King Jr. Day? Or Cinco de Mayo? How can you help the family celebrate or demonstrate reverence on these special days? As a Consultant, you need to be sensitive to a family's traditions and encourage and respect uniqueness without infringing on beliefs. (See Exercise 3.)

**5. Food preferences.** Food choices can be influenced by cultural differences. The variety of foods and ways meals are prepared can differ greatly depending on the family, and its ethnicity and upbringing. Some religions determine food preferences and prohibit certain foods. For example, Orthodox Jewish families do not eat pork or combine meat products with milk products. Shopping for these foods may be time consuming or difficult if certain types of food are not readily available in the family's neighborhood.

---

## Exercise 3: Your Holiday Traditions

On a separate piece of paper, list three family holiday traditions you enjoyed as a child.

1.

2.

3.

List three holiday traditions your partner or a friend enjoyed while growing up.

1.

2.

3.

How do these differ? How are they the same?

---

At times, a parent's vocation will determine food preferences. Many farm families prefer their heaviest meal at noon since they need more calories for hard outdoor work early in the day. Urban families, especially those in which the parents work outside the home during the day, usually have their biggest meal in the evening.

The traditional American diet has undergone tremendous changes in the last few decades. While we once enjoyed regular, big family dinners, most of us now eat out more often than ever before. Dining out means eating everything from gourmet food to fast food. Many families follow the "grab-what-you-can" philosophy, and children learn how to microwave snacks and even meals.

These are just a few of the many areas of family life that can vary greatly and be highly influenced by the culture. That's why it's so important not to make any assumptions when you work with a family. Understanding and respecting a family's values, traditions, and preferences is vital to working in the family's home. To disregard these may create a breakdown in communication and may cost you time and information that could be essential to your work.

## Changes That Affect Families

As we discussed earlier, a family's unique differences come from many sources within and outside a family. These differences form a family's self-image. Because they are tied to identity, family differences are a profound influence and help determine preferences, traditions, and family rules in all areas of family life. They are such an intricate part of a family's fiber that a change in the family (brought about intentionally by the Consultant or accidentally by an event such as the loss of a job, financial changes, a move, etc.) can meet with a lot of resistance. While families often resist changes, they are sometimes forced to change their rules, traditions, and preferences. When this occurs, a family experiences stress, which can contribute to crises in the home. As a Consultant, you need to be aware of these factors when they occur so you can help stabilize the family during the crisis, help the family make necessary adjustments, recognize when the family's value and belief system is being threatened, be sensitive to the family's need and desire to hold on to certain values, and understand the family's feelings about the change.

### Example 4

*The mother of a family dies. Since she had handled most of the family management chores, the family is lost when it comes to organizing finances, household schedules, child-rearing, etc. The father was taught growing up that those tasks should be done by the mother, and he is having difficulty adjusting to his new role.*

As a Consultant, you need to understand that new situations and changes often pose difficult challenges that can be perceived as threatening to the family. Therefore, it is not uncommon for families to resist change. This resistance should not be interpreted as a lack of concern or motivation.

Let's look at other family situations that may threaten or change a family's values or lifestyle:

1. **The family must move.**
2. **The family's income changes or the parents change occupations.**
3. **The children reject the family's values.**
4. **The family's child-rearing values and behaviors conflict with the law.**

**1. The family must move.** Families move much more frequently now than they once did (The World Almanac and Book of Facts, 1994). This, and the fact that families often move far from other relatives, contributes to a breakdown in supportive relationships. As a result, long-held family traditions, values, and rules may change or be weakened dramatically. If a family moves far away, members must adjust to a different regional culture, with possible differences in climate, recreation, cost of living, styles of dress, accent, etc. Language problems and changes in immigration status are additional sources of stress for children of immigrants and refugees, who must cope not only with adjustment to a strange new culture but also with the loss of their native land and indigenous culture (Gibbs & Huang, 1990).

**2. The family's income changes or the parents change occupations.** These changes include the loss of a job, a union strike, loss of income when a spouse dies, fading occupations, jobs lost to industrialization or computerization, jobs lost in a recession or depression, and having both parents working outside the home.

## Example 5

*You are working with a family in which the father works and the mother stays home. The father was recently laid off, and because he is in his late 50s, he is having a hard time finding work. He becomes despondent, stays at home, sleeps in late, and yells at the children. To meet the family's financial needs, the mother has taken a job. In what ways might these changes affect the family? What adjustments might this family have difficulty making?*

**3. The children reject** This type of forced chan called "the generation gap." specifically between a parent a many cultures, parents believe tain traditions that must be passed to their children. Parents want their children to value these traditions in the same way the parents value them. In order for parents to teach these values, the child has to live a life that conforms to the parents' values. Oftentimes, the parents insist on forcing the child to accept these values or traditions and the children rebel.

To illustrate how this situation might develop, let's consider a family in which the parents are Jehovah's Witnesses. This religion does not celebrate holidays and birthdays. Due to societal influences, a child in this family may rebel against his parents' beliefs by giving and receiving gifts on holidays, going to a friend's birthday party, eating a holiday meal with a neighbor, or participating in holiday activities at school.

Another example might involve parents who believe their daughter should only date boys of her own race. The girl's friends have interracial relationships and the daughter may rebel by sneaking out, lying to her parents, or defying their rules.

**4. The family's child-rearing values and behaviors conflict with the law.** Occasionally, you may work with a family that has certain child-rearing values, rules, or behaviors that conflict with local, state, or federal laws.

For example, some parents believe in excessive physical discipline for children. Does this type of discipline constitute child abuse? What about parents who believe that children are independent and should be able to take care of themselves at a young age?

What if parents who believe this leave their child at home alone for several days at a time? Though the age factor varies from state to state, there are laws against leaving children home alone.

Families who recently immigrated to the United States or whose parents were raised in another country may find that many of the child-rearing practices they use are in conflict with the law. Changes will need to occur so that the parenting practices fall within the limits of the law and the children are not in danger of being removed. Sensitivity to the family's values and beliefs is necessary to help the family adjust to the laws.

# Your Role as a Family Consultant

Any of these types of forced change can cause high stress in a family, which can create problems or add to the ones the family is already experiencing. Who can help?

The simple answer is you. Now that you have learned how important family differences are, their origins, and what areas of family life they influence, let's discuss your role as Family Consultant.

Your ability to recognize and understand cultural and family differences is a valuable tool. Strengthening this ability will help you further define your role in working with a family. To be effective, you will need to:

1. **Identify and understand the family's traditions and values.**
2. **Encourage the family's normal routine.**
3. **Follow the family's agenda.**
4. **Combine the agency's and family's goals with your own.**

**1. Identify and understand the family's traditions and values.** You will need to understand the basis for each family's beliefs. Above all, don't stereotype. Each family you will work with is unique in its own culture, and its strengths and weaknesses. Developing understanding of each family's beliefs and values is a continual process. As Consultants going into a family's home, we are eyewitnesses to a family's living conditions, interactions, and lifestyles. While this is invaluable in working with a family, it also makes it too easy for a Consultant to decide what the family needs and what its priorities should be. But the family should decide its own priorities. If you understand your own values and morals, you'll be better able to recognize when you are imposing them on the family.

You must be the one to bridge the gap if there are wide cultural differences between you and a family. That means that you also have to continually assess your values, traditions, and preferences, especially in the context of the family you are currently serving.

**2. Encourage the family's normal routine.** As you gather more information about a family through observations, active listening, participation, and exploring, adapt your treatment to the family's routine. Many simple mistakes can be made by not respecting or understanding the family's perspective. You may find after a few visits that you are sitting in the father's favorite chair. If you appear or sound as if you are part of a bureaucracy, you may intimidate family members. Educate yourself about different cultural groups so that you can be aware if the family adheres to many of the dominant cultural values. Is eye contact valued or devalued in this family's culture? If so, does the family adhere to that cultural norm? Follow the family's lead. Dress casually if they dress casually.

Use their language, not professional jargon. Adapt your speech to the family's "jargon." If you're working with a father who uses the word "tinkle" instead of the word "urinate," then start using the word "tinkle." If you need to discuss a temper tantrum, and you're not sure what family members call one, ask, "What do you call that?" They may use terms like "going ballistic," "pitch a fit," or "Tasmanian devil." Use their terms when you discuss their situations or describe behaviors.

Remember that you are not a guest in the family's home, so don't assume that role. Your job is to encourage the family's normal routine and be active in it, and to adapt to the family's culture while in the home. For example, if the family loves the television show *Rescue 911*, and the household stops to watch it, then visit the home at another time or watch the program with the family. If you arrive and family members are "spring cleaning," then pitch in and help rather than ask them to stop.

Observing a family during normal activities will provide you with information about a family's values and priorities, as well as help you to build relationships. In the Boys Town Family Preservation program, a Consultant may be in a family's home for up to 20 hours a week, but more typically about 8 to 12 hours. If you make the family change its routine by having members sit and talk the entire time, frustrations may build and the family may start to resist your intervention. At times, you may have to change your routine, such as helping family members while they do chores, meeting a parent at his or her job, attending a basketball game with the youth, or working on the car with a family member.

**3. Follow the family's agenda.** The focus of your treatment should be on the family's agenda. Help first with what the family wants to change. Ask family members what their problems are. Use what they say to determine why these problems exist and how they can best deal with them. If a family doesn't think something is broken, you can't fix it. For instance, if an agency asks you to deal with the family's communication skills, but the family doesn't think there is a problem, don't begin your treatment with communication. Ask the family members, "What can I help you with today?" Deal with the problems they give you first. If a child answers, "My dad says I have to do all the chores," you begin treatment by helping the family address chores. After making progress on that issue (the family's agenda), you can address the caseworker's concerns about communication skills.

The exception is when severe behaviors in the family are harmful to the children. If these behaviors are not addressed immediately, they will endanger the child's safety. Once you've deterred the threat, return to the family's agenda as soon as possible. You can return to the issue that created the threat after helping the family with its agenda problem.

Beware of the temptation to avoid the family's problems because they go against your own values. For example, sexual abuse is an issue that can be difficult to discuss. If you are uncomfortable about this issue, you will have to work against your feelings of discomfort in order to be effective as a Consultant.

Exercise 4 is designed to help you see how tempting it can be to attend to your goals

# Exercise 4:
# The Logan Family

It's your second week of working with the Logan family. The family was referred after the seven-year-old daughter Jessica reported that her 10-year-old brother Matthew had sexually abused her. The referring agency also would like Family Preservation Services to address several past substantiated neglect allegations.

The family appears very poor and lives in a dilapidated, filthy home. The only room in the house with a door is the mother's bedroom. A sheet is hung in the bathroom doorway for privacy. The family members include Stephanie, a 32-year-old single mother, and her three children, Matthew, Jessica, and Shona (age 6). The two girls are mildly mentally retarded. Matthew is in charge of babysitting his sisters when Stephanie goes to the store. The mom also has a 67-year-old boyfriend, David, who is Shona's father. David lives several miles away.

Strengths you have noted include Stephanie telling the children to do things she needs done and using time-outs when the children don't obey; Stephanie's attempts to meet her children's basic needs (food, clothing, and shelter); and Stephanie getting fun things for her children and doing fun things with them.

As you've gotten to know the family, you've learned that Stephanie receives Social Security for herself and her two daughters, and income assistance for her son. This totals about $1,200 a month. You are shocked to learn that the family has such a substantial income, considering that the heat was almost turned off in the house because the gas bill wasn't paid and that Stephanie asked for assistance so she could buy Matthew a Boy Scout uniform. Stephanie also tells you she automatically turns her money over to her boyfriend David, who gives her an allowance to pay bills. Today Stephanie said she is going to get a washer and dryer from the rent-to-own store. She knows about the interest rates because she already has two televisions, a video cassette recorder, and a dishwasher from the store. She also has furnished David's house with furniture she rented.

Let's take a look at the different issues that may be at work in this example. Can you identify what some of the differences in agendas might be? List them on a separate piece of paper:

## Family's Agenda

## Referral Agency's Agenda

## Consultant's (Your) Agenda

How are these three groups' agendas different and how are they alike?

In the next section we will talk about how to combine these three sets of agendas and goals when working with a family.

instead of the family's, thus disregarding the family's unique differences and rights to self-determination.

**4. Combine the agency's and family's goals with your own.** An important part of your role as a Family Consultant is being a combiner, meshing the family's goals with those of the referring agency. Being a combiner takes skill, but it helps to remember that the family's issues and the agency's issues usually are compatible.

## Example 6

*You are working with parents who are charged with medical neglect because their child needs a portable respirator but refuses to wear it. The caseworker's goal is to get the child to wear the respirator. The family's goal is to deal with the child's angry outbursts and refusal to do what the parents want.*

*Respect the family's agenda by helping the parents work with the child on controlling his anger, then on complying with his parents' requests. When the child starts to comply more with his parents' requests without having angry outbursts, teach the parents that having the child wear his respirator is a "parental request." Show them how to use the same skills they used to gain compliance earlier to gain compliance in this area. Then utilize this same pattern in teaching them how to control his angry outbursts with this request. Soon he will begin wearing his respirator without any angry outbursts.*

Your success at combining goals will improve your effectiveness when helping a family in a short amount of time. You will successfully maintain the relationship with the family because members will perceive you as respecting their values, opinions, and agenda. This will aid you in any further necessary treatment, as well as increase the probability that the family will maintain gains.

# Summary

Your role as a Family Consultant calls for you to join with a family to help its members achieve their goals. Assessing and respecting a family's traditions, values, rules, and role dynamics will enable you to adapt to meet the family's needs, equip family members for their tasks, and ultimately satisfy the goals of both the family and the referring agency.

The philosophy of Boys Town Family Preservation Services is for a Family Consultant to gain cultural competency, and to work within cultural and family differences. This enables the Consultant to:

- **tailor his or her teaching to fit each family.**
- **stabilize existing skills quickly.**
- **build on existing values to combine family and agency goals.**
- **build better relationships with family members.**

People develop family differences from relationships in their environment, their family of origin, their religion, and their ethnicity. We agree with Gibbs and Huang (1990) that "cultural" influences are the overarching dimensions that provide the person with a framework for perceiving and responding to the world; shape the person's personal and social identity; establish values, norms, and expectations for appropriate behaviors; and define parameters for choices and opportunities for the person's social, educational, and occupational experiences.

Every family is unique in how it is affected by changes and challenges. Every family adopts specific values and beliefs that are influenced by its culture. Every family has differences. Your role as a Consultant is to ascertain the family's traditions and values, encourage the family's normal routine, follow the family's agenda, and skillfully combine the goals of the family and the agency with your own. You need to be ready to listen, cautious about coming to conclusions, and open to guidance and correction when it comes to your presuppositions of the family.

# Community Resources and Networking

"No man is an island." John Donne's statement could easily apply to Consultants and the families they try to keep together — neither could accomplish their goals without the help of resources in the community. In fact, every person relies on community resources throughout their lives. Taking a child to day care, visiting the credit union for an auto loan, and calling an attorney for information about establishing a will are some common ways people use and depend on community resources. For families in crisis, outside resources are even more important because the services they provide help develop stability and ensure the safety and welfare of each family member.

The term "community resources," as it is used in this manual, has a broad meaning. Essentially, community resources include anything that can be obtained outside the family and within the community to meet the needs of the family. Examples of community resources range from grocery stores to counseling agencies to local ministers. They can be people, places, or things. The school principal, the city swimming pool, and disability income all are resources that can be found in a community and used by a family to meet its needs.

There are basically two types of community resources: formal and informal.

Formal resources often come to mind first because they are used most frequently. They include agencies and places whose primary purpose is to help people.

Informal resources are found in a variety of forms in every community. They often are taken for granted because people use them to different degrees without considering them to be "helpful." Some families, however, may not be aware of informal resources or know how to obtain them. (Later in this chapter, we'll discuss how families can use formal and informal resources.)

Here are some examples of formal and informal community resources.

## Formal Community Resources
   State child welfare department
   Veterans Administration
   Mental health clinics
   County attorney
   Homeless shelters
   Schools, preschools
   Department of Housing and
      Urban Development
   Food banks
   Foster homes, respite homes
   Medicaid, Medicare
   Libraries
   Employment services
   Welfare funds

## Informal Community Resources
   Parks
   Neighbors, friends, relatives
   Grocery stores
   Bowling alleys
   City swimming pools
   Church quilting groups
   Thrift stores
   Ministers, priests, elders, rabbis
   Baby-sitting exchange club
   Shamans, faith healers, spiritualists
   Social clubs
   Skating rinks
   Newspapers

As a Consultant, one of the most useful and important tools you can bring to your work with a family is an extensive knowledge of the types of available community resources and how they can best be obtained and used. This is important for a number of reasons. First, Consultants have a primary responsibility to help families meet their daily needs and make sure that the children are safe. If you can help a battered mother and her two children locate a safehouse quickly, the children are less likely to be harmed and the mother's chances of keeping her children with her are greatly increased.

Another reason to be familiar with community resources follows Maslow's *Hierarchy of Needs* (1954). Families whose basic needs for food or shelter are not being met must find community resources that can meet these needs before they can focus on other issues such as discipline or anger control. The sooner resources are located and tapped, the sooner the family can address other critical issues.

Also, a Consultant who knows how to put family members in touch with resources he or she can't provide directly can quickly gain a family's respect and confidence. Consider the single father who is preparing for the return of his son from a residential treatment facility. The father is working only part-time, and is worried that the food he has won't last until he gets his next paycheck. Your willingness to take the father to an emergency relief agency or food pantry, encourage him to apply for income assistance, and provide him with information about job services not only will resolve the immediate crisis but also will likely gain the father's trust and help you to develop a strong relationship with him. The father is apt to see you as competent and willing to help by doing more than just providing the traditional "talk therapy." Simply put, a Consultant must sometimes take action to help a family meet its needs. By knowing what kind of help is available, you act as a broker of community resources so that families get what they need in order to stay intact.

The next section will examine two critical times — before and during family interventions — when knowing about community resources and how to obtain them helps Consultants serve families effectively and efficiently.

Before you begin your work with families, it is essential that you become familiar with a community's people, places, and services. After exploring some ways you can get acquainted with local resources, we will discuss how this knowledge can be applied during interventions with families.

## Before Serving Families – Networking

Whether a Consultant has been recently hired and is new to the community, or has been practicing for years and is a veteran of the area, it takes time and effort to establish a working knowledge of the various available resources. Boys Town teaches it Consultants networking skills, which enable them to develop relationships with service providers, and learn about local policies and programs, and how to obtain particular resources.

**Networking** is the process of establishing mutual lines of communication among relevant people and agencies so that information can be exchanged for the common good of the agencies and the families they serve.

Each time Boys Town establishes a program at a different site, networking is one of the first tasks that must be completed in order to build a presence in the community. How easily this presence is established depends greatly on how much networking is emphasized in the early stages of program development. Since Boys Town is historically known as a residential home for needy children, networking is even more critical in establishing nonresidential programs because service providers and community leaders must be made aware of the services the new programs will provide and how they differ from residential treatment. In this way, the programs are introduced into the community and community leaders know that a new service is available to help meet the many needs of area children and families. Many of the lessons Boys Town has learned about networking came from replicating programs across the United States and are reflected in this section.

At Boys Town, we believe that networking within the community gives our Consultants several advantages. This also is true for Consultants in agencies that have adapted the Boys Town Family Preservation program. First, by actively seeking relationships with service providers, community leaders, and civil servants, you can quickly establish a professional reputation that positively reflects on your program. The community becomes more open to working with your agency or organization, and will want to know more about the kind of work that is done with families in crisis. For many programs, this curiosity and interest can generate more referrals. And because Boys Town and other family preservation agencies depend on a constant supply of referrals, networking can mean program survival.

Another advantage to networking is that it allows the Consultant to determine the best ways to gain access to a resource and to identify key resource contacts. For example, the process of procuring mental health services is different in every community. By meeting with the admission specialists from three local mental health centers, you can learn about the criteria for admission, the funding assistance available, and the types of services provided. This process also may provide opportunities for you to explain the kinds of mental health crises families present. On occasion, mental health agency officials may be willing to work out a special arrangement for families to use their services, especially if they sense that the program may be a source of frequent referrals. Again, the more a Consultant knows about who to contact and how to obtain resources, the more efficient and effective interventions with families will be. And, the more efficient a Consultant becomes, the easier the work becomes.

Networking also enables Consultants to identify gaps in the service delivery system and to determine what resources are lacking in particular areas. As you become more familiar with the community, you will learn which resource needs are not being met. These observations can be shared with other service providers, and over a period of time, agencies can work together to generate additional resources that are needed. In the meantime, you will be challenged to fill resource gaps by using existing resources in creative ways to meet the needs of your families.

# Methods of Networking

Having examined the many advantages of networking, one can understand the importance of taking the time and effort to learn about community resources. But just how does one go about networking? In establishing Boys Town Family Preservation programs across the country, several methods of networking are used; some are more effective than others, depending on the community. Let's look at some of those methods.

## Community Contacts

Making community contacts involves a deliberate and systematic effort to contact service and resource providers to get program information. The process is outlined below:

1. **Identify and prioritize the agencies** or persons you want to contact for more information.

2. **Phone the first agency** on your list and ask to speak to someone who can explain the program and services it provides.

3. **Introduce yourself and explain** why you want to familiarize yourself with the agency's services.

4. **Make an appointment** to meet with the provider. If the provider offers to give you information over the phone, schedule a time to call again if the person can't talk to you at that time.

5. **During the meeting, briefly explain your position** and describe how your program works. Answer any questions the person

may have and explain the referral process if he or she is in a position to make referrals to your program. Provide the contact person with brochures about your program.

6. **Ask the provider to explain** his or her program. Ask how the service works, how it is funded, and how to obtain services or resources. Ask for a brochure or pamphlet about the program.

7. **Ask whether you can use the agency's services** in the future.

8. **Thank the provider** for his or her time and encourage the person to call you with questions. Follow up with a written thank-you letter typed on agency letterhead.

9. **Record the information** you obtained during the interview and include it in a file on community resources.

10. **Periodically update your community resources file** by contacting each of the agencies to see if any information has changed.

Making community contacts can be time-consuming and should be an ongoing process. To make the process more manageable, try to make a certain number of contacts each month. Dividing the task with coworkers helps build the resource file more quickly.

## Community Involvement

Another networking method is community involvement. Some informal ways to get involved include attending open houses at other agencies, going to Chamber of Commerce gatherings (especially in rural areas), and setting up information booths at local family fairs. A more formal way to network through involvement is to serve on community committees. Most communities have multi-disciplinary committees or task forces that focus on issues like child abuse prevention or family advocacy. To find out what types of committees are active in your area, start by contacting the local child welfare office, school counselors, the juvenile court department, or state associations that deal with children and family issues. Once on a community committee, attend the meetings and volunteer to help with projects. The more involved you are, the more opportunities there will be to network and learn about more resources. This can be a rewarding way to network since committees are usually working to advance a worthy cause.

Another method of networking is offering to do presentations at civic club meetings, parent support groups, and teacher in-service meetings. People like to hear about programs that are active in their community. The opportunity to describe how your program works is usually an excellent time to mention the types of resources families in crisis often need to maintain the welfare of family members. On occasion, civic clubs offer to sponsor certain resource needs or to "adopt" a needy family.

## Peer Contacts

Finally, a simple but useful method of networking is communication with coworkers. The value of another Consultant's past experiences is immeasurable. Because in-home Consultants have fewer opportunities to interact and discuss experiences with coworkers, it's important for them to set aside time to share information about community resources. Talking with coworkers about how they found particular resources saves time and prevents the new Consultant from having to "reinvent the wheel."

## Networking in Rural and Urban Settings

Naturally, the size of the community a Consultant is working in and whether it is located in a rural or urban setting will determine the networking methods the Consultant will use. It has been well documented that differences in population density affect the community resources base (Sullivan, 1989; Falcone & Rosenthal, 1982; Johnson, 1983). Let's look at how the differences in urban and rural settings affect the way a Consultant networks with community resources.

In rural communities, there are fewer resources available and they may be located many miles apart (Sullivan, 1989). It is not uncommon for small communities to be without medical facilities, a police station, or even a public telephone. People in rural areas often rely on neighboring communities, which may be miles away, for their daily needs. When networking in rural areas, you can become familiar, and even friendly, with almost all of the service providers and civil servants in the area.

A Consultant who is networking in rural communities also needs to realize that each community may have its own politics and turf issues. Service providers who have been in a community for a long time may be set in their ways on how to provide services. They also may be overburdened by the task of trying to meet a variety of needs with a limited budget (Falcone & Rosenthal, 1982). These providers often have long waiting lists and must prioritize how they will allocate their few resources. Respecting these agencies' longevity and importance to the community is essential to the networking process.

Besides networking in several rural communities, Consultants also should contact resource agencies in the nearest city. Often, a city that's an hour's drive away is the closest place where specialized but essential resources are available to residents of smaller communities.

In many small communities, government agencies provide several of these resources. State child welfare caseworkers who work in rural areas are well-acquainted with community resources and usually are quite familiar with the families they refer. It is important to establish a strong professional relationship with referring caseworkers because they can share their knowledge of resources and confirm that the services provided for the families on their caseloads are satisfactory. With only a few caseworkers serving a rural area, it's not uncommon for a Consultant to become dependent on these workers for frequent referrals.

Networking in urban areas poses different challenges for the Consultant. One may involve facing an overabundance of resources that are scattered throughout a metropolitan area. It would be unrealistic for you to try to contact or become familiar with most of these resources before beginning work with families. Instead, you should prioritize service providers and agencies and determine which ones you should contact and become familiar with first. Services and resources that would be most essential to the families you will be working with should be given top priority. Most urban areas have information and referral agencies that link people with the specific community resources that are being sought. Some of these referral agencies publish community resource directories that are quite helpful.

As a Consultant in an urban setting, you are likely to encounter new and unfamiliar agencies regularly. When working to locate a particular resource for a family, you may be contacting agencies for the first time. This is a good time to do a form of abbreviated networking. Besides asking about the resources available for the particular client-family being served, you also can get information about the types of services and resources the agency provides in general, how to obtain these resources, and eligibility requirements. You also can provide information about your program, explain how families can be referred, and offer to send the agency additional information. Taking advantage of brief, first-time contacts with agencies not only benefits the family being served, but streamlines the networking process in the urban area. Over time, you will become more familiar with the community resources as part of an ongoing networking process.

Sometimes agencies do not provide the type of services or resources that their names or advertisements may imply. For example, an agency might offer to provide free prenatal services, but its primary goal is to screen young expectant mothers for its infant adoption program. You may need to screen agencies and resources in the urban communities before linking them with families.

Also, networking in the urban communities oftentimes is equated with advocating for families. Once you've contacted an agency, you are likely to encounter problems with waiting lists and strict guidelines for obtaining resources because there is such a high demand in densely populated areas. If a resource is critical to the maintenance of the family, you must attempt to convince the agency that there is an urgent need for the resource. Perseverance and persuasion are key components of obtaining resources.

Although there are different challenges to networking in urban and rural communities, networking in any size community is important in order to identify which resources are available and which ones are not. Whether you are working in the country or the city, networking requires creativity where resources are limited, inaccessible, or nonexistent.

One way to be creative is to know as much as possible about potential funding sources. With money, it may be possible to create and purchase a resource that isn't available. Consider Example 1 (next page).

While knowing about funding sources can help Consultants be creative, it is possible to be creative without spending any money. Consultants have networked in communities to get stores to donate food and household supplies, and to get mechanics and carpenters to donate labor. When it appears a resource cannot be immediately located or is seemingly inaccessible, creative planning can often generate resources that will adequately meet the needs of the family (Sullivan, 1989). "Never say never" is the motto for the Consultant who accepts the challenge of creating resources where none exist.

So far, we have discussed why and how Consultants network prior to working with families. We've described how networking

## Example 1

*A single grandmother and her three grandchildren lived in a trailer park on the edge of a large city. The 11-year-old grandson suffered from depression and had attempted suicide twice in two years. The grandmother complained that the grandson spent most of his free time in his bedroom and did not have any friends. She had tried to enroll her grandson in the Big Brother/Big Sister program so that he could go out and enjoy activities with a positive role model. But she was told the waiting list was long, and it could take up to a year before an opening became available. The Consultant who was working with the family knew of a government grant that was available for purchasing recreational services. She helped the grandmother acquire the grant, then suggested hiring someone from the family's church to take the grandson on outings and be his friend and role model. The grandmother talked to a young male adult from the church's college Sunday school class and he was thrilled to work with the grandson while earning a little extra money for himself.*

enables a Consultant to become knowledgeable about community resources, and prepares him or her to do effective and efficient interventions with families. Now let's look at how the networking process and knowledge of community resources can be applied as a Consultant works with families.

# Community Resources and Family Interventions

Once a Consultant has a good foundation of knowledge about the resources available in the community, it's time to apply this knowledge to interventions with the family. This application can be broken down into a three-step process called the Triple A's: Assess, Assist, and Advocate. Each step in the Triple-A process will be explained in this section.

## Assessing Families' Needs and Strengths

The first step in this process is to thoroughly assess the family's community resource needs and strengths. Among areas to focus on are the family's past and current use of resources, the formal and informal resources used, the family's social support network, the strengths the family exhibits in using resources, and the barriers that hinder the family in obtaining resources. Each of these areas will be discussed to clarify how a family's resource needs are assessed.

Many families you will work with will have resource needs that you can help the family meet. First, however, you should explore what the family considers its resource needs. (More details on the preliminary stages of an intervention are included in Chapters 4, 5, 8, and 9.) Discuss the family's problems, how family members think certain resources could help, and the family's current and past utilization of resources to meet its needs. Identifying resources a family has used before and is currently using will provide a great deal of information about the family's knowledge of resources, its skill in obtaining resources, and the family's level of reliance on resources. You'll also want to find out how much longer the family can rely on these resources. A family that is receiving income assistance, living in subsidized housing, and sending a child to a Head Start program probably has substantial knowledge of government-funded resources, has the ability to obtain some resources with assistance, and is fairly reliant on community resources to meet basic needs.

Sometimes you will encounter families that will tell you that they know about the resources in their community and how to obtain them, and that they don't need any help to link up with them. But the majority of families you will work with has at least one resource need. And families that have a history of substantiated neglect may have several resource needs (Nelson, Saunders, & Landsman, 1993).

While assessing the resources a family is using or has used, ask first about formal resources. Does the family use government programs, health clinics, schools, or counselors? How did the family find out about these resources and to what extent are they being used?

Next, discuss informal resources. Does the family have relatives who are willing to provide assistance? Does the family have a membership at the city pool? Are family members active in a church, synagogue, or fellowship group? When the family needs a baby-sitter, who is contacted? Where does the family shop? What activities are the children and the parents involved in? How did the family learn about informal resources and to what extent are they used?

In addition to gathering useful information, these questions can help determine the ratio of formal resources to informal resources. Knowing this can help you link the family with appropriate resources as part of the intervention plan.

In assessing the family's resource needs, it helps to know who is in the family's social support network. The people whom families interact with on a regular basis often provide various types and forms of resources that promote the well-being of the families (Zigler & Black, 1989; Dawson, Robinson, & Johnson, 1982). A neighbor may provide transportation, a child welfare worker may provide advice and referrals, a coworker may fix broken appliances, and a child's best friend may provide recreational opportunities. Each family member may rely on a variety of professional and personal relationships to meet his or her needs and alleviate stress (Cohen & Willis, 1985).

One way to assess a family member's social support network is to complete a social support network map like the one designed by Tracy and Whittaker (1990). This assessment tool was designed to explore the extent to which informal and formal resources are being used and relied upon in an individual's social network. The information gained from this assessment can help Consultants develop an individualized intervention plan that builds on social support resources already being used by the family. Whether you choose to use a formal assessment tool or just ask the family, knowing who forms a family's social support network will provide valuable information about how the family obtains resources.

Throughout the assessment process, the Consultant will be identifying the family's strengths. (See Chapter 20, which focuses on identifying strengths.) All families have strengths when it comes to identifying, obtaining, and using community resources.

The Consultant's task is to figure out what those strengths are. Examples of strengths include the use of many community resources, assertiveness in asking for help, community involvement, problem-solving skills, and the ability to identify and prioritize needs and meet basic daily needs. No matter how isolated and needy families may seem at referral, there will always be strengths to identify in their use of community resources.

Finally, the Consultant assesses the barriers that are keeping a family from using resources. Even when a family can clearly identify its resource needs, these barriers exist. Knowing what they are enables the Consultant to plan an individualized intervention that can work around them. Some common barriers are listed below:

1. **The family does not believe in accepting charity**, or believes that a family should "take care of its own." This barrier is based on the family's values and beliefs regarding receiving help from others.
2. **The family simply doesn't know that certain resources exist.**
3. **The family isn't able to obtain or use a resource**. This can include not having transportation, not having enough money, having too much money to qualify, or not having a way to contact the resource (e.g. the family does not have a telephone).
4. **The family lacks skills needed to obtain a resource.** Examples: The family does not know how to locate resources by using a telephone book; family members don't have the communication skills to explain their needs to the provider; the family doesn't know how to ride a city bus or call a taxi to get to an appointment.

5. **The family may be afraid to use certain resources.** Oftentimes, families are afraid to ask for help or leave their familiar neighborhood to go to an office, or are intimidated by talking to professionals. Family members may even fear for their lives if they have to venture out in an unsafe neighborhood to obtain the resource. They also may fear that it will appear that they are unable to care for their children.
6. **The family may have had negative experiences dealing with informal and formal resources** (e.g. betrayal, rejection, etc.).
7. **The family may have personal characteristics that alienate resource providers** (e.g. belligerent, lack of social skills, poor hygiene, etc.).

To practice your resource assessment skills, see Exercise 1 on the next page.

## Assisting Families in Meeting Community Resource Needs

The second step in the Triple-A intervention process is assisting the family. Again, the decisions about how best to help a family are based on the assessment of the family's resource needs and strengths.

In order to help a family meet its resource needs, several factors must be kept in mind. As a Consultant, you first should remember that one of your goals in working with families is to have them solve problems independently. This doesn't mean a Consultant should never provide a family with a needed resource. It simply means that you should teach families how to meet their resource needs on their own.

# Exercise 1:
# The Giovanni Family

Consider the example below and assess what the family's resource needs might be. Then, on a separate piece of paper, answer the questions that follow the example to see if you can remember the components of assessing a family's resource needs:

*The Giovanni family consists of two biological parents, Ellen and Marcus, and their two children, three-year-old Melisa and eight-year-old Jordan. Two months ago, Marcus was fired from his job as a farm hand and the Giovannis moved to a large city 60 miles away to be closer to Marcus's brother. The family was referred to Family Preservation Services after a neighbor reported that Jordan was not attending school. Ellen did not enroll Jordan in school because she and Marcus felt that the last three schools Jordan attended did not care about him and were always giving him failing grades. One teacher even told Ellen that Jordan might be mildly retarded. Ellen does not believe Jordan is retarded but thought he might have a reading problem like his father's. Marcus reads at a second-grade level.*

*The Giovannis wanted to set up a home school for Jordan and asked for help in getting a curriculum they could use. Marcus also stated that he wanted to find a better job than the night-shift janitorial job he started the week before. He admits that his job skills are limited because he worked on a farm most of his life. Ellen contributes to the family's income by doing sewing and alterations for people in the neighborhood.*

*Ellen enrolled Melisa in a preschool program at their church, but Melisa won't start until the next session begins in six weeks.*

*Although the family's income is tight, Ellen said she is used to living under a tight budget and has learned many ways to cut corners, such as using coupons and shopping at garage sales.*

What community resources have the Giovannis used in the past?

What community resources are the Giovannis currently using?

How many of these resources are formal? Informal?

Who are some of the people in the Giovanni family's social support network?

What are some of the Giovannis' strengths in using resources?

What barriers may be hindering the Giovannis from getting the community resources they need?

During the first several visits of the intervention, you should work with the family to identify and assess its problems, needs, and strengths. As you get to know the family, family members may discuss community resource needs they have. You and the family should decide which of these needs are most important and which needs, if not met, could endanger the well-being of family members. Depending on the family's values and beliefs, family members may prioritize their needs differently than you will. For example, a mother may think it's more important to buy cigarettes with her last few dollars than to make sure she has enough milk for the week. Or, a family may have these needs: The father needs a divorce attorney to finalize custody issues; the son needs a physical so he can play on the baseball team; and the family needs to get energy assistance to help pay overdue utility bills. During the intervention, you may be able to help the family meet all these needs. But the resource needs that are most important to the family and that will help the family achieve its goals will take top priority.

If at anytime during an intervention the Consultant and/or the family identify a resource need that must be met in order to ensure the family's welfare and safety, the Consultant should immediately help the family obtain that resource. For example, if a family reports to you on Friday night that it does not have enough food to last until the food bank opens again on Monday, you should help the family get food. If no community resources can provide food on such late notice, you should buy food to get the family through the weekend. Some family preservation programs have an emergency fund for such situations.

Another factor to consider when helping a family is the potential barriers and problems the family might encounter in obtaining resources. Does the family have a telephone, reliable transportation, enough money, sufficient communication or assertiveness skills, or sufficient knowledge of the system to obtain any resources it may need? If there are obstacles, the Consultant should help the family overcome them. For example, an 11-year-old boy who wants to be in the Cub Scouts will need more than just the time and date of the next meeting. He'll probably need transportation, uniforms, and money for dues. The boy also may be afraid to go to a meeting where there will be strangers. In this situation, you could help by taking the boy to the first meeting, or by introducing him to the pack leader.

Every family a Consultant works with will be different. But Consultants should remember these three guidelines when helping a family obtain resources: 1) Let creativity flow when conventional resources cannot be found; 2) Build on a family's strengths by finding out what resources it has obtained in the past and have family members repeat their successes to get other resources; and 3) Let family members do for themselves what they are capable of doing for themselves — do not interfere when a family can act independently.

As a Consultant, you can use several approaches to teach a family how to obtain community resources on its own. These approaches, which will be discussed in detail in the chapters on intervention skills, include modeling, providing rationales, explaining the process of obtaining resources, practicing how to contact providers, giving families assignments, and reinforcing families for attempting to get resources. Through the use of a variety of intervention skills, you can teach families skills such as assertiveness, how to locate resources, how to barter for resources with neighbors, time management, and problem-solving.

## Advocating for Families to Get Community Resources

The final step in the Triple-A process of intervention is advocating. A Consultant who has networked and become familiar with community resources prior to working with families has already begun advocating for families. By bringing together the knowledge of community resources and the knowledge of a family's particular needs and strengths, the Consultant is in the best position to advocate on the family's behalf.

As a Consultant, your role as an advocate is extremely important in interventions with some families. For example, a family that has been in the system for a long time often needs an advocate. It is not unusual for caseworkers, service providers, and even relatives to tire of consistently working to meet this family's resource needs. They may feel that the family is too dependent on the system, is lazy, or is no longer deserving of certain resources that have been overused. Whether these perceptions are valid or not, the Consultant who has assessed the family's resource needs and is assisting the family to independently meet those needs is going to be able to use sound rationales to convince resource providers that resources should be made available to the family. When the Consultant's primary goal is to help preserve the family, his or her opinion will carry much weight when it's clear that a resource is necessary for the maintenance of the family.

When advocating for the family, you should be guided by two principles: persistence and creativity.

Helping families obtain community resources can be a time-consuming and seemingly fruitless task. If the first several providers contacted cannot provide the resource, hopelessness can begin to set in. However, if you are persistent in advocating for resources, you will find and obtain resources more often than the Consultant who gives up after only a few tries. A family's well-being depends on your willingness to go the extra mile.

Creativity is the other guiding principle for the advocating Consultant. If conventional resources are not available in a community, you can advocate so that alternative resources can be considered. For example, using creativity, you may be able to convince the director of a senior citizen volunteer corps to find a volunteer who will provide child care for a family if you can arrange to have the family's caseworker reimburse the volunteer for mileage. If you advocate on a professional and well-informed level, you have a good chance of getting providers to accept creative approaches to providing resources for families. A Consultant who advocates with creative ideas is much more likely to help families meet their resource needs.

# Summary

The importance of community resources to families in crisis cannot be understated. A Consultant who can effectively network with resource agencies and providers has an inside track on helping families obtain the outside help they need. Effective networking involves learning about available resources, identifying a family's needs, and working creatively to find the resources that can best meet those needs.

Before and during the intervention process, Consultants must become proficient in the areas of assessment, assistance, and advocacy. This means effectively applying the information garnered through networking so that families receive the greatest benefit possible. Consultants who are creative and persistent in their work are more likely to help families achieve their goals of getting needs met and staying together.

One of the goals of intervening with families is to help them learn to meet their needs on their own by independently identifying, locating, and obtaining community resources.

# 4

# Family Assessment

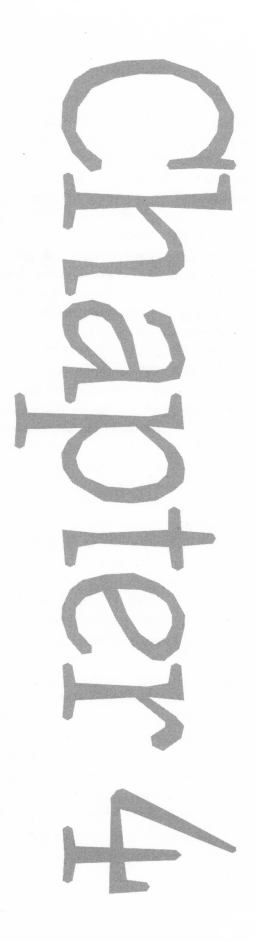

In large part, your success as a Consultant will depend on your ability to assess families as you work with them in their homes. It is this process that guides your interactions with every member of a family, each and every time you work with them. A complete assessment enables you to help chart a direction for a family to follow, alter it whenever necessary as the family begins its journey, and track the course each family member is taking.

What does it mean to assess a family? Above all, it means observation — thorough observation — of all that a family is. It means watching for bits of information, patterns in relationships, and evidence of the distinct differences we discussed in Chapter 2. It means listening to each family member and the family as a whole, and discovering their roles as well as those of people outside the family. Assessment also involves observing the family's environment — its housing, workplace, neighborhood, and community.

In many ways, family assessment is like a system of navigation. Imagine that the family is a ship. Family members have some idea of where they want to go during therapy, but little idea about how to get there. As the Consultant, you are the navigator, familiar with different courses to take and skilled in using the navigational tools of assessment. You advise the captains and crew on how to follow the course you have charted for them. Once a family begins therapy, your navigation — just like your assessment — continues throughout the journey. All the while, you check your compass, watch the stars, and gauge the wind and the currents. If the ship is blown off course, you're ready with new coordinates. Because you're always watchful, always monitoring the advice you give and the direction the ship is taking, you can help the crew make adjustments if the ship suddenly takes on water or loses sight of land.

Just as navigation is crucial for sea travel, family assessment is a pivotal concept of Family Preservation Services. Very few professionals will be able to spend the amount of time with a family that you will. Few will be seeing so many facets of a family's life. By applying the ideas and techniques presented in this chapter, you'll learn more with your eyes and ears each time you work with a family.

It is important to have an understanding of cognitive and behavioral theory if you are to help family members make progress in this treatment program. Boys Town Family Preservation Services uses the Social Learning Theory in its work with families. This outlook integrates the behavioral theory, which provides an understanding of reinforcement and punishment and the manner in which they shape behavior, with the cognitive model, which enables you to understand how beliefs about events affect the way people behave, including the ABC Model of antecedent events, behaviors, and consequences (Bandura, 1977; Martin & Pear, 1988). The ability to understand and employ these approaches is essential when working in this program.

## Family Consultant Skills

Let's begin our discussion of family assessment with a look at the types of skills required for assessment and for family therapy as a whole. In this way, we can lay a foundation for understanding how assessment affects all that you do as a Consultant.

According to Alexander and Parsons (1982), assessment is conducted by utilizing three types of assessment skills: conceptual, technical, and interpersonal. These three types of skills are interrelated, with each skill area complementing the other two.

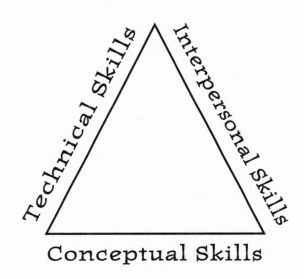

**Conceptual skills** are those dealing with how to think about families. These are the core skills of family assessment. Conceptual skills help you view the family accurately, giving you a clear picture of how the family functions. In our illustration, conceptual skills form the base of the triangle because they are the foundation for all other family therapy skills. How you conceptualize a family and its situation determines which technical and interpersonal skills you will use to improve the family's functioning. Conceptual skills allow you to look at a family and identify, among other things, who the parent figures are, who manages the home, who everyone looks to in times of crisis, the hierarchy in the home, the most serious issue or problems the family faces, and approaches that have been tried before and the family's response to them. You will be able to conceptualize the whole family system. The use of conceptual skills is necessary to elicit the greatest amount of change in the shortest amount of time. If you cannot work with a family and assess what the family members' functions are and how the family system works, you will continually hit roadblocks in your work.

**Technical skills** incorporate two modes of teaching. The first involves a variety of techniques the Consultant uses in order to promote positive change within a family. These are techniques you will need to be proficient at so you know how to teach families new skills. They include active listening, exploring, reframing, metaphors, confrontation, and mediation. (Each of these skills is described in later chapters.) The second teaching mode incorporates skills that a Consultant will use to teach family members how to solve problems such as neglect, physical abuse, domestic violence, and juvenile delinquency.

Every educator draws from these two types of technical skills when teaching students new skills. For example, a piano instructor must know how to use the teaching methods of modeling, having students rehearse, lecturing, and giving assignments to help students learn to be pianists. Also, the music instructor must have the technical skills to know what to teach the students. In order to prepare students for a performance, the instructor must understand the skills the students must learn. The instructor must be proficient at reading music, playing notes, using the pedal, establishing a tempo, and using proper posture to be able to teach the students these skills. Any instructor needs to know the best ways to teach (how) and the kinds of skills to teach (what) before he or she can pass on the knowledge to a student.

**Interpersonal skills** are those that enable the Consultant to strategically teach skills through relationships, creating and maintaining a rapport with family members while enhancing their skills through the use of technical and conceptual skills. Some specific examples of interpersonal skills include convincing parents to try a new skill, rewarding them for learning it, building trust, empathizing with the feelings of family members, and supporting them through family successes as well as family setbacks. These skills also involve knowing when to praise a parent and when it's most effective to give a suggestion, understanding the strategy of using concrete services, and the subtlety of nonverbal and verbal cues. Even though each category of skills is equally important, any lack of interpersonal skills can seriously hamper or halt the progress of a family. If the relationship is negative and there are bad feelings — hostility, defensiveness, uneasiness, mistrust, disrespect, discord, psychologically threatening feelings — between a Consultant and family members, there is less desire and readiness to hear what is being said (Kadushin, 1983). Sensitivity, intuition, openness, and respect are building blocks for strong interpersonal skills.

Some approaches to family preservation rely heavily on only one category of skills. Boys Town's approach, as the triangle illustrates, assigns equal importance to each category. Your work as a Consultant will involve all three categories of skills. Sometimes, you will need to combine sets of skills. More commonly, you'll be shifting from one category to another. For example, let's say that you are teaching a mother a problem-solving skill (using your technical skills) and you sense that she is reluctant and afraid to try new ideas. You decide to build her trust in you by helping her three-year-old learn how to somersault and talking about how much fun it is to gain a new skill (using your interpersonal skills). Then, after assessing the family's "system," you revise your view of the mother's leadership role in the family, realizing you need to give her more encouragement or rewards when she does try a new skill (your conceptual skills help you make this assessment). In one interaction, during one visit, you have utilized all three of the assessment skills discussed.

Consultants who master all three areas in their work are tapping into all their resources and will find the most success in assessing families. Like the master craftsperson, your best work can be done when you know how to use every tool in your belt.

## Assessment Guidelines

Now that we've looked at the different types of assessment skills you will need as a Consultant, and how they are interrelated, let's discuss some guidelines for assessing a family. We have found that Consultants can often become enmeshed with the myriad of family issues going on in a home. Following the guidelines listed here will assist you in staying focused on the issues that most endanger the children. These guidelines also will help you assess how to use your conceptual, technical, and interpersonal skills effectively.

**1. Treat each family as unique.**
**2. Focus on the present.**
**3. Meet the family's physical needs first.**
**4. Validate through observation.**
**5. Make assessment a continuous process.**

**1. Treat each family as unique.** From our discussion of cultural and family differences in Chapter 2, you know that each family has its own values, beliefs, and cultural priorities. Families are unique in the particular mix of problems they want a Consultant to help with, the number of problems they may have, and how willing they are to share their problems with outsiders and accept help in return. Families also have different skill levels and intellectual levels. For all these reasons, you must individualize treatment plans for each family. Avoid comparing one family with another family you may have worked with in the past. This will help you keep an open mind and enable you to better discover the unique strengths and problem areas present in each family. For example, don't assume that because a family was referred for neglect that you need to teach them house-cleaning strategies. Remember that in assessing a family, you are looking for what is endangering the child. Don't start your intervention with preconceived ideas of what needs to be "fixed." Just as each family system is unique, so are the problems each family experiences.

**2. Focus on the present.** Knowledge of a family's history can help you understand how family dynamics from the past influence the patterns you see today. You must, however, focus on the present in order to teach families the skills they will need to address their current issues. Perhaps a 14-year-old who throws tantrums today was once a two-year-old who threw tantrums. If the parents gave in when the child was two, they started a pattern that still may exist today. It may help to know how long a pattern has existed. Interactions among family members can change over time.

Families also experience interactions with their environment, which can change as well. For example, a family that recently moved into a neighborhood where there are crack houses may begin having problems with drug addiction or experience fear because of crime and gangs. Two months earlier, these problems may not have existed for that family. Conversely, if a family reports that the father used to abuse alcohol but stopped drinking and has been sober for three years, don't assume that issues of alcoholism or codependency will never come up during the intervention. Through your assessment you may find that current issues are more relevant to the endangerment of the child than issues from the past. Use information from the past to help you understand the present situation, but focus your intervention on what is presently occurring in the home that is endangering the child.

**3. Meet the family's physical needs first.** Families function at their best if the basic needs of family members are met, i.e. food, clothing, shelter, safety, health (Maslow, 1954). If these needs aren't being met in one or more of these areas, other problems may be intensified. Sometimes it's easy to assume that parents are feeling stressed out because of their children's misbehaviors, when in fact the real stress is rooted in the fear that the food stamps are late and the parents have no idea how to feed the children. Often it is easy for us to overlook how the basic needs of the family affect stress. Assessment is crucial here to determine what is creating the stress and assist the family in dealing with it.

As a Consultant using the Boys Town Family Preservation Services program, you can provide concrete services to families to help meet these needs. If there's no food, help the family get it; if someone is sick or malnourished, don't work on parenting problems until you have obtained the necessary medical help; if the roof is leaking or the furnace doesn't work, help the family get them repaired. Once the physical needs are met, then you can better assess how the other problems are affecting the family. If a Consultant determines through assessment that a family's basic needs aren't being met, he or she can arrange to provide these services while simultaneously teaching the family how to acquire the services for itself in the future.

**4. Validate through observation.** Indirect observation — information provided by family members, caseworkers, and other outside agencies — is critical in your work with families. This information will provide you with perspectives of both the family and the outside agencies involved with the family. However, there will be times when what you directly observe will contradict what someone else has said. For example, a caseworker may tell you that a family is neglecting a child's physical needs. You spend several days in the home and see that the family is frugal, that members pinch their pennies, but that there simply aren't enough pennies. You determine that the family isn't neglectful; it just needs basic services in order to supplement its income. Trust what your eyes tell you. Constantly be watchful so that you can feel confident that the information you receive from other sources can be verified by what you observe. You may be better able to assess the family's progress through your critical observations than through verbal reports from others.

**5. Make assessment a continuous process.** Remember that assessment is like assembling the pieces to a puzzle. You will seldom get all the pieces together at the beginning of the intervention. For example, you may begin working with a family whose children are having problems at school. After two weeks, the teenage girl tells you she doesn't like the way her stepdad looks at her. This new issue or puzzle piece arrives two weeks after you begin services.

It's not uncommon for family members to begin to trust you more and thus reveal more as time goes on. Assessment is a fluid and dynamic process that involves receiving, analyzing, and synthesizing new information as it emerges during the entire course of working with a family (Hepworth & Larsen, 1990). You must continually reassess not only what you know about a family, but also the techniques and strategies you are using to keep the family intact and the children safe. Assessment continues as long as you are working with a family.

These guidelines provide a framework for the assessment process. Following them will make your assessments more accurate and effective. We often work with families who have been labeled as "uncooperative," "resistant," "unmotivated," "noncompliant," or "uncaring." By using these guidelines, we can determine what may be occurring in the home that creates such perceptions. Family members may have their own ideas of what the problem is. They may be concerned about their next meal. Past interventions may have focused on an issue that is no longer occurring, rather than a current issue. Whatever the problem is, the guidelines we've discussed will enable you to make a clear assessment of the family situation.

## Assessment Process

Now that we have discussed skill areas for working with families and guidelines for assessment, let's examine an overview of the assessment process. As the guidelines help keep you focused and provide a framework for using your skills, the assessment process provides the framework for what areas to assess. The following three areas will help you gain an overall picture of what is going on in a family and help you decide how best to begin and tailor your intervention. Thoroughly assessing these areas will save you time and energy in the long run by preventing the need to "start over" because you have misunderstood the family roles, family situation, or family capabilities. Like the navigator of a ship, you will want to understand how your ship runs, what its structure is like, how the ship handles, its capabilities, and the relationship between its working parts.

### Three Basic Steps for Assessment

1. **Determine the family's "system"; how it works as a unit, its roles and structure.**
2. **Determine the ABC's (Antecedent, Behavior, and Consequence) for each of the goal-oriented problem areas.**
3. **Determine the family's capabilities.**

**1. Determine the family's "system."** Each family member is part of a system that determines how he or she works within the family and how the family works as a whole. This system is dynamic in that if one family member changes, the other family members can't help but be affected because they all are interconnected in the system. How each family system works and is affected by outside influences depends on a number of factors, including past family experiences, learned styles of interacting, and culture. Determining such things as the role of each family member in the home, how the family structures its time, the family's rules, customs that influence family roles and structure, and the boundaries the family sets for itself will provide a picture of how the family system works. Some family systems are more open and able to adjust to change, while others are more rigid and closed, and highly resistant to change.

Determining a family's system is important because it will tell you how the family operates, much like an operator's manual describes how a machine works. Determining the family roles and structure is also vital to the assessment process. Together, they are like the girders of a bridge. You cannot evaluate the strength or makeup of a bridge without a thorough inspection of its supporting girders. Likewise, you cannot accurately assess the family's functioning without knowing its underpinnings. (For more about family systems, consult *Families and Family Therapy* [1974], by S. Minuchin.)

**2. Determine the ABC's.** It will be necessary to assess the driving force behind a family's behaviors and the behaviors of each family member. To do so, the Consultant must acknowledge that behavior does not occur in a vacuum. Events that occur in the environment — something that happens before and after a behavior — can have a major impact on that behavior. Thus, it is important to understand all the circumstances surrounding a behavior if it is to be fully understood.

The ABC Model provides a method for observing and describing what people do, making reasonable assumptions about why they do it, and developing strategies to maintain positive behaviors and change negative behaviors. It is based on the idea that we learn most of our behavior. The ABC Model comprises these components:

**ANTECEDENTS (A)** — **the events or conditions present in the environment before a behavior occurs.**

**BEHAVIOR (B)** — **what a person does or says.**

**CONSEQUENCES (C)** — **the results, outcomes, or effects of a behavior.**

Let's look at these three areas more closely.

**Antecedents** are the events or chain of events that occur prior to a behavior. When assessing a behavior, it helps to know what might have helped "trigger" or "signal" it. You should pay particular attention to the four "W's" to determine the antecedents:

**Who** — with whom does the behavior occur or who is present when the behavior occurs?

**When** — the time of day the behavior occurs (before bed, after school, during dinner).

**Where** — in what location does the behavior usually occur (classroom, bedroom, kitchen)?

**What** — what activity is the family member engaged in (e.g. watching TV, fixing supper, playing with friends)?

The four "W's" can work in combination or alone to set the stage for particular behaviors to occur.

As we discussed earlier, becoming familiar with a family member's history to get a feel for how much previous learning has occurred can help you understand how the past may be influencing the present. But you should remain focused on the present. While the antecedents for a behavior may be a complex chain of events (the alarm doesn't go off in the morning, which makes dad late for work, which makes his boss angry and results in loss of pay, which makes dad so irritable that when he gets home he hits his daughter when she whines for a snack), it is often a more simple stimulus that immediately precedes a behavior. For example, a telephone ring immediately precedes someone answering the phone; a red light at an intersection precedes someone stepping on the brake in the car; and a mild argument between a parent and a child precedes the child walking out of the house.

**Behaviors** are anything a person does or says that can be directly or indirectly observed and measured. This includes body movements, facial expressions, and verbals that are occurring as part of the behavior that has been identified as problematic. While behavior is the second component of the three ABC components, it is necessary for you to focus on this component first in order to understand the other two. You must determine what the behavior is before the relevant antecedents and consequences can be known. It also is important to have a clear picture of what the behavior is. We all have a different definition of "aggressive" behavior — "going nuts," "wild," or "out of control." Asking clarifying questions and observing closely, when possible, will provide you with an overall picture of what the behavior is and what smaller behaviors make up the "aggressive"" behavior so that effective teaching can occur.

**Consequences** are the outcomes that result when a person engages in a behavior. The events in the environment that follow a behavior can be pleasant, unpleasant, or neutral. That is, events that follow a behavior can make the behavior stronger or weaker, or have no effect. An event that follows a behavior that makes the behavior stronger increases the likelihood that the same behavior will occur again in the future. Events that follow a behavior that make the behavior weaker decrease the chance that the behavior will occur again. Thus, knowing what happens right after a behavior occurs will help you analyze the behavior and predict its future course. For example, answering the telephone can result in a pleasant event like talking to a friend; stopping at a red light can lead to a pleasant outcome like avoiding a traffic ticket or a collision; and teaching a parent effective discipline techniques can result in less frustration over a child's inappropriate behavior. In each of these examples, the behavior results in a pleasant consequence and, in each case, the behavior is more likely to occur again under those same antecedent conditions.

Let's summarize the effects of consequences on behavior:

- **Behavior can be positively changed, or occur with more frequency or more intensity.**
- **Behavior can occur less often or with less intensity.**
- **New behaviors can be learned and old behaviors can be improved.**
- **Behavior can be changed so that it occurs at a different time or place.**

Determining the antecedents, behavior, and consequence of a situation helps in understanding a behavior, focusing treatment strategies, and determining skill deficits. This process is particularly useful in assessing the occurrence of especially negative events between family members such as verbal and physical aggression, violence, and depression.

Working in the family's home, you can help change behavior by changing the antecedents, the behavior, or the consequences, or all three.

Antecedents often can be changed. For example, if a child uses foul language when asking for money to go out, the parent may respond by saying "No" or hitting the child. However, if the child learns to ask for money using appropriate language, the parent may say "Yes."

Behaviors can be changed by changing the antecedent events, the consequences, or by teaching family members a different way to do things. Take a situation in which a child breaks curfew. The parent responds by yelling, screaming, calling the child names, and grounding the child for one month. The child then yells, screams, and stomps off to his room. Changing the antecedent event by teaching the parent to calmly tell the child that he is grounded and then walk away may decrease the child's yelling, screaming, and stomping-off behaviors over time, without dealing directly with the child's behaviors.

Consequences also can be changed. A parent can learn to walk away after giving a child a consequence rather than arguing, stick to grounding a child rather than giving in when the child cries, show approval or notice appropriate behavior, or give rewards only after appropriate behavior has occurred. By showing family members how to change the consequences to behaviors, you can help them change the behavior itself. (Ways in which changing the ABC's can help teach skills and address problem behaviors will be discussed in more detail in later chapters.)

**3. Determine the family's capabilities.** A family's capabilities are determined by the limits on the members' willingness or ability to learn, their strengths, and the pace at which they learn and operate. Treatment plans and goals are based on a consideration of the family members' capabilities. The ultimate goal of therapy is to equip family members with enough skills to meet their particular needs, skills that can be generalized across places and people. This goal requires you to teach skills that reflect the family members' limits, strengths, and pace, and to assess the quantity and quality of these skills for successful acquisition and retention.

Let's look at the three areas of capabilities more closely.

A family's limits may be determined by its members' intellectual abilities as well as their physical and emotional abilities. In some families, the abilities of a parent or a child may be limited by age, mental retardation, autism, developmental disabilities, a mental illness, cerebral palsy, muscular dystrophy, Alzheimer's, hyperactivity, or some other factor. The emotional limits of a family may be created by such things as cultural differences, values, and beliefs. All of these limits need to be thoroughly assessed so that intervention can be individualized, thus preventing frustration on the part of the family members and the Consultant. Limits may require creativity in the development and implementation of your treatment plans. By assessing what these limits are, you can determine how to work with the family member, make suggestions to other family members, and set realistic expectations.

You can identify a family's strengths by becoming a partner with your family. Strengths also can be identified by assessing what the family is already doing correctly through observation of the family dynamics, how family issues are dealt with, and the family's day-to-day activities. Strengths also can be identified through active listening and exploring (techniques that will be discussed more thoroughly in Chapters 8 and 9) to determine how the family has handled similar situations with different people, in different places, and at different times.

As mentioned in other chapters, families are the experts on themselves and their situations, and a Consultant needs to assess this expertise in order to understand each individual family member's strength. Developing a skill that is based on the family's strength is impossible to do without assessment of the family's expertise. Determining the family's strengths in areas the members identify as problematic provides you with the foundation for helping to build on skills. Constantly assessing a family's strengths will reduce resistance that may arise within the family. Focusing on the strengths of family members helps them see success and feel good about the changes occurring in their home. Identifying strengths and building upon those strengths is a critical component of the Boys Town program and will be discussed in more detail in a later chapter. However, it is important here to understand that assessment is critical in determining strengths within the family's problem situations and goals.

Along with a family's strengths, it is important to determine its pace. A family member's pace is his or her rate of progress toward an established goal. In other words, it's the rate at which a family member chooses to move through what is being discussed and taught.

A family's pace is as individualized as the family itself. As you build on strengths and teach family members new skills, continue to assess the rate at which they are acquiring new skills. Some families like to analyze and try out each new step of a skill a dozen times before taking on the next new step. Others can be taught by having the entire skill presented at one session. Respecting the family's pace will help reduce both the family's anxiety and your anxiety over promoting change that will last over time.

These three basic steps of assessment are just an overview of what should be an intricate process in your work with a family. Remember that the family's treatment can only be effective if your assessment is accurate. These areas — determining the family system, the ABC's to goal-oriented problems areas, and family capabilities — are very much inclusive of each other, and assessment often occurs simultaneously in all three areas.

In order to gather information about a family, our Consultants use an Assessment Questionnaire. This questionnaire can help you start identifying the who, what, where, when, why, and how of a family's situation as you begin your intervention. Sometimes you may need to ask these questions directly; other times you may obtain the answers by observing the family. You will gradually gather more information as you build relationships with family members. Often, family members will change their answers and will frequently reveal more as you gain their trust.

The Assessment Questionnaire is not inclusive, but it will help you in your observations of the family and its environment. Like a puzzle, you must fit each piece of information into an assessment that makes sense and is a workable tool for treatment. Continually assessing and reassessing a family throughout your intervention with them provides an assessment process that is compatible with change and that will monitor the behaviors that brought you into the home in the first place. Assessment also allows you to focus on the family's strengths as well as its problems. It allows you to look for the potential in each family and prioritize goals. Asking thorough questions about each family and family situation reduces the need to "interpret" what is going on in the home.

The Assessment Questionnaire and an exercise on how to use it are at the end of the chapter. After reading the questionnaire, move to Exercise 1 and follow the directions.

# Summary

Family assessment is a continuous process that relies on thorough observation of the family, other significant people, and the family's environment.

Three types of skills are essential for your success as a Consultant. They are conceptual skills, technical skills, and interpersonal skills. Conceptual skills, which deal with how to think about families, form the core skills for assessment. Conceptual skills serve as a foundation for all other family therapy skills because how you conceptualize a family and its situation determines what technical and interpersonal skills you will use.

Five guidelines that will help make your assessments more accurate and effective are: 1) treat each family as unique; 2) focus on the present; 3) meet the family's physical needs first; 4) validate your observations; and 5) make assessment a continuous process.

The process of assessment can be divided into three basic steps: 1) determine the family's system and how it functions as a unit, and identify the family's roles and structure; 2) identify the ABC's of goal-oriented problem areas; and 3) identify the family's capabilities.

Using a set of thorough assessment questions will help you observe and gather all the crucial, specific information you need to accurately assess a family. Items of information should fit together like the pieces of a puzzle into an assessment that makes sense and is a workable tool for treatment.

# Assessment Questionnaire

## 1. How does the family's system function?

List the family members' activities, places they go, and the significant people around them to discover how they interact with their world.

- Which people are considered members of the family?
- What role does each person play?
- Who holds the most power in these relationships?
- Are there any spoken or unspoken rules for interacting with others?
- Do some rules apply to some family members but not others?
- How are decisions made?
- Are conflicts resolved? If so, how?
- Are emotions expressed? If so, how? Which emotions are acceptable?
- How well does the family communicate?
- How does the family organize to get tasks done?
- Do the tasks get accomplished?
- How does the family structure its time?
- Does one parent or the other have a greater strength in imposing order in the household?
- What customs may be influencing family roles and structure?
- What kind of internal boundaries does the family set for itself? Between generations? Between individual family members (e.g. do the children ever act as the parents, and vice versa)?
- How clear and/or tight are the boundaries between the family and external systems (e.g. extended family, neighbors, friends)?
- Do outsiders know about the family's secrets and problems?
- Do any neighbors act as extended family, lending support and advice?
- What is the physical environment of the home and how does it affect interactions?
- How does the location of the home or surroundings in the neighboring area affect the family (e.g. isolation, crowding, safety)?
- Does the home and neighborhood offer sufficient resources for the family (e.g. recreation, employment)?

## 2. What are the ABC's?

### Antecedents
- What happened prior to the behavior?
- What was each family member doing prior to the behavior occurring?
- Were there any non-family members present? If so, what were they doing?
- Were there any indicators that the behavior was going to occur?

### Behaviors
- What was the behavior?
- What specific behaviors, including verbal, made up the behavior?
- When and where does the behavior occur?
- Has the behavior ever been worse or better?
- How often does the behavior occur?
- When does the behavior occur more or less frequently?
- Did the behavior stop? If so, how?

### Consequences
- What happened immediately after the

behavior occurred? What was the "pay-off" of the behavior?

- Who reacted to the behavior and in what way?
- Who is concerned about the behavior? What is their typical response to the behavior?
- What effect, if any, does the reaction of others to the problem behavior seem to have? Does the behavior increase or decrease in frequency, intensity, duration?
- Are responses to the behavior consistent or inconsistent?
- Are reactions to the behavior stronger or more frequent at certain times of day or in different locations?

### 3. What are the family's capabilities?

#### Physical limitations
- Are there any physical disabilities?
- Is anyone unemployed due to a physical limit?
- Does anyone in the family have a physical illness?

#### Emotional limitations
- Has there been any emotional traumas within the family?
- Do any family members have mental health problems?
- Are there any impending emotional traumas (terminal illness, job loss, eviction, etc.)?

#### Intellectual limitations
- Are there developmental disabilities?
- Do family members learn through auditory, visual, or hands-on instruction?
- What is the variation, if any, among family members' intellectual levels?
- What is the extent of their capabilities within their limits?
- How, if any, do their limits affect the family system as a whole?

#### Family strengths
- What are the family members already doing right within the problem area?
- What is each member doing that affects the family system?
- What else is the family doing right that might affect the problem area?
- What has the family done in the past with a similar problem?
- Does the family react the same way or differently regardless of which family member is involved in the problem-area behavior?

#### Family pace
- What rate of learning skills is each family member comfortable with?
- Does the actual rate of learning coincide with the rate at which the family members say they can or want to learn?
- Are you continuing to teach based on the family's rate of learning?

# Exercise 1:
# The Chen Family

The following section contains observations of the Chen family. Read carefully for details and then use the Assessment Questionnaire to prepare as complete an assessment as possible with the information that is provided. You should be able to answer many of the questions, but not all. Record the questions you are addressing and their answers on a separate sheet of paper. Remember that actual assessments require the use of your eyes and ears, working directly with the family involved. This exercise is only an approximation of how you would assess the Chen family.

*The Chen family consists of Nick and Joyce, and their three children — Ramone, 15, Kayla, 12, and Lee, 6. This is the second marriage for both Nick and Joyce. They have been married for one year. Ramone and Kayla are from Joyce's first marriage. Their father has visitation every other weekend and lives in the same town. Lee is from Nick's first marriage. Nick has joint custody of Lee. Lee lives with Nick every other week; Lee lives with his mother the rest of the time. Lee's mother lives only one mile away and calls him frequently while he is with his father. You have noticed that these calls cause friction between Lee and his stepmother, Joyce.*

*You have been working with the family for one week now. The family was referred for services because neglect charges were filed against Nick and Joyce by Lee's school. Lee has arrived at school in frigid temperatures with only a spring jacket. His teachers have said he comes to school dirty during the weeks he lives with his father. They said Lee has complained about not getting breakfast at his father's house. He also has complained about being home alone after school until 6:30 p.m. Joyce usually returns home then after picking up Ramone and Kayla at gymnastics practice.*

*Nick and Joyce both leave for work at 7:30 a.m. They ask Ramone and Kayla to make sure Lee gets on his bus on time for school in the morning. Both parents arrive home from work about 6:30 p.m. Nick has complained that his ex-wife doesn't pack appropriate clothes for Lee to wear when he stays with him. Nick and Joyce told you that the next-door neighbor, Mrs. Lopez, is always home during the day and that Lee can go to her house for help in case of an emergency after school.*

*You have seen the children ignore their parents' requests until they've been asked to do something three or four times. They do, however, go to bed on a schedule at the same time every night. Nick is always the one to enforce bedtimes. When the children disobey, there is a lot of yelling by the children and the parents. You have not seen any physical punishment used. When the children fight, Ramone and Kayla usually team up against Lee. If Joyce comes to Lee's aid, he recoils from her touch. You have seen the two older children sent to their rooms for fighting, but not on a consistent basis.*

*Nick and Joyce have asked for help making the children "mind better." Since they both work, they especially want the children to help put things away at the end of the day. Items needed for the next day are frequently lost. When the children are asked to help straighten up the house, they ignore the request and watch television. Then the shouting begins. Once Nick became so angry, he left the house and didn't return until 2 a.m.*

*The Chens live in a small, rented duplex with little built-in storage space. Most of the basement is crammed full of items that are not in boxes. There is a neighborhood park two blocks away with playground equipment and a basketball court.*

*You've noticed that Joyce does needlecraft projects every evening. She likes to shop for craft supplies on Saturdays when she gets the chance. Nick enjoys fishing on the weekends and bowls in a Tuesday night league. Everyone in the family likes popcorn, which the family has every Sunday night instead of a regular meal.*

How many questions from the Assessment Questionnaire were you able to answer from this example? Did you identify the family's strengths in these areas: discipline, monitoring, meeting basic needs of children, and nurturing? Also, what conceptual skills and technical skills might you use? What interpersonal skills might you use to draw out more information as you continue your assessment?

# 5

# Building Relationships

*Webster's Dictionary* defines a relationship as a logical or natural association between two or more things or people. At Boys Town, building a relationship is a process by which trust and positive regard are developed between two or more people. Developing a strong relationship with the family you are working with not only is essential to your work but also is the foundation upon which change is made. Without a good relationship, families are likely to withhold pertinent information, cancel sessions, resist using techniques they have learned, and/or drop out of treatment (Fleischman, Horne, & Arthur, 1983). Building a strong positive relationship with a family creates an atmosphere that will foster the family's cooperation and help you determine what to do in order to enhance this cooperation.

Building a relationship is an essential component to a successful intervention. At Boys Town we view the relationship that a Consultant establishes with a family as a product or an outcome of using the intervention techniques correctly and adhering to several principles. Building relationships is not a technique in which the Consultant can simply follow the steps and utilize them. There is a process to building relationships, but the process is more general and cannot be broken down into specific steps. Building relationships is much more than a process; it is a goal that the Consultant must strive for so that the intervention can be successful.

Much of the effectiveness of the Boys Town Family Preservation program is based on having a strong therapeutic relationship with the family. This relationship must be founded in a sense of mutual respect, trust, and understanding of each other's strengths. Throughout the intervention, the Consultant will be assisting the family to make many changes so that goals can be achieved quickly and effectively. A relationship that will facilitate this change must be developed and maintained. There are several guiding principles that the Consultant can follow that help establish a therapeutic relationship. These principles will be presented in this chapter.

Showing that you understand a family's situation is an essential ingredient in building a relationship. If you demonstrate an awareness of the family members' feelings, concerns, and views of the world, they will feel that you understand them. You must communicate a respect for each individual's worth, integrity, and abilities. This includes seeing each person as unique, and not part of the stereotypes connected with his or her race, sex, age, religion, or group affiliation (Ivey & Authier, 1971).

While respect by itself cannot establish a relationship, it is the basis upon which the relationship is built. Respect is showing that you value the other person, and you should communicate it in everything you do and say. In 1967, Truax and Carkhuff empirically validated the importance of empathy, respect, and genuineness. By the 1970s they had amassed more than 100 studies relating these three characteristics to constructive change in families. Lazarus (1993) believes that an effective Consultant, in order to enhance treatment compliance and to offset resistance, needs a wide range of techniques at his or her disposal (intervention techniques), and a flexible repertoire of relationship styles and stances to suit families' different needs and expectations. These would include being able to work with families at different levels of formality or informality, knowing how much personal information to disclose, knowing when to initiate topics of conversation, and knowing when and how to be directive, supportive, or reflective.

## Principles for Building Relationships

Building relationships can be accomplished through:

1. **Understanding and respecting the family's beliefs and values.**
2. **Recognizing the family members as experts.**
3. **Showing support for and being empathetic to the family.**
4. **Building on strengths and praising.**
5. **Providing concrete services.**
6. **Using the family's "lingo."**
7. **Knowing when and how to self-disclose.**
8. **Effectively using intervention techniques.**
9. **Reframing hopelessness into hopefulness.**
10. **Normalizing a family's situation and a child's behaviors.**
11. **Using humor .**
12. **Understanding and adapting interpersonal behaviors.**

Let's look at these areas more closely.

## 1. Understanding and respecting the family's beliefs and values.

As discussed in Chapter 2 (Cultural and Family Differences), you are not in the home to impose your beliefs and values on family members but to respect and accept theirs. Instead of looking at a family as being resistant and a caseworker as being impartial, Consultants must assess whether or not their cultural values and lifestyles might present opposing goals and expectations to the family (Berg, 1994). Have an open mind and give the family members the benefit of the doubt; look at things from their point of view. Instead of expecting the family to adopt your way of thinking and doing things, remind yourself to adapt to the family's way of thinking and doing things.

Remember, respect is acknowledging that different perceptions of the same situation are being heard, honored, and appreciated. You must respect the clients' autonomy, and personal, familial, and cultural boundaries. You must positively value the family members' experiences, and if there are differences of opinion, appreciate their right to be different and actively support these differences. In developing a relationship with a family, it is important to remember that there are more similarities than differences between you and that family. At some time, we have all needed help, we have all become angry, we have all been unfair, and we have all had dirty, messy houses (Kinney, Haapala, & Booth, 1991).

## 2. Recognizing the family members as experts.

When working with a family, you must accept that the family members know more about their family than you do. They are the experts on their family, family situations, and circumstances; you are the expert on interactions, behaviors, and solutions within family situations. As a Consultant, you need to join these two areas of expertise to elicit the best long-term change in a family (Patterson, 1971). You must join the family at its level, its culture, and its expertise.

Recognizing the family's expertise is vital to establishing a relationship. Sometimes it may be necessary to postpone knowing the "facts" about the details of the family's situation. In other words, you will want to avoid giving suggestions, making verbal assessments, or advising the family even if the family asks for your input. Allow the family members to feel as if they are the experts and state that you cannot possibly give advice without learning from them all that they know about their situation. It's like going to a medical doctor for unusual and painful symptoms you are experiencing. You might want the doctor to quickly diagnose your problem and prescribe medicine that will help you get well. However, if your doctor diagnosed the problem without allowing you to first fully describe your symptoms, you would likely be skeptical of what he tells you. You would question the accuracy of the diagnosis because your doctor did not take the time to hear your concerns and understand the problem you were experiencing.

Look at the family as your partner in change. Actively involve family members in problem identification, goal-setting, and intervention strategies. This active involvement will empower family members to recognize their roles in bringing about change and assist them in internalizing the change once it occurs. This does not mean that you condone the antisocial, illegal, or unhealthy belief system or behaviors the family may have. The relationship must be a collaborative venture between you and the family. There must be a belief that the family is competent enough to know what is good for its members and that the family can solve problems and has solved problems in the past (Berg, 1994).

**3. Showing support for and being empathetic to the family.** Supporting a family means being there and providing encouragement during difficult times. Being empathetic means telling a family that you understand and that you are there to help. In building a relationship, you will want to avoid the appearance of siding with or against any particular person or faction within the family. By supporting each individual family member equally you can uncover each perspective of the situation and how it affects each member emotionally and behaviorally. At Boys Town, we find this guideline useful in situations where there may be conflicting issues. We believe that if you find something positive about one family member, you should try to identify something positive about another family member and point it out when you can. By supporting each family member with encouragement and suggestions, your relationship will remain strong with each member. Your support should reflect confidence in the ability of each family member to fix his or her own problems.

As you build on a family's strengths and skills, the family will face new and different stressful situations. You can show your support by being available to the family 24 hours a day, seven days a week, answering calls from your families as quickly as possible, and advocating for families when necessary while apologizing for your mistakes or misunderstandings. You can show support by being flexible and scheduling visits when the family states it needs you most. It's important to believe that families are doing the best they can with the resources they have. If you believe this, then it's easier to provide support to families each and every time they encounter a crisis.

**4. Building on strengths and praising.** Once you have accepted the family's expertise on itself, find out exactly what that expertise is and build on it. Determining what family members are doing correctly within the family's agenda, problem areas, and other areas of life will assist you in building a strong relationship with them. (Identifying and building on family members' strengths will be discussed in more detail in Chapter 20.)

Understanding that encouraging and praising family members when they are doing things correctly will enhance your relationship when you first begin to work with a family and throughout your intervention. Frequently complimenting family members for appropriate behaviors, even those behaviors that are not related to the problem (the way parents interact with their child, the cleanliness of the home, family members taking time for themselves, the children doing their homework or leaving notes when they leave the home), will help enhance their self-esteem and competency, thereby helping you build a strong positive alliance with the family.

Be aware of the expertise of the family members within their environment; for instance, skill at woodworking, knitting, putting puzzles together, or sportsmanship (fishing and hunting). Demonstrate positive regard for your families. Demonstrate faith and trust in your family's ability to change. If you are going to help your families, you must believe they can be helped. Identifying a family's positive assets and praising them, then helping the family to build on those strengths will assist in creating a strong working relationship between you and the family.

**5. Providing concrete services.** Providing a concrete service means helping family members by doing specific tasks for them and with them that they deem necessary and important. These services may include helping a parent cook dinner, cleaning animal feces off the floor, organizing closets or financial records, mowing the grass, or taking a family member to the doctor or to the store. They also can include playing cards with the family, helping a teenager clean her car, or baby-sitting so the parents can take a few hours off.

There are many advantages to providing concrete services to a family.

First, it helps strengthen relationships. It is crucial in building relationships with a family to avoid being so therapy-oriented that you do not help with the everyday tasks the family needs to accomplish. When you help with dinner or wash dishes or bathe the children during your visits, the family will become more comfortable with you and view you and your visits as positive rather than negative. If family members don't need anything done in the home or they insist that they don't want help, then talk about their interests, hobbies, occupations, pictures of kids on the wall, or what they do on their days off. Homebuilders (Kinney, Haapala, & Booth, 1991) refers to this as "chit chat" therapy — noticing items of interest in the home, or commenting on the weather or the drive home.

Second, providing concrete services makes your visit less intrusive. It is difficult for any individual or family to have people come into their home for several hours five to six days a week. Having you in the home more than a few hours a week can be overwhelming to a family. A family can begin to feel resentful if your presence prevents the members from taking care of their daily routine. By providing concrete services, you encourage the family members to continue with their normal routine. Assisting them in this routine helps break down barriers and allows you to see the family engaging in activities that might provide insight into areas that need to be addressed.

Third, providing concrete services provides insight into the family's lifestyle. By working with and for the family, you can observe family members engage in daily activities in their natural environment. This is one of the advantages of doing therapy within the home. When you become an active part of the family's day-to-day routine, the family becomes more comfortable with your presence and the "masks" and "costumes" often come off. The family is more likely to interact naturally, allowing you to more easily identify strengths and problems.

**6. Using the family's "lingo."** Every family has its own language — words, phrases, nicknames, and ways of saying them that are part of how the family communicates. As part of your intervention, it is important that you attempt to match your communication style to that of the family's. This is done by using the gestures and words the family uses. By avoiding professional jargon and using simple everyday language, you will enhance your relationship by talking to family members in a way they can relate to. For example, let's say a parent calls any positive behavior by the child "a miracle"; when you observe the child engaging in a similar positive behavior, report to the parents that "a miracle" just occurred. Or, if a family tends to give long detailed explanations of situations, you would want to match this manner of communication by giving detailed explanations of the skills you are teaching. Some families use the terms "unattached," "codependent," or "reinforcers"; other families use words like "cold," "needy," and "prizes" instead.

When using a family's "lingo," you must be careful not to appear demeaning. You also should not imitate inappropriate language that family members might use; if family members call each other derogatory names, you don't want to condone this by imitating this behavior. But by communicating with family members using their own words, you can establish an added measure of respect in your relationship with the family.

**7. Knowing when and how to use self-disclosure.** Self-disclosure means revealing to family members similar personal experiences from your own past that relate to their current situation. Sharing these feelings, thoughts, and problems will help the family feel more comfortable about working with you. Disclosures should be brief and should be made only when they directly relate to the family's situation. That way, you don't distract from the family's issues and are able to remain focused on the family and its situation. In disclosing information about yourself, you should refer to the past rather than the future and, when possible, allude to a positive out-

come. Referring to the past shows families that you have had a similar experience and made it through; it gives no "maybes" about the future. Disclosing only those situations that had a positive outcome allows the family to see light at the end of what might seem like a very long dark tunnel.

**8. Effectively using intervention techniques.** Building and maintaining therapeutically strong relationships is accomplished in part by effectively using intervention techniques with the family. In the next section, the intervention techniques used in the Boys Town program will each be fully described. These techniques are the tools that the Consultant uses to assist a family in making the changes it desires. But like any kind of tool, if not used correctly, these techniques will not help to fix the problems and the relationships will become strained. It would be similar to a carpenter using a saw incorrectly or opting to use a hammer when a screwdriver is needed; the project being worked on will likely be flawed or unsalvageable. The Consultant needs to know the correct way to utilize the intervention techniques and how they work to bring about change. Not all techniques will work to fix all problems. The Consultant needs to know which techniques to use, and when and how to use them. When working with the family, the skilled Consultant varies the use of intervention techniques and assesses the impact that each technique has on each family member. Being sensitive to the family members' learning styles and adjusting the techniques accordingly strengthens the relationships between the family members and the Consultant.

**9. Reframing hopelessness into hopefulness.** Reframing means taking a basically negative situation, trying to decide what is positive about it, then tying it back into the family's treatment goals. For example, Mom is very anxious about her daughter returning home from the hospital after a suicide attempt and is saying things like, "What if she tries to kill herself again?" Using reframing, you can restate and validate mom's fears while changing the hopeless statements into hopeful ones. For example, you could respond by telling Mom, "You're well prepared now. You know what to look for and I'll be here to help you." Often, families view their situations negatively and feel hopeless about change. Your ability to change their hopelessness into hopefulness by restating their negative comments as positive comments will enhance your relationship with the family. Keeping the family members focused on positive action-oriented statements will help them buy into services, thus reducing resistance during your initial visits with them and later in times of crisis. Reframing will be discussed in more detail in Chapter 12.

**10. Normalizing a family's situation and a child's behaviors.** Some families you will work with will believe that their situation is unusual, that they are the only ones who have ever faced the problems they face. Parents also may not understand what behaviors are age-appropriate for their children. These parents may think that their children are the only kids who behave the way they behave.

Assuring these families and parents that their problems are common and that others face the same situations can help parents see themselves and their children in a more posi-

tive light (Fleischman, Horne, & Arthur, 1983). In offering reassurance, it is important that you are sincere and sensitive to the family's perspective of the situation and the behaviors occurring in the home; don't belittle the problem. Many families start counseling services with feelings of hopelessness, guilt, anger, or fear. Sometimes, assuring family members that other families have been in similar situations and that some of their children's behaviors are age-appropriate will help reduce their anxiety and improve your relationship with them.

It is important to note that normalizing statements are used to respond to and acknowledge the family's feelings and situation as normal. Normalizing should never be used to discount or minimize a family's perceptions.

**11. Using humor.** Using humor and seeing the lighter side of things can help clients relax and view their problem as less than hopeless. It also can reduce anger and defensiveness. Be sure not to make fun of the family's problem; don't try to make a joke out of something that is not funny and don't try to force humor on a family.

Many Consultants have the natural ability to see the humor in situations. Appropriately sharing the lighter side can help family members put their problems in perspective and show that you accept that human beings can make mistakes.

**12. Understanding and adapting interpersonal behaviors.** A Consultant often shows sincerity, respect, and acceptance of the family and its situation in his or her verbal and nonverbal behaviors. These include such things as eye contact (Is it appropriate and positive?); body language (Is it effective? Does it communicate assurance?); voice tone (Is it positive and assured?); and gestures (Are they congruent and confident?). Your proximity, volume and rate of speech, facial expression, and in some cases, the act of physically touching the family members, all are components that reflect the quality of your sincerity, respect, and acceptance of the family.

While assessing a family's values, be sure to determine how members feel about the verbal and nonverbal behaviors you might use during treatment. Some family members may resent physical contact or avoid direct eye contact while others might lean in very close to talk or speak in loud voice tones. Understand and adapt how you interpersonally relate to the family members according to what will make them feel most comfortable. This adaptability will build a strong relationship.

## Summary

Having a good relationship is vital to change. Often, however, families are leery of change. This is probably most evident when family members are being asked to replace old patterns of behavior with behaviors that will allow the children to stay in the home. Many families have been doing the same thing year after year. They are used to having agencies come in and go out of their lives. Serious resistance has a major impact on the Consultant's behavior and can often lead to burnout and can slow, if not stop, the family's progress toward goals. Noncompliance and abrasive refusal to cooperate in treatment are often a result of a family's cautious attitude toward change. Sometimes, families will show

resistance and be unwilling to participate in treatment because of the Consultant's disregard for establishing a therapeutic relationship. If you encounter resistance, lack of motivation, or noncooperation from a family member, evaluate your own behaviors while realizing the difficulties many people have in making changes. More than likely, there is something you can do to improve the relationship so that the family becomes less resistant to the intervention process. Building relationships by adhering to all the principles discussed in this chapter will help you establish and maintain relationships that foster change, not hinder it.

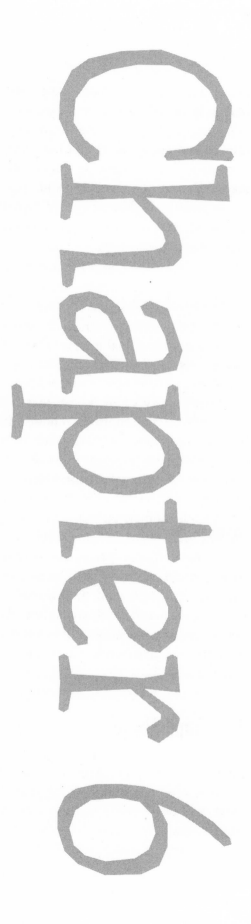

# Detecting Child Abuse and Neglect

More than half of the families that Boys Town Family Preservation Services has worked with have been referred because of child abuse or neglect. That's why it is vital for Consultants to have a strong foundation in understanding child maltreatment, as well as knowing what to look for and what to do if abuse or neglect is suspected.

Abuse occurs when a caretaker who is responsible for a child's welfare commits an act that harms the child or allows an event to occur that causes harm or puts the child in danger. The caretaker acts knowingly and willingly, and the act that harms or endangers the child is not an accident. Neglect occurs when "a caretaker responsible for the child, either deliberately or by extraordinary inattentiveness, permits the child to experience avoidable present suffering and/or fails to provide one or more of the ingredients generally deemed essential for developing a person's physical, intellectual, and emotional capacities" (Polansky, 1987, p. 15).

This chapter will discuss the primary categories of child maltreatment, defining them and identifying indicators that can help you recognize and assess actual as well as potentially dangerous situations. It also will explain the importance of knowing state regulations and policy concepts that are necessary for the protection of children. Every state has a legal definition of child abuse; some are more specific than others. Each state law also specifies how reports of abuse are to be made. It is important that Consultants know their own state's definition of abuse and reporting requirements. The information in this chapter is generic and generally valid regardless of jurisdiction.

## Physical Abuse

Physical abuse is defined as an act that causes a nonaccidental injury; for example, a violent assault by a parent, caretaker, or guardian that results in an injury to the child. An abuse injury often is one that leaves a mark that can be seen up to 24 hours after the incident; other abuse injuries, such as broken bones or brain damage, can be internal. Examples of external injuries include cord burns, a burn inflicted by an appliance such as a hot iron, submersion burns (a child being dunked in hot water), cigarette burns, bruises in the shape of hand prints, and injuries that would be difficult for a child to receive accidentally (bruises behind the ear, welts, fractures, or bite marks). Spanking also can be considered physical abuse if it leaves a visible mark that remains 24 hours after the spanking occurred.

## Emotional Abuse

Emotional abuse occurs when a parent or caretaker treats a child in ways that cause emotional or psychological damage to the child. Emotional abuse includes situations in which a parent, caretaker, or guardian belittles or verbally and emotionally assaults a child. This would include frequent and excessive use of statements like: "You're stupid," "You're ugly," "You're fat," "I wish I never had you," "Your mom/dad left because they couldn't stand you," "Everything is your fault," or "I hate you." Violently cursing at a child or calling a child names also is a form of emotional abuse.

There are other types of emotional abuse. Confinement is when a child is tied up, or locked in a closet, attic, basement, or car for hours as punishment. Inadequate nurturing is the failure to provide proper care that children need to thrive and grow. Knowingly permitting a child to engage in or act out antisocial behavior, such as delinquency, and not dealing with such behavior in a responsible and proper manner is a form of emotional abuse. Refusing to provide mental health care for a child who has been diagnosed with a serious emotional problem is yet another form of emotional abuse, and this also can be considered medical abuse.

It is important to understand that of all the types of abuse, emotional abuse is the most difficult to prove because the injury it inflicts is internal rather than external. Because it is difficult to prove emotional abuse, child protective service agencies may classify such reports as unfounded or charge a parent with another type of abuse (e.g. physical abuse or neglect).

## Sexual Abuse

Finkelhor (1986) defines child sexual abuse as any interaction, contact, or noncontact between a child and any adult in which the child is being used for the sexual stimulation of the adult or another person. Sexual abuse can be committed by a parent, caretaker, or guardian, or by a neighbor, stranger, or family friend. A child also can sexually abuse another child.

When charges are filed in such cases, the terms used and even the agencies responsible for investigating the incidents may vary from state to state. Often, the way charges are filed or investigated is determined by the identity of the alleged perpetrator. As a Consultant, it is essential that you learn the regulations of the state in which you are working.

A sexual crime committed by a neighbor, stranger, or non-caretaker is generally reported to law enforcement and is prosecuted under the criminal code as a sexual assault or rape. Crimes committed by guardians usually are first reported to the state child protective agencies. This same rule generally applies to physical abuse as well.

Physical signs of sexual abuse include: hickeys and/or bruises on the face, neck, groin, buttocks, or inner thigh; underwear or diapers that are stained, torn, or bloody; and complaints by a child of pain, itching, cuts, bruises, or burning in the genital areas. A clear indicator may be the evidence of a sexually transmitted disease, especially in very young children.

## Neglect

Neglect can involve the abandonment of a child by the parent; the refusal of the parent to seek or allow medical treatment for illnesses or disabilities; inadequate monitoring, either intentional (i.e. knowingly letting a child take drugs, drink alcohol, engage in sexual acts, etc.) or unintentional (i.e. through caretaker inattentiveness, a child is sexually abused by others, plays in traffic, falls downstairs, drinks toxic substances, etc.), that places the child at risk of being harmed; and failure to provide adequate nutrition, clothing, or shelter, creating a health risk to the child.

Contrary to some people's beliefs, a messy house, a missed meal, or a meal that is not nutritiously balanced are not necessarily signs of neglect; neither is forgetting to pick up a child from day care for several hours. What needs to be considered is whether there is a pattern of such activities. Is the house so unkempt on a daily basis that it poses a health risk? Did the family miss one meal or were there several days when no meals were prepared and there was no food available for the child? Do the parents consistently leave their children at day care or with others for unreasonable lengths of time and sometimes forget to pick them up at all? These all are issues that need to be assessed before a neglect charge is considered. Also, a family can be charged with neglect only if services or monetary means that can prevent a neglectful situation from occurring are made available and the parent or guardian does not utilize them.

Neglect also includes educational neglect, a situation in which a parent, caretaker, or guardian knowingly permits chronic truancy, repeatedly keeps a child home from school without cause, or fails to enroll a child in school. Laws regarding educational neglect vary from state to state. Most states have a law that requires children to attend school until they are 16 years old. Some states, however, have exceptions to such requirements, such as allowing a child to quit school after he or she has completed the eighth grade, regardless of the child's age. These differences make it cru-

cial for you to become familiar with the laws in your state. Understanding these laws will assist you in appropriately assessing a family and its needs.

## Accountability and Documentation

Before working with families, be sure to review your agency's policies and procedures concerning abuse and neglect, or begin to develop a set if none exist.

State laws mandate that professionals who deal with the care of children are required to report any suspicions of child abuse or neglect. These professionals are considered "mandatory reporters." Because Consultants provide professional services to children, it is essential for family preservation programs to develop some basic policies for staff members who deal with potential child maltreatment situations. One policy is to require Consultants to notify their supervisor and the referral agency about suspected abuse or neglect as soon as possible. If, with the supervisor's consultation, child abuse or neglect is suspected, a report to the local child protective agency is necessary.

It also is recommended that in all cases you keep clear and specific documentation of your suspicions and/or observations, and any contacts you make. If a report is filed, the state in which you provide services may require you to file relevant documentation. You also should document all injuries to a child who is receiving services from your agency whether the injuries are suspicious or not. Investigate all injuries and explore every incident from both the parent's and the child's perspectives. If you suspect abuse, refer to the subsequent policy. If abuse is not suspected,

document the injury on an injury log to protect the child, your agency, and possibly the family. This information also can be helpful in determining whether a pattern of injuries is developing.

## Consultant's Role in Reporting

Working with families that have mistreated their children is a difficult and delicate endeavor. For Consultants, several values may be in the balance while providing services. For example, when does the safety of the children outweigh the rights of the parents to raise their children? If parents have physically abused their child, you may question whether those parents still have their rights. How much emotional abuse must a child endure before out-of-home placement would be more beneficial to the child than remaining in the home? How can one focus on a family's strengths when the primary problems are the parent's neglectful or abusive behaviors? Shouldn't the focus be on stopping the abuse? These are difficult value questions to consider, and must always be weighed carefully in the Consultant's mind. These questions force the Consultant to constantly evaluate if the children's needs are being met in the home and if the intervention is effectively protecting the children.

In order to provide family preservation services, the Consultant needs to hold to the fundamental belief that most parents, whether they have been charged with abuse or not, are doing the best they can with the skills they have. That is to say, abusive parents have skill deficits that prevent them from raising their children without mistreating them. But these parents can learn alternative skills necessary to raise their children in safe and nonabusive environments. They can learn to replace physically harmful or neglectful behaviors with alternative behaviors that are useful in caring for their children safely. The goal of family preservation services is to provide parents with the skills they may need to remedy the problems of child maltreatment while simultaneously ensuring that the children are free from harm.

Consultants must keep in mind that it is never their full responsibility to determine if abuse or neglect is occurring. While providing services, the Consultant is responsible for being aware of any potentially dangerous or abusive situations that may have occurred, are occurring, or may occur in the future. Being aware of "red flags" that indicate child maltreatment, the Consultant has a responsibility to report those "red flags" of suspicions to the child protective agency authorities so that they can decide whether or not child abuse or neglect occurred. The Consultant must follow the reporting guidelines of the state, and allow the child protective agency or law enforcement authorities to make the determinations of abuse or neglect and rule whether the child is in imminent danger at the time of the report.

Sometimes, it is difficult for the Consultant to make a report of abuse or neglect against a family member with whom a relationship has been established. Making allegations of child abuse or neglect can damage the relationship with the family. Family members may react with anger, mistrust, and avoidance. But you can minimize the potential problems that may arise if an abuse report must be made against the family. When you first begin services with the family, the report-

ing guidelines should be discussed with the family. The family needs to understand that you are mandated by law to report any suspicions of abuse or neglect. Also, when a report must be made, you may opt to inform family members that it is necessary for you to make the report. This is permissible as long as this action doesn't hinder the investigation or potentially endanger the child further. Many families feel a sense of relief when you communicate honestly with them and offer to provide support during any investigations that may result from your report. It is essential to minimize the negative effects that reporting abuse and neglect can have on your relationship with the family because you will most likely continue working with the family after a report is made.

Sometimes, you might hesitate to make such allegations because you want to give the family the benefit of the doubt. When you've invested a lot of time and energy in an intervention and seen a family make progress, it can be difficult to report suspicions of abuse or neglect. After all, you have been working hard to focus on the family's strengths and not to fixate on its problems. But you must keep in mind that in order to make services successful, any potentially harmful behaviors must be addressed. This includes making reports to the proper authorities. The most successful intervention is when children remain safe from harm.

Information on issues surrounding abuse and neglect is readily available. Because we have limited ourselves to the basics in this book, we are including at the end of this chapter a short list of books that may be helpful to you in detecting child maltreatment and in working with the victims of abuse, as well as with their families. We also would encourage you to attend local training workshops and seminars to learn more about the child abuse and neglect standards in your service area.

Bolton Jr., F.G., Morris, L.A., & MacEachron, A.E. (1989). **Males at risk: The other side of child sexual abuse.** Newbury Park, CA: Sage.

Brassard, M.R., Germain, R., & Hart, S.N. (Eds.)(1987). **The psychological maltreatment of children and youth.** New York: Pergamon Press.

Finkelhor, D. (1979). **Sexually victimized children.** New York: Free Press.

Garbarino, J., Brookhouser, P., & Authier, K. (1987). **Special children, special risks: The maltreatment of children with disabilities.** New York: Aldine de Gruyter.

Helfer, R.E., & Kempe, R.S. (1987). **The battered child** (4th ed.). Chicago: University of Chicago Press.

Laird, J., & Hartman, A. (Eds.) (1985). **A handbook of child welfare: Context, knowledge and practice.** New York: Free Press.

U.S. Department of Health and Human Services, National Center on Child Abuse and Neglect (1993). **Child neglect: A guide for intervention** (The user manual series). (Contract No. HHS-105-89-1730.) Washington, DC: Westover Consultants.

U.S. Department of Health and Human Services, National Center on Child Abuse and Neglect (1993). **Child sexual abuse: Intervention and treatment issues** (The user manual series). (Subcontract No. S105-89-1730.) Washington, DC: Westover Consultants.

U.S. Department of Health and Human Services, National Center on Child Abuse and Neglect (1992). **A coordinated response to child abuse and neglect: A basic manual** (The user manual series). Single copies are available free through the Clearinghouse on Child Abuse and Neglect Information, PO Box 1182, Washington, DC, 20013-1182.

# Intervention Techniques

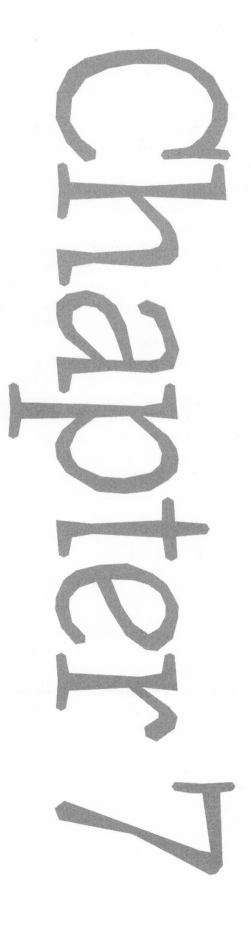

# Introduction to Intervention Techniques

Boys Town Consultants use a variety of intervention techniques to help families meet their goals and stay together. Intervention techniques are the heart of Boys Town Family Preservation Services. As the human heart keeps the body functioning and provides essential blood to the body, techniques provide the Consultant with essential skills that help keep a family functioning and intact.

By being skilled in a variety of proven intervention techniques, a Consultant can more easily advocate for the family to keep its children in the least restrictive environment possible, the family's home.

Therapists are not born with a set of characteristics or traits that enable them to effectively treat families. At Boys Town we believe Consultants can build rapport and join with a family, but that is just one essential element of working with families. As a Consultant, you need to know what to teach family members and how to teach it effectively in order to meet the family's goals, as well as those of the referring agency and your own. A fundamental belief at Boys Town is that you can empower family members by teaching skills based on their strengths so they have the capability to handle future crises or problems with little or no outside intervention. Having a repertoire of intervention tools will assist you in enhancing the families' strengths and increasing the learning process.

In 1989, the School of Social Work at the University of Utah undertook a project called the National Child Protective Services Competency-Based Training Project. One of the underlying principles of this project was that the successful demonstration of professional behavior that is intended to achieve a desired result is predicated on the **knowledge** a person has, the **skill** a person applies, the **qualities** a person possesses, and the **values** a person holds. Earlier chapters have addressed the importance of your knowledge of the family and family situations, and the importance of understanding how your values may influence your work. The chapters in this section will continue to stress these elements, as well as the skills and qualities you must possess to effectively work with families. For now, let's look more closely at the techniques a Consultant needs and why they are important.

## Tools of the Trade

At Boys Town we rely on two basic premises concerning intervention techniques:

1. **It is necessary to have a set of tools (intervention techniques) to work with families.**
2. **A variety of intervention techniques allows the Consultant to adapt treatment to meet each family's individual needs.**

It is necessary to have a set of techniques prior to working with a family in order to help the family discover its own resources and strengths. Going into a home without intervention techniques would be like sewing without a needle and thread or playing baseball without a ball and bat. Your heart and your desire may be in the right place but you won't accomplish much without the necessary tools. When you are actively involved in working with a family using a variety of intervention techniques, you can directly influence the process of change.

Teaching a family enough necessary skills to keep the children safe and at home is a Consultant's most important task. One way to enhance these skills is to bring about behavior change in an in-home therapy situation. Obviously, Consultants must be trained in methods that can teach families new behaviors.

What does this mean? First, it means you must have a network of techniques that are designed to bring about positive changes (Ivey & Authier, 1971). Second, the techniques must enable you to address a wide variety of problems. Providing service to multiproblem families continues to challenge and frustrate Consultants. Only techniques that give a Consultant a number of options in planning and carrying out an intervention can be effective. Third, families must learn skills that they can continue to use long after the intervention is completed. Consultants must be skilled in teaching skills in such a way that they have a long-term effect on the family. And finally, you must be seen as an "expert" on family systems when you start to work with a family. A family will have greater confidence in you and the intervention if you can demonstrate your expertise in this area.

# Summary

With a foundational knowledge of intervention techniques, you will have the freedom to act in the best interests of a family and in accord with the family's goals and agenda. When working with families, we often become bogged down in their many problems and situations. This creates stress and occasionally burnout. Using a diversity of techniques helps prevent burnout. Such techniques enable the Consultant to fall back and regroup, identify specific problem areas, and look for specific intervention techniques that may be applicable for that situation.

As Consultants, we know that just because a family completes our program does not mean it will never have problems again. However, we do know that because of our intervention, the family has solved small but significant problems and in the process has learned a great deal about how to find solutions in the future. Since you don't know what you'll find when you go into a family, Boys Town has a treatment strategy that uses Phases and specific intervention techniques that work in many types of family situations. Phases provide the structure for interventions while intervention techniques are the tools we use for direct treatment. In other words, the family is like a house we have come to build. Phases make up the framework of the house, the structure we work within (walls, floors, etc.). Intervention techniques are the tools we use to build with (hammer, drills, saws etc.)

Phases will be discussed in more detail in the next section. In this section, we will discuss the following intervention techniques:

**Active Listening**

**Exploration**

**Relationship-Building**

**Effective Praise**

**Metaphors**

**Circular Refocusing**

**Criticism by Suggestion**

**Reframing**

**Role-Playing**

**Confrontation**

**Mediation and Behavioral Contracting**

**Crisis Intervention**

**Modeling**

**Assignments**

**Ignoring**

**Prompts**

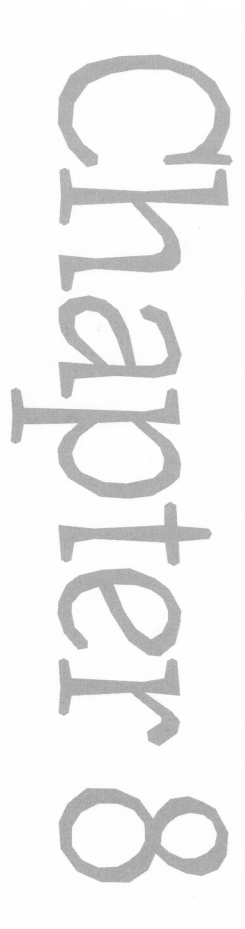

# Active Listening

If you think listening is a natural ability that depends only on a good set of ears, this chapter is for you. Active listening is one of the most critical intervention techniques and it requires trained use of not only the ears, but also the eyes, the head, the face, and the body.

To help a family, you must have accurate information about the family's problems, relationships, and affective experiences (Fleischman, Horne, & Arthur, 1983). Active listening is your tool for eliciting this information. You will want to obtain information about existing problems and gain a sufficient understanding of the family and its situation so that problems can be solved effectively (Garrett, 1942). Most of this information will come from talking with or "interviewing" family members. In 1942, Garrett wrote a book on interviewing techniques that are still useful today. Among them is the technique of active listening, the focus of this chapter.

Active listening is the ability to be attentive and selective during a conversation. As a Consultant, you need to listen not only to the family's requests but also to the undertones that may give you clues to perhaps even more serious situations that are not immediately evident. These undertones may be the nonverbal behaviors of the family, or problems or emotions that are hinted at but not openly discussed. Sometimes family members communicate without speaking. They may choose not to verbally share information with someone outside the family or may communicate with each other through body language or gestures. You must pay attention not only to the words that are spoken but also to the nonverbal messages that are given.

Listening to family members discuss their perceptions of a situation or problem in the home is a way to communicate your respect for the family. This communication is probably the most essential factor in establishing a relationship. Unless family members think their viewpoints are being understood, listened to, and taken seriously, and that their feelings and opinions are valued, they will not trust you enough to disclose personal and vulnerable information.

For instance, a mother you are working with begins a session by telling you that her caseworker is threatening to take her children away, the school is going to report her for educational neglect, and her 14-year-old son is staying out all night. She believes all of these problems stem from the move the family made one year ago. Since then, the mother and father have split up, the children are not minding, and the mother doesn't have enough money to survive without state assistance.

In this situation, you must listen not only to the facts the mother is giving you about the current situation but also to her explanations of the problems. You need to show the mother that you recognize that she knows her family and the family's situation better than you, and that you respect her expertise.

In order to create the openness that is essential to demonstrating respect, you must show a willingness to listen in a concerned, nonbiased, nonjudgmental way. Assess the situation, don't judge it. Accept the family and its perceptions just as you accept reports from other agencies, and the referring workers. Your keen ability to actively listen will allow you to understand the family's perceptions as the family chooses to present them. Active listening demonstrates to family members that you respect and are interested in their situation and their perceptions of problems. By using good active listening behavior to enhance the family's self-respect and to establish a secure atmosphere, a Consultant facilitates free expression of whatever is on the minds of family members (Ivey & Authier, 1971).

## Skills and Components

When working with a family, it is vital to find out as much information as possible before responding to what family members say or giving suggestions. While some family members may engage in much spontaneous sharing of information, others share information sparingly or not at all. When a family member is quiet, it is important for the Consultant to be comfortable with the silence. In these situations, you may be tempted to "fill the space" with words. Resist that temptation and use the silence. Being silent often encourages the family to continue talking. By respecting and observing the silence, you will be more likely to engage the individuals at their pace. Sometimes the silence is the result of reluctance to talk about painful feelings or experiences. If that seems to be the case, you might want to show empathy by using a statement like, "I know it's hard to talk about...." Then allow the individual to share what he or she is comfortable disclosing.

Interrupting family members when they are telling their "story" may cause them to stop talking. If you are talking, then you are taking up time that the family members could be using to teach you about themselves and their situation.

Consider this example: You are referred to a family in response to a physical abuse allegation. The parents begin telling their "story" of how they were raised and disciplined. If you interrupt them to get them back to your agenda (the abuse allegation), they might stop talking and you might miss some important clues about the alleged abuse: What parenting style were they raised with? Is physical discipline a cultural norm? Did their parents value physical discipline as a means of gaining respect? This is all vital information that can help you determine the direction of intervention and piece together the current issues in the home. Learning about the parents' past behaviors will help you understand the family's present behaviors.

Even when your primary interest in talking to family members is to obtain answers to particular questions, you can profit from letting the family talk freely at first. They will usually reveal the answers to many questions and often will suggest the best way to obtain other necessary information (Garrett, 1942). Once family members are talking, you won't need to say much to encourage them to continue. Simple acknowledgments (nodding your head, saying "I see," etc.), repeating one or two words the speaker has said, and one-word questions ("Then?", "And?", "Oh?") usually are sufficient.

Be sure you understand that their perspective is their perspective. If you try to redefine the perspectives of the family members, you may find yourself in an argument. This can lead to misunderstandings and mistakes on your part that can damage your relationship and your intervention with the family. If you respect the family's opinions, you can identify successes and the motivation behind the family's behaviors. Family members will most likely respond with pleasant, positive behaviors.

Even though the emphasis is on listening, there are times when you can make short statements of empathy and understanding to demonstrate to the family that you are hearing what is being said. The use of empathy and statements of understanding helps the family feel more at ease and demonstrates your concern and interest. These statements also encourage the family to talk more about difficult or emotional topics. Empathy is conveyed through statements that acknowledge the family members' feelings and experiences. Empathy is expressed when you "feel with" the individual and accurately relate that back to the individual. Empathy and statements of understanding can be words that reflect back the family members' feelings or affirm what is being said.

Nonverbal cues — especially body language — also can affect your effectiveness. How you express your interest in what the family is saying is most apparent by the way you nonverbally respond to the family. Head nods, eye contact, posture, and use of hands can be cues that indicate whether or not you are listening. Does your facial expression show interest or boredom? Does the way you're making eye contact with family members make them uncomfortable? (Are you looking at someone too long and too directly, or not at all?) To show that you are paying attention, lean forward to encourage talking, turn toward the person who is speaking, and use gestures that are appropriate and comfortable. Also, use gestures that are similar to those the family members use. (Are their gestures expansive or subtle? Do they "talk" with their hands?)

## Summary

In general, you will make more progress obtaining information by encouraging family members, showing empathy, and allowing family members to talk freely than by bombarding them with questions. This doesn't mean you sit back and let everyone talk about whatever they want. Skilled Consultants always assume an active role in listening, continually making conscious decisions about how to allow family members to express themselves and conveying those decisions through the use of the active listening technique.

Let's review the components of active listening.

1. **Limit how much you say.**
2. **Be comfortable with silence (gaps in the conversation).**
3. **Keep the conversation going by letting family members talk.**
4. **Acknowledge what is being said.**
5. **Offer statements of empathy and understanding.**
6. **Be aware of nonverbal cues.**

# 9

# Exploration

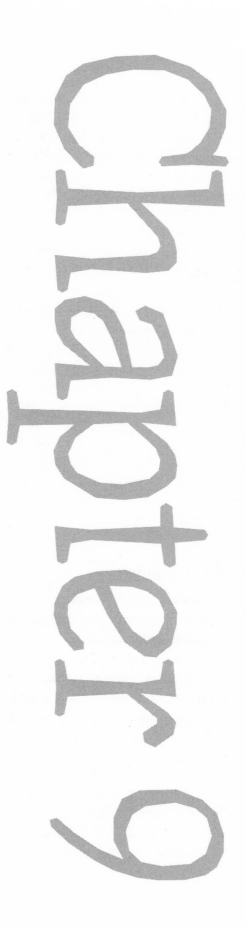

What do Christopher Columbus, Lewis and Clark, and Ponce de Leon have in common? They all were great explorers whose diligence and perseverance brought about growth and enrichment to others. As a Consultant working in the homes of families, you also need to be a great explorer in order to uncover a family's strengths, possible problem areas, and goals, and to help bring about growth and enrichment.

Exploration is another intervention technique that can be used to gather information for assessing and understanding a family. This technique involves asking questions in a friendly, warm, respectful, and sincere manner to determine how the family can be helped.

During exploration, the Consultant should move at the family's pace, listen actively, ask a variety of questions, and use mostly open-ended questions. Open-ended questions give the respondent many options for answering. They work best because they are specific enough for families to understand what's being asked and general enough for them to answer as they wish. Open-ended questions also require thought and elicit more complete information.

Exploring is a more direct technique than active listening. It is a process in which general topic areas are discussed more and more specifically so that details and pertinent information necessary for developing and carrying out the treatment plan can be obtained. Exploring allows the Consultant to funnel information from the family members by asking questions that go from general problem areas to one problem area, to the specifics of the problem, and to the family's desired goal in fixing that problem. A Consultant's decision to ask certain questions and to not ask others may appear haphazard and random, but each exchange has a purpose. Thus, the questions the Consultant decides to ask; how, when, and why they are asked; and whom is asked has significant impact on the continuous assessment process (Berg, 1994).

Exploration is used to uncover information about the family in two basic areas: the family's agenda and the situation that is endangering the child and his or her placement in the home. Let's look at these two areas more closely.

## Family's Agenda

As described in earlier chapters, a family's agenda is a problem that a family member believes the family has; usually, it is a problem that is causing the most stress in the lives of family members. These problems are the family's perception of what needs to be fixed. In working with families, stay as close to the family's definition of the problem as you can because in the end, the family will have to make any necessary changes (Berg, 1994). Some examples of a family's agenda might include, "My paycheck doesn't last until the end of the month," "Fred will not go to school," "My husband yells at me all the

time," or "My parents never let me do anything." By focusing on the family's agenda, a Consultant can reduce resistance and begin treatment based on what the family perceives as necessary.

A family's agenda may differ greatly from the situation that is endangering the child. The endangering situation is whatever is going on in the family's home that could lead to the removal of the child. For example, the parents may see Fred's refusal to go to school as the endangering situation. But the caseworker may see the parents as abusive because they use physical discipline to get Fred to school. You may assess that the parents don't know any other type of parenting technique besides physical discipline. At Boys Town, we believe all of these perceptions are important. If the child is not in imminent danger, you should focus on the family's agenda first.

There are many open-ended questions you can ask to identify a family's agenda — "What can I help you with today?", "How can I help?", "What problem, if solved, would have the greatest impact in keeping your family together?", "What bothers you most about your family?", or "What do you want to accomplish today?"

Be sure to help the family narrow its scope by asking, "If you had the ability to fix one problem, what would it be?" This helps the family focus on one problem at a time, something that is difficult for many multiproblem families. Many multiproblem families can have one or more pressing issues: chronic unemployment, frequent job changes, frequent address changes, chronic physical and mental illness, marital conflicts, truancy, delinquent behavior or poor academic performance of one or more children, long-standing intergenerational conflicts, overinvolved extended families of origin, drug and alcohol abuse, sexual abuse of children, and so on (Berg, 1994). By exploring what family members see as the most distressing, urgent problem to fix, you stay focused on their issue or agenda. Because some families have a tendency to jump from one problem or crisis to another without resolving a single issue, they feel overwhelmed and immobilized most of the time. You may feel overwhelmed and immobilized along with the family if you do not discipline yourself to maintain a focus. By modeling how to stick to one issue at a time, you help the family develop that skill also. By staying focused on one agenda item at a time, you help the family to see progress more quickly.

## Situations That Endanger the Child

The second area we want to explore is the situation that is endangering the child. As mentioned earlier, an endangering situation consists of behavior(s) that is occurring in the home that could lead to the removal of the child. The Consultant, the referring agency, and family members all can have a different perception of these behaviors. It is important when working with a family to ask the members and the referring agency how they perceive the family situation (e.g. "What has occurred that made it necessary for me to come into this home?"). Using exploratory questions like, "Could you tell me more about that?", can get the family or agency to elaborate on a point. This produces examples of specific behavior so that you are better able to understand what the family or agency is describing (e.g. "Can you give me a specific example?", "What do you mean by 'going ballistic?'", "What is the family doing that makes you feel it is being uncooperative?", "You said your dad is a jerk. What does he do when he acts like a jerk?"). These exploring questions help you define the situation that is endangering the child, using the perceptions of family members and the referring agency. You also may find that the family's agenda is the same as the situation that is endangering the child.

Be aware that families often have many agencies involved in their lives: schools, mental health agencies, hospitals, etc. All of these agencies will probably have their own views on what the endangering situation is and their own agendas on what needs to be "fixed." Your job is to listen to all of these perspectives, explore them to gain further understanding, and use the information to develop your treatment intervention. As mentioned in earlier chapters, being a mesher of goals and a sifter of information is one of your responsibilities as a family preservation Consultant.

## Antecedents, Behaviors, and Consequences

The ABC Model is a format that often is used to acquire facts about the family members' agenda and the perceptions of the situation that endangers the child. As discussed in Chapter 4, A stands for antecedents, B stands for behavior, and C stands for consequences. The purpose of using this model is to determine in what context a particular behavior is occurring. In other words, what was happening prior to the behavior (Antecedent), what exactly the behavior was (Behavior), and what happened afterwards (Consequences). Knowing what happened before and after a behavior can help the Consultant determine why the behavior occurred, and even more importantly, can help him or her change the behavior in positive, effective, and efficient ways (Father Flanagan's Boys' Home, 1990).

You might think that a family should easily be able to recognize a problem behavior, but you often will need to ask exploring questions to determine what the behavior is. For example, a mother and father tell you that their 16-year-old daughter, Karen, is "unmanageable." What does this mean? The term "unmanageable" is vague and could include numerous behaviors. Remember that your perception of "unmanageable" may differ greatly from the family's. At this point you might ask the parents to role-play how Karen acts when she is "unmanageable." Ask more questions to define the behavior more specifically: What is Karen like when she is "unmanageable?" What does she do? Anything else? Tell about a situation when Karen was "unmanageable."

Then begin exploring the entire situation to get a clear overall picture. Ask the parents to tell you what happened prior to the situation (antecedent). What was the parent doing? What was Karen doing? What was the first sign that Karen was becoming "unmanageable?" What do the parents think caused Karen's behaviors? Does Karen behave this way everytime this occurs?

Finally, make sure you understand the "payoff" or consequences of the behavior. How did the parent respond to Karen's behavior? What did Karen do then? Then what did the parent do? Did anyone else deal with Karen? What made Karen stop her behaviors?

Remember that your questions are trying to pin down the before-and-after behaviors to the problem behavior. In the following situation, determine what questions you would need to ask to identify the antecedent, the behavior, and the consequence. Write down the questions in the spaces provided.

## Exercise 1:

*When you arrive for a visit, the mother tells you that her husband yelled at her again last night. (This is not much information but often this is where visits start with families.)*

Using the categories below, think of what questions you could ask as part of your exploration of this particular problem behavior.

List the questions on a separate piece of paper.


Antecedent Questions



Behavior Questions



Consequence Questions

## Identifying a Family's Strengths

Another way to further explore the family members' agenda and the situation that is endangering the child is to identify the family's strengths in these areas. By using exploring questions, you can determine what the family is doing right within its agenda and the endangering situation.

You can use exploring to identify possible strengths within any problem areas the family or referring worker has identified. Ask questions that elicit information about the family's past successes in dealing with this problem prior to getting help. Ask about the times the problem wasn't occurring; how are those times different from now? Using exploratory questions that focus on the family's successes can help you identify possible strengths in both the family's agenda and in the situation that is endangering the child.

For example, if a family's agenda is running out of money before the end of the month, you could ask these questions: "Has the money ever lasted to the end of the month? What was that like? What is different about your family when the money lasts to the end of the month? What happens when the money is gone before the end of the month? How do you make ends meet?" Be sure to ask all the family members these questions in order to get a clearer picture of everyone's strengths within the agenda. Asking these questions as part of your exploration will allow you to go beyond the facts you gathered through the ABC questions. By identifying a family's strengths, you create building blocks on which to construct an effective treatment intervention.

## Goals

Understanding the family members' agenda and their views of the situation that is endangering the child is imperative to developing goals. It also is important to understand the referring agency's view of the situation, as well as your own view. As the Consultant, you will want to determine what the family wants to accomplish and what behaviors the family wants changed.

The family's agenda and the differing perspectives on the endangering situation are areas that focus on the problems and what needs to be fixed. Goals focus on how things will look when the agenda or endangering situation is fixed. Goals are solution-oriented and describe the positive outcomes to the agendas and situations that are identified. Let's look back at some of the agendas described earlier in this chapter and what goals may be related to them.

**Agenda** — My paycheck doesn't last until the end of the month
**Goal** — To be able to pay monthly bills

**Agenda** — Fred will not go to school
**Goal** — Fred attends school

**Agenda** — My husband yells at me all the time
**Goal** — One evening where my husband has a pleasant conversation with me

**Agenda** — My parents never let me do anything
**Goal** — My parents let me go out without asking me 20 questions

Now let's look at the different perceptions of a situation that is endangering the child that were described before and see how these may be translated into goals.

Earlier we discussed the family agenda of Fred not attending school. The referring agency's perception was that Fred's parents are abusive, so teaching the family alternative discipline techniques may become the referring agency's goal. Your perception is that the parents don't know how to maintain Fred's school attendance except by using physical discipline. Your goal may become having the family learn alternative ways to keep Fred in school. As discussed earlier, combining the family's goals with those of the agency and your own is essential to your work. By fully exploring these areas, you often will be able to identify compatibility. Remember, however, that if these goals differ and the child's safety is not at risk, the parents' goals as well as their agenda are a priority.

You need to ask enough questions to arrive at a goal that is measurable, concrete, and specific to the family. Having goals that meet these criteria will aid both the family and you in recognizing success and make it possible to teach family members how to be specific when they encounter problems in the future.

For goals to be concrete and measurable, they should describe an outcome that can be gauged and not just sensed. The following goals would be difficult to measure: "I will feel happy," or "My dad will mind his own business," or "She will be less codependent." They can be made more concrete by identifying specific behavior changes that can be observed or gauged within the goal statement:

"I will laugh when I'm watching television"; "When my dad calls, he will talk only about his problems, not mine"; and "She will go shopping for herself and by herself one afternoon a month." These goals can be measured because one can determine whether or not they occurred.

Let's look again at the goals we arrived at earlier and see how these can be made measurable and specific.

**Goal** — Be able to pay monthly bills
**Measurable** — Pay rent, utilities, and get groceries and gas for a month

**Goal** — Fred attends school
**Measurable** — Fred goes to school four or five days a week from 8:30 a.m. to 2:30 p.m.

**Goal** — My husband has a pleasant conversation with me
**Measurable** — One evening where my husband doesn't yell, and talks with me for at least 20 minutes before watching television

**Goal** — Parents let me go out without asking 20 questions
**Measurable** — I tell my parents where I am going and with whom and they say "Yes" or "No" without asking any more questions

# The "Miracle Question"

Often families are unsure of what they are trying to accomplish and will give vague answers such as, "We want everything to be okay" or "We just want things to get better." Insoo Kim Berg (1991) suggests using the "miracle question" to get families to start discussing their goals. Asking the "miracle question" at this point will give you insight into both the family's goals and current agenda. Ask family members to imagine that a miracle has happened and their problem is solved. What will be different? How will they know the miracle has occurred? What will things look like after the miracle happens? Continuing with exploration along these lines may help you clarify the path the intervention takes. Ask questions like, "What would it take to make a miracle happen?" These proactive questions suggest to the family members that they need to do something to bring about changes, that the family members themselves can bring about changes, and that they must act if change is to occur (Berg, 1994).

Let's summarize these areas again:

**Agenda**
  A. Family's Agenda
    1. Explore ABC's
    2. Explore Strengths
    3. Explore Goals

**Situation Endangering Child**
  A. Family's Perception
    1. Explore ABC's
    2. Explore Strengths
    3. Explore Goals

  B. Referring Agency's Perception
    1. Explore Goals

As a Consultant, you need to remember that exploration brings to light new knowledge of agendas and possibly endangering situations as well as new information about relevant facts. This would imply that you should not let the intervention plan be unalterably fixed in advance as flexibility is always desirable (Garrett, 1942).

# Summary

Utilizing exploration throughout the intervention will assist the treatment process with families in many ways. Staying on the family's agenda will help reduce the resistance families feel in many instances. You will be able to identify the family's strengths. What do the family members do well? Maybe they negotiate rules, maybe they monitor the children, maybe they praise one another. You will be able to identify and build on these.

Exploration of the ABC's of both the agenda and the situation that endangers the child's placement will provide you with a clearer picture of the context of the problems along with the family's identified strengths. Together these will give you and the family a place to begin the intervention. You will identify clear, family-oriented goals. You will understand what the family wants out of treatment and be able to construct the treatment plan accordingly. Understanding these goals will give you a clear picture of whether the family members view intervention as successful. This will provide opportunities to strengthen the family as it progresses toward its goal.

# 10

# Effective Praise

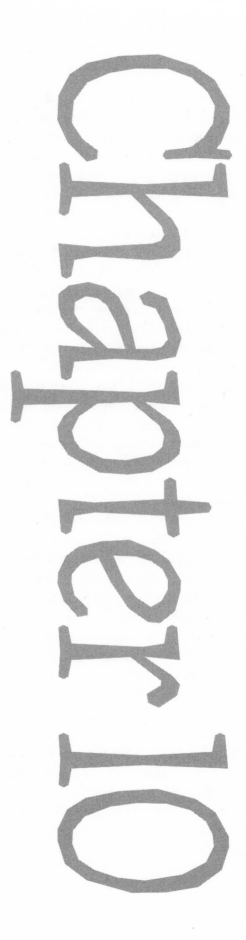

Human beings thrive on attention from other human beings. In fact, the most powerful reinforcers for a child or an adult are found in the behaviors of another person (Patterson, 1971). Even though this attention might sometimes be negative, people need touch, words, approval, a glance or a smile, and recognition of accomplishment in order to become happy, healthy individuals. These "little things," which we call social reinforcers, occur hundreds of times a day and cost nothing to give. But they are found only in the behaviors of another person.

One of the most important and effective social reinforcers is praise. At Boys Town, we give praise in abundance for appropriate behavior so that these behaviors are repeated. Praise is a big factor in teaching people how to change their behavior for the better.

This chapter will focus on how to use praise effectively to bring about change in family behavior.

Praise must be used carefully. Research (Black, 1992; Brophy, 1981; Meyer, 1979; Kamii, 1984) indicates that praise can be very effective in strengthening or increasing good behavior in children or adults. Praise can be one of the most powerful tools you use. Or it can be one of the most misused if you misunderstand what it can accomplish. Praise can be just words without meaning or it can actually be a therapeutic tool. But praise can be a helpful tool only if it is used correctly.

Indiscriminate praise is praise that is given at random, without apparent purpose. It often can be predicted because of its casual abundance. This type of indiscriminate praise can create confusion in a family and inadvertently increase undesirable behaviors. Too much praise also can have a detrimental effect in that it can create a satiation effect, a condition in which a family member receives so much praise that it is no longer rewarding. When this happens, the praise is no longer effective in bringing about change. For example, during a visit with a family, the Consultant tells the parents, "That was great!", "Good job!", and "Okay!" approximately 27 times without connecting the statements to the parents' behavior. The parents have no idea whether the Consultant liked the way they grounded or yelled at their child, or simply thought they grilled hamburgers with great skill!

Praise is effective if it is given immediately after the desirable behavior. In order to have the most powerful influence on strengthening a behavior, praise should be given as soon as possible after the behavior occurs. For example, a Consultant who notices a father calling next door to check if his son is still playing at the neighbor's wants to encourage the father to keep checking on his son periodically. If the Consultant wants the father to continue making these phone calls, he or she should praise the father for making the call as soon as he gets off the phone. If the Consultant waits until the end of the visit or remembers the next day to mention how well the father checked on his son, the praise will not be as powerful.

The size of the praise also is important. Size refers to the amount of praise that is given. For example, a child who argues and never follows through with a task has just completed the chore of cleaning his bedroom. Simply saying "Good job" wouldn't come close to being adequate praise for what this child has done. He deserves some big praise! A more appropriate statement might be, "All right! Way to go! You finished cleaning your room!" In determining the size of the praise, make sure it matches not only the behavior but the effort behind the behavior.

## The Effective Praise Interaction

Effective Praise® is crucial to developing relationships and is very important in strengthening appropriate behavior. Effective Praise allows the Consultant to sincerely and enthusiastically recognize the progress each family member is making. How the praise is given is what makes it effective in developing relationships and in strengthening skills. At Boys Town, we use a five-step process called the Effective Praise Interaction, which incorporates all the principles of praise to accomplish its intended goal. The steps of the interaction are:

1. **Praise statement.**
2. **Description of the behavior/skill you want to see repeated.**
3. **Rationale for using the skill.**
4. **Tasteful routine statement to present the reinforcer (for use with tangible reinforcers).**
5. **Present the reinforcer without describing skill/behavior (usually for adults when presenting a tangible reinforcer).**

**1. Praise statement.** Beginning interactions with family members by providing general praise about their accomplishments or efforts continues the relationship-building process between you and the family. It also increases the probability that the family will be open to suggestions you may have at another time. Simple, short superlatives paired with specific descriptions of the behavior or skill you want to see repeated can be quite effective.

**2. Description of the skill/behavior you want to see repeated.** Specifically describing a family member's behavior or approximation of behavior enables that person to see what he or she was doing, when the behavior occurred, and how well it was done. By being specific, you can verbally demonstrate or describe the exact behaviors the family member should repeat. This helps identify how the family member can successfully use the behavior in similar situations and in different situations.

**3. Rationale for using the skill.** Rationales are statements that explain to family members the relationship between their behaviors and the outcomes that may result. Rationales should include the natural consequences for engaging in a behavior or using a new skill; be personal to individual family members and their individual interests; be specific and brief, and believable; and, for some family members, point out the short-term consequences for engaging in a certain behavior.

**4. Tasteful routine statement to present the reinforcer (for use with tangible reinforcers).** Too much reliance on verbal praise alone will not have the desired effect of increasing the targeted behavior. Tangible rewards tend to give more "oomph" to your praise, especially after the family has tried to learn or succeeded in learning an especially hard skill. Tangible rewards are very individualized so it is vital to identify, explore, and listen for what family members enjoy before giving a tangible reinforcer. This is done by talking to them about what they like to do on their days off, what helps them calm down, what do they do for fun, and so on. You also can use what you've learned through your assessment of the family, what you've seen the family do for fun, what they enjoy talking about, etc.

**5. Prevent the reinforcer without describing the skill/behavior (usually for adults when presenting a tangible reinforcer).** When working with some adults, you might often observe a behavior or skill that you'd like to see repeated and casually present the parent with a tangible reinforcer such as a Diet Coke, a key chain, a fishing lure, bubble bath, or candy bars, depending on what motivates them.

You can individualize the reinforcer further by using a verbal praise statement. Such statements aren't always necessary; presenting the reinforcer immediately after a desired behavior or skill usually creates a strong enough connection between the behavior or skill and the reinforcer. In fact, some parents feel as though they are being treated like children when verbal praise statements and descriptions are attached to a reinforcer. For example, you are working with a mother who just followed through with a grounding she gave her daughter. This is the first time the mother displayed this behavior. After seeing this wonderful parental accomplishment, you may say, "Oh, you know what? I found your favorite bubble bath and it reminded me of you so I had to get it," and then present this tangible reinforcer to the parent. No praise statements, rationales, or specifics were made that directly related the behavior to the reinforcer (bubble bath). However, the bubble bath was given immediately after the appropriate behavior in hopes that the mother will use that behavior (following through on grounding procedures) more often.

It is important that you note how family members are responding to your use of verbal praise or tangible reinforcers. Every person is different and finds different things rewarding. Some people like to receive verbal recognition from others when they have done something well. Others tend to cringe when someone makes a fuss by praising them for something they have done well. Some people find that just doing something well is reward enough; they don't think it is necessary for others to acknowledge or comment on what they have done. You can determine the family members' response to praise or a tangible reward by asking yourself these questions: Is your praise increasing the behavior? Does giving a tangible reinforcer motivate the person to do more of the actions you want? Are any family members offended by your attempts to praise them, or do they try to negate your praise?

The use of praise and tangible reinforcers is effective only if the person receiving them feels rewarded and is motivated to keep up the desirable behaviors. Most people are motivated by some sort of verbal praise and/or tangible rewards. It is up to you to determine what these motivators are and how to present them tactfully.

Example 1 shows how these skill components work together.

## Example 1

*The Consultant has just seen 12-year-old Sarah arrive home at 9 p.m., her curfew time. The Consultant says, "Sarah, that was wonderful. You certainly are doing a great job of minding mom and dad (Praise). You came home right at 9 o'clock like your parents asked you to (Description of the skill you want to see repeated). That was great. Coming home on time is sure going to show your parents that you can follow the rules and will probably make it really easy for them to tell you "Yes" the next time you ask to go someplace with your friends or stay out a little later on a weekend night" (Rationale).*

*The Consultant might add a tangible reinforcer to the verbal praise: "You sure have earned going out for a hamburger tonight by coming home on time. Let's go now."*

Along with these skill components, O'Leary and O'Leary (1977) have identified three other ways to make praise effective: It must be contingent, specific, and credible.

### Contingent

In most cases, Consultants should give praise only when families meet a specific objective. Remember, behavior is strengthened when followed by a reinforcer. Therefore, the behavior must occur before the reinforcer is given. That way, the reinforcer (praise) is linked directly to the family's accomplishments. In your initial intervention with a family, reinforce any positive behaviors that occur within the skill areas you are planning to teach. Look for things the family already does well (strengths), improvements (even small improvements in problem areas), and positive attempts at new skills (Burke & Herron, 1992). As the family demonstrates skill in the area you're developing, praise becomes contingent on a higher level of skill performance. (Chapter 20, "Identifying and Building on Strengths" will more fully describe this). Effective Praise rewards the family for attaining specified criteria.

## Specific

Consultants should specifically describe the appropriate behavior or achievement in their statement of praise. Specific praise describes aspects of the family's accomplishments and conveys the value of the accomplishment. Effective Praise should be behaviorally specific and descriptive, and related to the skill being taught. The descriptive, specific nature of the praise serves to further increase the probability that those particular appropriate behaviors will occur again. Praising behavior that is related to the skill or approximation has several functions: It increases the sincerity and naturalness of your interaction with the family, it reinforces approximations to the desired behavior, and it helps the family recognize progress (Father Flanagan's Boys' Home, 1991). Using vague statements such as "Boy, you did a nice job" or "That sure was great" can leave a family member confused about what he or she did that was so nice or great. This vagueness may inadvertently reinforce another, less desirable behavior that the family member interprets as appropriate.

## Credible

Praise is effective only if it is personal, sincere, and focused on improvement. Effective Praise suggests that you have paid clear attention to the family's accomplishments and are attributing success to the family's efforts and ability while implying that similar successes can be expected in the future (Brophy, 1981).

As we discussed earlier, indiscriminately praising every move a family makes may create satiation, which makes praising the desired skill or behavior less effective. Also, make sure that your facial expression, voice tone, and mannerisms match the verbal praise. A bland, monotone voice is not very reinforcing and certainly doesn't lend credence to your words. Also, always try to use "you" statements rather than "I" statements. "You" statements focus attention on the family's accomplishments; "I" statements focus attention on you as the person judging the family's behaviors. For example, saying "You did a nice job of staying calm and quiet when your sister was talking," is better than saying, "I was impressed when you stayed calm and quiet when your sister was talking."

## Summary

As a Consultant, you must be vigilant for any signs that family members are trying new behaviors or skills. Developing a new skill is difficult and involves many behavioral steps. You must acknowledge, validate, and reward even the smallest steps. Effectively praising the accomplishment of each step encourages family members to keep trying, and lets them know that their efforts are worthwhile. When family members falter the first few times they try to make changes, praise their efforts and intentions. (We will discuss this change process that uses Effective Praise in Chapter 20, "Identifying and Building on Strengths.")

Everyone needs recognition and appreciation. The more ways and times you can find to effectively praise family members for how they are trying to learn, the faster they will learn. Families are not aware of what they routinely do; they need feedback about their success, especially from professionals. Families become reassured when the Consultant is highlighting and praising their strengths and successes rather than making more demands (Berg, 1994). Effective Praise allows you to sincerely and enthusiastically recognize the progress each family member is making and indicates to them that you recognize what they have accomplished and are continuing to accomplish (Phillips, Phillips, Fixsen, & Wolf, 1974).

Using praise effectively, either through verbal praise or tangible reinforcers, will help remove barriers the family or the Consultant may have set up and keep you focused on the family's accomplishments and strengths. Using praise appropriately, especially with the children in the home, models for the parents how to be specific and recognize the accomplishments, rather than the failures, of their children and other family members. Through the use of modeling, praise, and reinforcement, skills can be demonstrated to family members at the same time other skills are being taught. This creates more time for the Consultant to address those issues that may require more explanation, and allows change to occur in more areas in a shorter period of time.

# 11

# Metaphors

In Chapter 2, we discussed how each family has a unique cultural background that Consultants must acknowledge and incorporate into their therapy. Every person perceives and makes sense of the world around him or her in a different way. Education levels, cognitive abilities, and life experiences are just a few of the factors that influence how an individual processes information. And as a Consultant, you bring your own understandings and preferences for processing information to the therapeutic relationship. Herein lies the challenge. How can you best communicate your ideas, knowledge, and skills to families who may have a world view that is completely different from your own and who process new information in ways you may never have considered? One way Boys Town has found to be most effective in bridging the gap of understanding between the family and the Consultant is the metaphor technique.

Using the metaphor technique allows the Consultant to find a common ground of understanding so that new information can be passed on. Metaphors allow you to describe an experience or idea in a way that generates a new form of understanding. Metaphors work by assigning meaning in two ways: You can relate to what the family tells you, and the family members can relate to what you tell them (Hallock, 1989).

## What Are Metaphors?

Jooste and Cleaver (1992) define metaphors as a process by which meaning is "carried over" from a situation to which it ordinarily belongs to another situation that is somehow similar. Metaphors are so much a part of our everyday language that we often do not realize how much we rely on them to communicate our ideas to one another. In fact, trying to relate many of our thoughts without using metaphors could be as difficult as trying to learn a foreign language.

The use of metaphors in therapy is as common as traffic jams on a Los Angeles freeway, or cornfields in Iowa, or even tourists on Florida beaches in May. Many therapeutic approaches have been designed to incorporate the use of metaphors. Metaphors come in a variety of forms, from anecdotes to analogies, from brief figurative statements to objects that are used in treatment to represent something other than what they are (Barker, 1985). At Boys Town, metaphors often are used in the form of anecdotes, short stories, analogies, or similes.

Since there are several different types of metaphors and many different therapeutic approaches that utilize them, it is important to distinguish how Boys Town defines and uses the metaphor technique in interventions with families. In the therapeutic process, metaphors are defined as statements that compare the client's experiences with the concept or skill being taught. The emphasis in using metaphors is on finding a simple and understandable way to convey information to the family. Using experiences from the family's lives helps family members understand what you are teaching. The goal of the metaphor technique is to bring about an "Aha!" revelation to the family so that members can understand the metaphor's meaning and then apply what you have taught.

In the Boys Town approach, Consultants use metaphors in all phases of the intervention. Whenever a concept or idea or skill needs to be taught, a metaphor can be used to help convey understanding. Therapists use metaphors to establish and maintain a positive relationship with the family by using the family's language and metaphors. We have found that metaphors can be used with adults and children to relate information.

A good way to assess whether a person will be receptive to teaching that uses metaphors is to listen to his or her language. People who use metaphors in their language can usually understand metaphors. If a person uses simple metaphors or uses metaphors incorrectly, take this into account before using the metaphor technique.

## Skill Components of Metaphors

The metaphor technique consists of these five skill components:

1. **Through conversation, identify language or a topic area the person thoroughly understands.**
2. **Draw a comparison between the person's experience and the concept/skill being taught (the metaphor).**
3. **Personalize the metaphor to the family's goals or experiences.**
4. **Relate the metaphor back to the concept/skill.**
5. **Solicit understanding from the family member.**

**1. Through conversation, identify language or a topic area the person thoroughly understands.** When you are teaching a family member a new skill or idea and are unsure about how the person will receive your teaching or whether it will be initially understood, begin by having a conversation with the family member. During your talk, identify possible language or topic areas you can use in order to draw a comparison to the skill you want to teach. Listen to the person's use of language and search for topic areas in which he or she demonstrates an understanding or a mastery. Listen for any metaphors; these can often be used to develop more metaphors.

For example, you are working with a mother who complains that she is having trouble getting her three-year-old son to stay in his own bed at night. During today's visit, you want to introduce the idea of rewarding the boy when he does stay in bed, but you know the mom doesn't think it's right to give rewards for the kinds of behaviors she expects from him. From previous visits you know the mother enjoys betting on the dog races. You might want to begin by talking with her about the process of betting on races. This conversation should be very natural and flow easily. During this conversation, the mother tells you that she wins big only every third or fourth time she goes to the races, but generally wins a small amount every fourth time she bets.

She is demonstrating to you through her conversation that she has mastered an understanding of how gambling works at the dog track (positive reinforcement). She may even use a few metaphors that can be elaborated on later, such as "hitting the big one," "laying it all down on the long shot," and "don't put all your eggs in one basket."

**2. Draw a comparison between the person's experience and the concept/skill being taught (the metaphor).** Once the topic area or language where a metaphor can be used has been identified, introduce the metaphor into the conversation, relating it to the concept or skill being taught.

In the example, the mother's experience is with dog racing, but the concept area you are teaching is using positive reinforcement or rewards to get her three-year-old son to stay in his own bed at night. As a metaphor, you could compare the mom's experience with winning on her bets to the experience her son may have by winning a reward when he stays in bed.

In conversation, your metaphor can be introduced like this: "It's interesting that you keep betting at the dog races even when you only win every so often. You talk about how exciting it is to win big. The thought of winning keeps you interested in betting more. Actually, rewarding your son with extra privileges or a prize when he stays in his bed all night is a lot like winning at the dog races. You may not catch him staying in bed all the time he does it, but when you do notice it, you can reward him big with those privileges or prizes."

**3. Personalize the metaphor to the family's goals or experiences.** After introducing the metaphor, be sure to personalize it to the particular goals or changes the family wants. This component is critical to making the metaphor meaningful and connecting it with the family's goals in the intervention. To the mother in the example, you would want to personalize the metaphor to her goal of getting her son to stay in his own bed all night. You might say, "If you reward your son when he stays in bed, soon he'll be sleeping in his own bed all night, every night. He'll be anxious to sleep in his own bed because he gets a reward, just like you're anxious to go to the race track because you know you're going to win. Then you'll get what you've wanted, a full night's sleep without worrying about your son crawling into your bed."

**4. Relate the metaphor back to the concept/skill.** This component involves repeating, via the metaphor, how the concept or skill is similar to the person's own prior experiences. The metaphor is the bridge of understanding between the person's experience and the concept or skill being taught. To enhance understanding, be sure the metaphor bridges these two seemingly unrelated ideas. In the example, you might say: "So when you win every so often at the dog track, it has a powerful effect on you — it keeps you coming back for a chance to win more. Rewarding your son with privileges every so often when you can catch him staying in his bed at night has a powerful effect on him. Eventually, he will want to stay in his bed in hopes that you will reward him again. Occasionally rewarding a child for a behavior you want him to keep doing will motivate him to keep doing the behavior."

**5. Solicit understanding from the family member.** The last component entails making sure that the concept or skill being taught through the use of the metaphor has been understood by the family member. You may solicit understanding in several different ways. You could simply ask the person if what you said makes sense. You might ask the person to paraphrase what you just said to see whether he or she is making the connection. You also could ask if the person sees any other ways that his or her experiences relate to the concept/skill area.

As you solicit understanding, you will want to watch for nonverbal cues that indicate whether or not the person understands. If the family member has a blank look, is shaking his or her head, or is grimacing as if confused, the metaphor probably needs more clarification. Otherwise, it is not going to be effective in bringing about understanding. If, on the other hand, the family member nods approvingly with a smile, or if the person's eyes widen as if a bell went off in his or her head, the metaphor probably was effective in enhancing understanding of the concept or skill.

When soliciting understanding, look for any indications that the person has had an "Aha!" experience; this will tell you whether or not the person understands what you've related through a metaphor. In the example, you could ask the mother if she sees how rewarding her son will motivate him to stay in his own bed at night. If the mother indicates through both verbal and nonverbal cues that she now understands the power of rewarding good behavior, you have been quite successful.

## Summary

Using these five skill components, the metaphor technique can be effective in conveying a complex, abstract concept such as positive reinforcement in simple, meaningful terms and ideas to which the family can relate.

In the example, the mother now can understand the effectiveness of rewarding good behavior by relating it to how winning a few times at the dog track (reward) encourages her to keep making bets. This mother may never understand the complexities of behavioral theory and why reinforcement works, but she does get a sense of how effective this skill can be in getting her son to stay in his bed. And if the family members understand in their own terms how skills and concepts bring about the changes they are seeking, they are much more likely to apply this knowledge and use the skills.

Metaphors are effective only if they provide clarity and generate understanding for the family. Resist the temptation to use your own metaphors. Metaphors that are comfortable and clarify meaning for you may not enhance understanding for the family at all. The Consultant who uses metaphors should frequently evaluate whether the metaphors are helping to clarify the meaning of abstract concepts for the family or are just making the concepts more confusing, vague, or complex.

Learning to use the metaphor technique effectively takes time and practice. But once mastered, metaphors serve as a useful intervention technique that maintains a positive therapeutic relationship while teaching families ways to meet their goals.

# 12

# Circular Refocusing

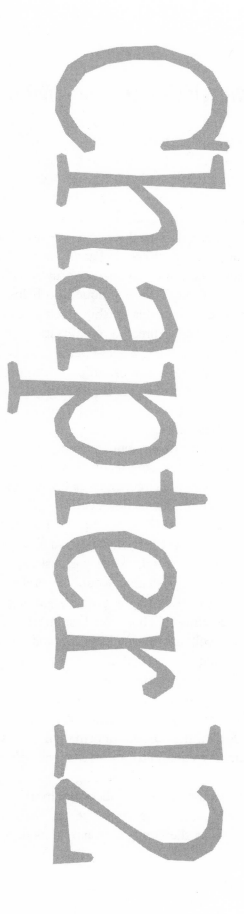

A Consultant who has been working with families for any length of time can probably recall working with family members who love to talk. And for the most part, having family members who openly disclose information and freely talk about their experiences contributes to the relationship-building process. But when a family member talks excessively, rambles on about anything and everything, or continually whines, a Consultant can begin to feel frustrated and lost. Family members who like to tell you every detail of their day at work, ramble on about Uncle Jim's children, or enjoy showing you every knick-knack, describing in detail when and where they got them, presents a unique challenge as you attempt to help the family achieve its goals.

Families who tend to ramble may take up so much time talking about seemingly irrelevant topics that little time is left to teach the skills that will bring about the changes they are seeking. Usually people who whine or talk a lot are not intentionally trying to avoid their problems, but merely enjoy talking to other people. When you realize that excessive talking is preventing you from doing your job — teaching the family skills — you may feel like time is being wasted because the family is not getting the help it expects. At this point, the circular refocusing technique can be most useful.

## What Is Circular Refocusing?

Circular refocusing is defined as redirecting a conversation that has strayed from a goal-related topic back to that original topic. Circular refocusing is a round-about way to get family members to discuss presenting problems and goal-oriented ideas. Boys Town Consultants use this technique to maintain the flow of conversation and to avoid shutting down communication by abruptly changing the subject. This technique also helps maintain a positive relationship when you need to frequently redirect a conversation back to teaching a skill in a goal-related area. By using this technique, you can utilize the information that family members are rambling about in a reinforcing manner to lead them back to the teaching topic.

Before we present the components of the circular refocusing technique, it is important to look at the circumstances under which you should use this technique.

Sometimes you do not need to intervene and direct the conversation; you need to allow the family to talk while you just listen. One time when listening would be preferable to circular refocusing is at the beginning of the intervention. When you first meet a family, you will use active listening and exploring techniques, as well as concrete services, to encourage a family to talk a lot. Listening during this time helps to establish a relationship, and rambling family members often will disclose much useful information about their interests and perceptions that will help you in your assessment. Providing concrete services helps the family members feel more comfortable with your presence in their home. Helping the family to maintain its day-to-day routine by your active participation also encourages communication and provides valuable insight into family dynamics.

Another time you may choose to listen without refocusing is when family members are eager to share information with you that they feel strongly about. For example, a teenage girl may want to tell you about an argument she had with a classmate, or a mom may be very excited to tell you about a date she had over the weekend. Although these topics may not relate to the family goals, they are important to the family members and once they share them with you, the family member is likely to be ready to talk to you about more goal-related topics. Similarly, if family members are extremely angry or upset, it may be necessary to allow them to talk so they can vent their frustrations. Attempts to redirect family members when they are angry may escalate the feelings of frustration and possibly shut down your relationship.

Finally, you may want to just listen to family members talk without refocusing the discussion when, during an intervention, you begin to feel uncertain about the direction your treatment should take. By letting the family talk for a while, you will likely discover the family's agenda as well as the best way to address it.

The circular refocusing technique is most useful in situations where a family member's conversation becomes counterproductive to the family's time with you. In many cases, circular refocusing is frequently utilized in the middle to later parts of the intervention. Sometimes, family members will begin to repeat stories or get so comfortable talking with you that they ramble on for a long time. Even though you may have used active listening or exploring techniques to encourage the family to talk freely about a variety of topics in the beginning, you will want to encourage the family to talk about goal-related topics as much as possible once you have begun to identify the family's agenda and goals.

Another time circular refocusing is helpful is when a family member gets into the habit of complaining or whining to you. A person may naturally enjoy talking about his or her problems and like having an empathetic listener. But listening to a family member complain about problems without discussing possible solutions becomes counterproductive to making changes. Your listening to "problem talk" might be inadvertently rewarding or reinforcing such talk when it is no longer useful. Therefore, your job as the Consultant is to bring the family back to a solution-oriented focus which is productive in creating changes within the home.

Knowing when to use the circular refocusing can be challenging. Fortunately, when the technique is used smoothly and correctly, the family may not even be aware that you are redirecting the conversation. Hence, using this technique produces many benefits that help the family progress more efficiently toward its goals while maintaining a positive working relationship.

## Skill Components of Circular Refocusing

The circular refocusing technique consists of these three components:

**1. Listen for and identify verbals in the conversation that can be linked back to the goals, presenting problem, or teaching topic on which you are working.**

**2. Use the identified verbals to tie the conversation back to the goal-related topic.**

**3. Continue to teach on the goal-related topic.**

Let's look at these components in more detail. An example of how they can be used in a dialogue with a talkative family member will follow (Example 1, Page 111). For purposes of discussion, a talkative or rambling family member is someone who continually redirects a conversation to his or her own topic for long periods of time. If not refocused, this person often will talk 20 to 30 minutes at a time about issues that are not related to the reason you are in the home.

**1. Identify verbals.** When a family member is rambling and you think circular refocusing is needed to bring him or her back to the goal-related topic, begin by listening to what the person is talking about. Try to pick out key words, phrases, and/or ideas that can be linked to the teaching topic or goals. These words, phrases, or ideas may be similar or related to the topic you are attempting to address. For example, a family member is going on about how the parents down the street never know where their kids are and how they let them run the streets at all hours. This idea can be used to question the parents you are working with about how they know where their kids are and what rules they have about their kids running the streets. Eventually, something will be said that can be used as an analogy for comparison with the goal-related topic.

Listen for phrases that can be turned into metaphors. For instance, if a father is telling you all about his fishing excursion and how he tried three different lures before he was able to catch a fish, mentally note that this story can be transformed into a metaphor. Then explore how he determined that he needed to change lures. Explore how he learned to develop the patience that fishing requires. Ask specific questions that allow the father to talk about his strengths as a good fisherman. In your mind, meanwhile, think about how to relate his strengths and skills in fishing to the kinds of strengths and skills necessary for raising a teenager.

Another way to refocus is to listen for verbals that describe a skill you are trying to teach. Let's say a teenager is going on and on about her cheerleading and how she has to practice a new routine several dozen times every day to get it right. This conversation reflects the skills of perseverance, patience, and practicing a new skill, things you have been working on with the teenager in dealing with her parents. Taking the teenager's statements and relating them into skill areas, then tying them back into her work with her parents refocuses her on the treatment issues at hand.

**2. Tie the conversation back to the goal-related topic.** Once you have identified verbals in the family members' conversation, the next step is to connect them to the goal-related teaching topic. One way is to praise the family members' strengths or successes in the area they are discussing and then explain how that same strength relates to the goal area. This will connect those past successes or life experiences to the skills the family is learning so that it can progress toward its goals.

Verbals also can be tied back through the use of metaphors, comparing how something or someone in the family's conversation relates to the skills or goals you are addressing, or tying an idea from the family's conversation back to the goal-related topic area.

For example, with the father who is rambling about his fishing trip, you could praise his ability to learn that it takes time, patience, and practice in order to be a competent fisherman. Then you could relate how learning a different discipline technique also takes time, patience, and practice. For instance, the father is trying to get his son to stop arguing with him all the time. You are teaching the father to walk away and not engage in arguing behaviors with his son. The father is frustrated at first and tends to get drawn into these arguments before he realizes what he is doing. This is an opportunity to break into the father's rambling with the metaphor from the fishing story to explain that just as fishing takes time, patience, and practice, so does learning to walk away from arguments. You also may want to include the comparison (from the father's earlier comments) that as he was able to figure out that the fish would bite only on a certain type of lure, he will eventually figure out which discipline techniques are most effective in getting his child to mind.

**3. Teach on the goal-related topic.** Once you have identified verbals you can use from the family's conversation and tied these back to the goal-related topic, you can continue to teach that topic. Now that you have opened the door to discussing the family's goals and skill areas, you can simply continue to elaborate on the verbals you chose and give rationales for why the metaphors you used hold true to the goal topic. Or you can teach on the

# Example 1

Here's how circular refocusing is used in a dialogue with a mother who has a tendency to ramble about her frustrations in running her small craft store. Keep in mind that the goal-related topic is finding a way to get her 14-year-old son Clete to get up and get ready for school on his own.

*Mom: (For the last 10 minutes, the mother has been talking about a customer who has overextended her credit at the store and the conflict that arose when she confronted the customer.) "And then when I told her over the phone that I expected her to pay her bill before I would let her sell any more of her stupid afghans at the store, she got really nasty. She said she wasn't going to buy any more of my goods. That was fine with me; I won't be threatened. I've got a business to run and sometimes I've just got to put my foot down."*

*Consultant: "I guess when you run a business you really need to know how to put your foot down and stand your ground."*

*Mom: "You ain't kidding. Everybody tries to take advantage of me. But I wasn't gonna take it from this lady. I mean, she even had the nerve to start cussing at me over the phone. I don't have to take that. So I hung up on her. And I told my cashier not to let that freeloader buy or sell anything in the store until her account is paid in full. I'm not going to let her run over me." (The Consultant has begun to identify verbals that can be used to refocus the mother.)*

*Consultant: (The Consultant begins to ask specific questions to identify the strengths the mom has in dealing with business matters.) "How did you learn to manage your business and put your foot down with people who try to take advantage of you?"*

*Mom: "It comes from years of experience and learning that if you give an inch to some people they will take a mile. This woman would rob me blind if I just looked the other way and didn't put my foot down."*

*Consultant: "When you put your foot down and expect the lady to pay her account, will she pay?"*

*Mom: "You are darn tootin' she'll pay if she ever wants to make money selling her blankets in my store."*

*Consultant: (The Consultant praises the mom's strengths in business management and relates these strengths to the goal-related topic.) "You have quite the business sense, it sounds like. When someone isn't meeting your expectations, you are very clear about it by putting your foot down. You managed this business problem with such a creative and effective approach. If that lady doesn't pay her bill, you won't let her sell her product in your store. That's real similar to the approach you are trying with Clete to get him to get up for school. If Clete sleeps late, you clearly state your expectations. In fact, you put your foot down when you wouldn't let him watch TV yesterday because he slept in. You were using your business sense to not let him take advantage of you. Now Clete will know that if he wants to watch TV, he has to get himself up for school because you have made your expectations very clear. He's not going to run over you." (From this point on, the Consultant has the mom back on the goal-related topic and can continue to teach the skills for dealing with Clete's oversleeping.)*

goal-related topic using other intervention techniques, such as Criticism by Suggestion. (See Chapter 13.) In our example, you could teach the father that the next step in learning how to get his teenager to mind better is to try to use natural consequences and observe what effect this discipline technique has on changing his child's behaviors.

## Summary

The circular refocusing technique can be a very useful tool for intervening with families. When used with other techniques, it can make your teaching more effective as well as more efficient. However, it is important to remember that when using circular refocusing you need not always rush a family back to the goal-topic. Be patient, remain calm, and wait for the right opportunity to use circular refocusing. We have learned over time that the more a Consultant hurries to redirect the conversation, the more likely he or she is to abruptly change the subject and cut off the flow of communication. Circular refocusing keeps the communication flowing, leads the family toward goal progress, and fosters strong relationships.

# Criticism by Suggestion

"Criticism by Suggestion" is a term that is unique to Boys Town Family Preservation Services. It refers to another technique of teaching families new skills and building on existing strengths. By definition, it means observing a family engage in an approximation of a desired skill and intervening in a reinforcing way to shape the skill by giving a suggestion that will enhance it. Criticism by Suggestion was adapted from the Boys Town Family Home Program's Teaching Interaction®, a technique that has been used since 1972 to teach youth new skills.

What does this mean? It means that in working with families, you will be teaching new skills, building on existing skills, and providing feedback to family members who have just engaged in a skill you feel could be enhanced. In these situations, you will want to come across positively, recognize a family's progress and efforts, and suggest a more effective way of handling a situation or improving on a skill. In the Boys Town program, Criticism by Suggestion is used only in Phases II through V. In Chapter 21 on Phases we will discuss how you will avoid using this skill in Phases I and VI. This helps to ensure that you have identified the family members' strengths to foster their abilities and expertise.

# 13

Giving criticism in the form of a suggestion has several advantages over simply giving criticism. For one thing, it is nonthreatening to families and emphasizes their partnership role in your relationship. By making suggestions to family members, you are letting them know that you still consider them the experts in their homes and family situations, and that you are providing ideas for change, not telling them what to do. Adults generally do not appreciate being told what to do or how to do something, especially when it comes to their own family. Criticism by Suggestion makes it easier for families to accept suggestions because there is little emphasis on the criticism, praise is incorporated, and ideas are offered in a suggestive manner.

## Skill Components of Criticism by Suggestion

Let's look at the skill components of Criticism by Suggestion. An explanation of each step follows. An example using all of these components is presented at the end of the chapter.

1. **Provide praise/empathy.**
2. **Describe behaviors surrounding the attempts.**
3. **Suggest the alternative/next approximation.**
4. **Provide a rationale.**
5. **Solicit understanding.**
6. **Practice if needed.**
7. **Discuss the practice.**
8. **Provide general praise.**

**1. Provide praise/empathy.** Each suggestion you give a family should begin on a positive note with specific, sincere praise that describes what a family member did correctly. Praising a behavior that is related to the skill you are trying to teach increases the sincerity and naturalness of your interaction, augments similarities to the behavior you want family members to learn, and helps them recognize progress.

Sometimes, however, it is very difficult to find something within a particular skill, at a specific time, to praise. In situations like this, you can use an empathy statement. An empathy statement lets family members know that you understand what they are going through and recognize the difficulty of their situation. Empathy statements can help build relationships, quiet an agitated family member, and help you approach the situation in a positive, calm manner. By consistently using praise and/or empathy when giving a suggestion, you can strengthen appropriate behavior and skill usage. You also can build relationships by recognizing accomplishments; this can help family members to become more receptive and open to the entire therapeutic process.

**2. Describe behaviors surrounding the attempts.** It has already been made clear that building on strengths is a crucial element of the Boys Town program. (This element will be discussed in more detail in Chapter 20.) Therefore, the second component of Criticism by Suggestion — describing behaviors surrounding the attempts — is focused more on what the family members attempted to do correctly instead of what they did incorrectly. In fact, it is important to describe what was done correctly even if it involved simply responding to the behavior or situation. Letting family members know that you recognize even their smallest accomplishments starts you off on the right foot in making suggestions. The family is less resistant to your ideas and more open to implementing your suggestions.

**3. Suggest the alternative/next approximation.** Now the family members should be ready for your suggested alternative to what they were doing or the next approximation toward the skill you are teaching. Specifically describing the alternative behavior or next step will result in quicker understanding by the family of what to change or do next. Without clearly describing the behavior you want family members to try, they may be left guessing and you will find yourself repeating the same steps.

**4. Provide a rationale.** As discussed in Chapter 10 (Effective Praise), rationales are statements that show family members the relationship between their behavior and the various outcomes that may result. For example, the rationale for practicing a sport is that the players probably will do better in a game.

Most people prefer suggestions that are accompanied by explanations. It would be ludicrous to tell family members who argue a lot that they should walk away from an argument without explaining the rationale that walking away ends the argument without power struggles and gives each individual time to calm down and return to talk later.

As discussed earlier, it also is very important to use rationales that are individualized for the family member you are working with.

Rationales that relate the family members' behavior change to achieving their own goals and solving their own problems will be the most individualized. We all seem to be more motivated to change our behaviors if we see the connection between behavior and the personal gains that changing will produce.

**5. Solicit understanding.** Once you have explained the possible outcomes of using your suggestion, make sure the family members understand what you have suggested. Soliciting understanding is very important to promote dialogue and avoid lecturing. It lets you know how well you are teaching and how much the family is understanding. This also gives the family members opportunities to comment on your suggestion. They often will state whether or not the suggestion is realistic enough for them to try, or they may ask questions because they are confused about what you are suggesting. This helps you evaluate how receptive the family is to your suggestion.

**6. Practice if needed.** If you feel that family members do not understand the skill you are discussing or what the next step is, practice with them. We all learn better by doing something rather than by just listening. Practice gives the family more opportunities to learn. This practice may involve talking through a situation that is similar to one in which the skill would be used, or acting out (role-playing) the situation. In role-playing, you can play the part of a family member, teacher, friend, spouse, etc., and the other person can play himself or herself. If you think the family member is still having problems, you may want to play his or her part and have them play the other family member, teacher, friend, spouse, etc. That way, you can model the skill and how it is used. (Role-playing will be discussed in more detail in Chapter 15.)

**7. Discuss the practice.** After each practice, discuss what the family did correctly and give any suggestions you may have, then practice again if necessary. How often you practice is not important; what is important is how well the family members understand the skill you are trying to teach them.

**8. Provide general praise.** Be sure to remain supportive and positive throughout the time you are providing Criticism by Suggestion by praising family members for things they are doing during your teaching, such as listening, being patient, and showing interest in helping the family's situation. General praise throughout the process will enhance and continue your relationship-building with the family while making it easier for the family to listen to suggestions you may have in the future.

Throughout this intervention skill, remember to continually assess your verbal and nonverbal behaviors so that you don't offend the family or create a distraction to your treatment.

At this point you would go through the practice with both parents, using humor to lighten the mood and choosing a nonthreatening subject for the argument, such as the color of the sky. Afterwards, you would discuss the practice with them. When the parents feel comfortable enough to try using the alternative behavior or next step, be sure to praise their cooperation and effort, and assure them that you will be with them when they use the new skill.

## When Family Members Resist

When giving suggestions, you often will run across a family member who resists your suggestions or responds negatively. That is why it is crucial to continually assess your behaviors to make sure you are not judging the family, and that you are working within the family's culture, values, norms, and agenda. One way to avoid negative responses is to give two acceptable options and let the family member choose the one he or she prefers.

If you try these methods and it still appears that the person is resisting your suggestions, it may indicate that you need to further explore with the family members their agenda and perceptions of the problems that are occurring. The relationship also may have become strained because the suggestions/ steps are unclear or too difficult for the family to handle, or because the family's goals have been misunderstood.

## Summary

The Criticism by Suggestion technique is designed to provide a gentle yet effective means of creating change within the families with whom you are working. Consistently using it will make your teaching more efficient as well as more effective. Suggesting an alternative behavior instead of telling a family what needs to change keeps the family's perspective and agenda in focus and empowers family members to actively participate, developing skills that will bring about the most efficient changes in their home.

# Example 1

The family you are working with consists of a mother (Wendy), a father (Tom), and their 5-year-old son (Carl). The parents report that they are having difficulty getting along and have often pushed or hit each other during arguments. On occasion, their son has been injured while trying to stop the fighting. You have worked with the parents on taking time away from each other when they feel that an argument might turn into a physical fight.

During one of your visits, the parents get into an argument that lasts about 10 minutes. Then dad pushes mom and leaves the house. Mom goes into her bedroom to cool down. Later when dad comes home and both parents are fairly calm, your conversation with them may go something like this:

*Consultant: "Boy, you guys did great! I know you were really angry with each other but Tom, you left the house, and Wendy, you went to your room before anything really physical occurred. That took a lot of self-control! What would you think of walking away from each other without any physical contact whatsoever — not even a touch on the arm — during your next argument? I know that may seem silly, but sometimes when you are really angry it only takes one shove or even one touch to push you over the edge so you get into a physical fight. The more you can stay away from physical fights the less chance there is that Carl will get in the middle and get hurt. What do you think? Would you try that?"*

*(Both parents agree.)*

*Tom: "Yeah I guess. But it really is hard not to want to get that last jab in."*

*Consultant: "You bet it is, and you are trying so hard now and I know you're doing this because you are really concerned about the injury Carl got when he jumped into your fight. Maybe it would help if we tried a dry run while we are all calm now. What do you think?"*

*(Both parents agree.)*

*Wendy: "Yeah, okay. What do we have to do?"*

*Consultant: "Well, how about if I pretend I'm Wendy and you be yourself, Tom, and we'll practice. Then I'll be Tom and Wendy can be herself. Then the two of you can try it together, okay?"*

*(Both parents agree.)*

*Wendy: "Okay, we'll try."*

# Reframing

Imagine working with family members who are extremely angry about having the local child welfare department involved in their lives. The parents are hostile toward you and are talking with you only because they believe it's the only way to keep the authorities from removing their children from the home. While talking to you, the mother expresses her negative thoughts and feelings about the welfare worker and even says she doesn't think she needs the services you have to offer. She contends that she is tired of everyone telling her what to do.

How could you respond to this mother's negative outlook? What kind of approach could you take to break through this family's resistance to your services?

Working with hostile, resistive, negative, or overly worried families can be difficult. Active listening, exploration, and Effective Praise techniques provide some avenues for working with these families. Another technique that can be used to help establish and maintain a positive working relationship with families who show some resistance is "reframing."

## What Is Reframing?

Reframing has been defined as "altering the conceptual, emotional, and/or perceptual view of a situation so that the same 'facts' take on an entirely different meaning" (Watzlawick, Weakland, & Fisch, 1974). In other words, negative thoughts and problematic situations are cast in a new light by changing the way the thoughts and problems are viewed in order to gain a more open, positive, or solution-oriented perspective. Gordon (1978) sees reframing as a way of "taking a previously painful or unwanted experience and recasting it as valuable and potentially useful."

Many therapeutic approaches incorporate the technique of reframing. Systems theory utilizes reframing as a strategic technique that is designed to shift the conceptual framework within which family members view their situation. Some of the ways the reframing technique can be applied to change a family's perspective from the negative to the positive will be highlighted in this chapter.

Regardless of the way the reframing technique is applied, there are numerous benefits for using it. As mentioned earlier, Boys Town Consultants have found reframing to be a particularly effective technique with families who are demonstrating resistance, negativity, and hostility. Reframing is a gentle, yet powerful way to alter the perceptions family members have about a problem situation without alienating them. First, it allows the Consultant to validate and empathize with the family's view of the situation while offering a broader or different interpretation of the situation. Second, reframing can help clients consider new ways to conceptualize their problems so that more goal-focused, solution-oriented options can be introduced (Hartman & Laird, 1983). Reframing also can minimize resistance. Instead of directly confronting a family, you can use reframing to turn the family's perception of a problem into a strength by drawing out the positive aspects within the family's negative viewpoint.

Reframing can be applied to alter conceptual, emotional, and perceptual views in a variety of ways. One method highlighted in the literature (Hepworth & Larsen, 1990; Feldman, 1992; Hartman & Laird, 1983) is positive connotations. In this method, the Consultant attributes positive intentions to what might otherwise be regarded as the family's undesirable or negative behavior. The goal of positive connotation is not to condone the family members' distorted perceptions or resistance, but rather to minimize their need to defend themselves. In the situation described at the beginning of this chapter, positive connotation could be used to reframe the mother's feelings about child welfare services. Placing a positive connotation on what this mother has said would involve describing her negative feelings as a demonstration of her assertiveness and desire for independence in wanting to keep others from telling her how to live her life.

Another way reframing can be applied is by helping the family redefine its problems as an opportunity for growth. Rather than having the family and the Consultant view problems negatively, reframing can be used to reconceptualize the problem as an opportunity for growth and goal obtainment rather than an uncomfortable situation that will be too difficult to change. Reframing does not need to minimize problems or ignore the family's fears about trying new behaviors. But it can enable family members to see their problems in a new context that may stimulate altered responses and new options.

# Skill Components of Reframing

The reframing technique consists of three skill components. An explanation of each step follows.

**1. Provide empathy to the family members as they describe their perceptions of the situation.**

**2. Rephrase a verbalized negative perception as a positive perception.**

**3. Relate the rephrased positive perception to the family's goals.**

**1. Provide empathy to the family members as they describe their perceptions of the situation.** When a family member is describing his or her perception of a painful or problematic situation, the first step is to validate that person's perspective by showing empathy. Empathy statements can help build relationships, calm an agitated family member, and help the Consultant deal with the family's agitation in a positive, calm manner. Empathy is a way to validate the family members' feelings and concerns about what is occurring in their lives.

Using both verbal and nonverbal communication, tell the family member that you are listening and that you understand the situation as it is being described. Ways to show empathy include assuming the same type of facial expressions the person is displaying, head nods, saying "Uh huh," and maintaining eye contact. You also can convey empathy by paraphrasing or summarizing what the person has said, and by reflecting back the feelings that are being communicated. For example, if you are working with parents who are frightened and worried about their depressed daughter coming home after a two-month stay in a psychiatric hospital, show empathy for their fears and concerns. Obviously, having a family member who is possibly suicidal in the home can generate these kinds of emotions.

**2. Rephrase a verbalized negative perception as a positive perception.** By providing empathy to the negative statements and validating these perceptions, you have placed yourself in a nonthreatening position to offer another interpretation of the situation. At this point you'll want to cast a new light on the situation by showing the family the potentially positive aspects. As described earlier, this can be done by placing a positive meaning on the situation, or by having a family member look at the situation as a potential source for growth and movement toward goal attainment.

In the situation with the parents and their depressed daughter, the parents may be telling you that they're afraid their daughter will get depressed again living at home, and that they are worried about what she might do. You can reframe this fearful perspective into one with a positive meaning — that the parents are concerned about their daughter and want to help her. The negative verbals can be rephrased like this: "When you talk about your concerns about your daughter's return home, it's comforting to know that you want your daughter to be happy and safe. Because of your fears, you are going to more carefully watch for changes in her moods and behaviors. This will help you monitor her to make sure she is safe."

**3. Relate the rephrased positive perception to the family's goals.** This skill component emphasizes the importance of connecting the rephrased perspective to the family's goals. Because reframing allows you to cast the family's perception into a new perspective, you can influence the perspective in a number of ways. Reframing is most productive when it ties the new, positive viewpoint in with the family's goals. Families are more likely to consider and accept the reframed perspective if it is connected with resolving their problems and meeting their goals.

In the earlier situation, you might tie in the rephrased positive verbal with the parents' goals of having their daughter live at home and having her learn how to manage her mood swings without threatening to harm herself.

It might sound like this: "Because of your increased watchfulness and concern for your daughter's well-being, she can return home as the psychiatrist has recommended. By being more aware of her moods, you'll be prepared to help her take preventive steps when you first see the signs of depression. You will be able to encourage her to get help before she gets to the point where she threatens to hurt herself. How can I help you feel more comfortable about monitoring your daughter's moods when she comes home?"

## Summary

Reframing is useful at any stage of the intervention. When reframing is utilized correctly, family members will feel that their concerns, opinions, and viewpoints have been heard and understood. Reframing makes it possible for family members to hear a different interpretation of their situation without feeling threatened or ignored. This technique will help you establish and maintain a positive working relationship with families that express hostility, frustration, negativity, and resistance. Reframing works with all families by helping them to find ways to focus on solutions when they may get "stuck" focusing on the problems.

122

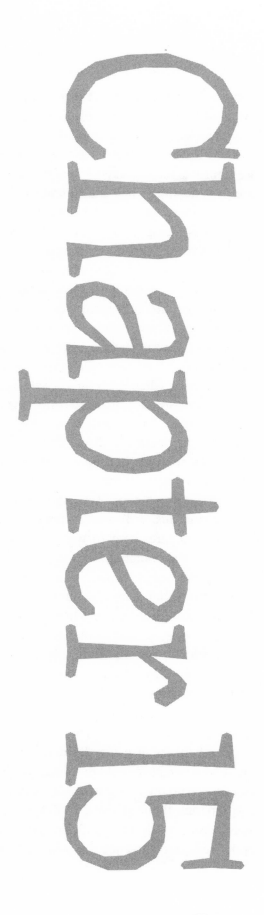

# Role-Playing

The age-old adage, "Practice makes perfect," has proven its validity time and again at Boys Town. Every time a new skill is taught, a youth is expected to practice that skill in order to demonstrate that he or she understands it and can use it in real-life situations. The research literature supports the effectiveness of having children practice skills to ensure that they have fully learned the skill (Timbers, 1975; Sarason & Ganzer, 1973).

At Boys Town, the importance of practicing new skills is emphasized with caregivers and employees as much as it is with the youth. Training incorporates the use of practice and role-plays at every opportunity possible. Role-play is an invaluable way to teach new skills to people. Role-plays help people break away from old, habitual responses to a situation by providing them with opportunities to practice and improve their new responses to a situation. Boys Town Consultants have found that the role-play technique enhances a family's ability to learn new skills.

## What Is Role-Play?

Role-play is defined as a technique where families or family members practice a skill or behavior to make sure they understand the skill or behavior and how to use it. This technique is based on the tenet that people learn more by doing than by merely listening. Role-play enables the Consultant to teach new skills by setting up learning experiences that are similar to real-life experiences the family is likely to encounter. The Consultant can assess through the role-play how well the new skill or behavior is being understood by the family members by observing how they use the skill.

The role-play technique can be employed when teaching a family a new behavior or skill, and is sometimes incorporated with the Criticism by Suggestion technique. (See Chapter 13.) It can be used when introducing a new skill that the family has little or no experience with, or when the family is anticipating a particular situation in which the new skill could be used. For example, if parents are expecting an argument from their teenager when they confront him about ignoring curfew, and you are working with the parents on how to confront their son, give a consequence, and then walk away, using a role-play will help prepare them to use the new skill during the confrontation.

Role-plays also can be used to enhance your relationship with the family. Because role-plays can be done in a light-hearted manner and convey to family members that you understand their situation, this technique strengthens your relationship with the family. The family sees that you understand the problem thoroughly when you "act it out" with them through a role-play.

The benefits of using the role-play technique as a teaching tool are numerous. First, you can set up the family members for success by preparing them to use the skills correctly. Role-plays provide the family members with opportunities to practice the skills until they feel comfortable using them. The more comfortable family members feel about using the skill and understanding how it works, the more likely it is that they will successfully use the skill in a real-life situation. Second, role-plays serve to help the Consultant better understand the family's problem. When the role-play is being set up, family members often guide the Consultant by telling him or her how the problem generally presents itself. As the Consultant acts out or talks through the role-play, the family indicates whether it truly reflects the family's situation.

Role-plays are beneficial in assessing and evaluating how well the family understands the new skill. This is done by observing family members use the skill during the role-play. Are they using all the behavior steps of the skill? Is the family choosing the best time to use the skill? Can the family generalize the skill in a variety of situation role-plays? When the skills are taught only by suggesting to the family how to implement them, it often is difficult to determine whether the family understands how to actually use them.

Also, role-plays help Consultants assess and evaluate their own teaching. By observing a role-play, the Consultant can decide whether more teaching is necessary and what parts of the skill need to be clarified. Using role-plays helps the Consultant to be behavior-specific in his or her teaching. (Behavior-specific means breaking down a skill into the individual behavioral steps that must be followed.) For example, a Consultant who is teaching the family to clean the home more regularly will have to make the concept of home management more behavior-specific in order to carry out the role-play. Even skills like using a chore chart or budgeting money must be broken down into behavioral components so they can be taught through role-play.

Finally, the role-play technique allows the Consultant to have fun with the family. The process of setting up role-plays and acting out family situations can be humorous. Many parents enjoy playing the part of their children so they can demonstrate how they think their children act during tantrums. Children enjoy getting a chance to act like their parents, too.

When using the role-play technique, it always is important to first determine which kind of role-play — verbal or physical — is best suited for the family. In verbal role-plays, the Consultant talks family members through a situation step-by-step, guiding their responses with a series of questions. Physical role-plays call for the Consultant to act out or demonstrate how the family can handle a situation using the new skills. Family members can be "actors" in the physical role-plays, or can watch the Consultant act out the situation and provide input as needed. Some families are more reserved and will feel more comfortable using verbal role-plays. Other families are very animated and will have no reservations about participating in a physical role-play.

As the Consultant, you must determine how receptive the family is to using role-plays and which approach will work best. Note the responses of family members when you begin a role-play because their nonverbal cues will indicate whether they feel comfortable with the scenario you are attempting to set up.

## Skill Components of Role-Play

The role-play technique consists of five skill components. An explanation of each step and examples of how to use it follows.

**1. Specifically set up the role-play situation.**

**2. Incorporate humor.**

**3. Practice the skills through role-play to the family's limits.**

**4. Provide feedback to family members about how they implemented the skills during the role-play.**

**5. Praise family members for their efforts at incorporating the skills in the role-play.**

**1. Specifically set up the role-play situation.** When teaching a new skill or behavior to a family, always consider using role-plays to enhance the family's learning. Once you have determined that a role-play will work, decide whether to use verbal or physical role-play, or both types. Next, specifically set up the role-play situations with the family. This involves telling the family members that you are going to show them a way to practice the skill you are teaching. With the family's input, you can set up a scenario that is realistic. Decide who will play which roles and discuss possible responses. It is important to specifically describe and explain how the family can incorporate the new skill into the role-play scene and to emphasize that the purpose of the role-play is to practice the skill.

For example, here is how you might set up a specific role-play for a family that is learning communication skills:

You may already have taught the family members how to recognize when they are using inappropriate communication such as yelling, blaming, and name-calling. Now you want them to practice stopping the conversation for five minutes so each person can think through what he or she wants to say using "I" statements. You have decided a physical role-play will work best with this family. To begin, tell family members that you want them to practice their communication skills. Explain a realistic scenario in which the mother, father, and youth are discussing housework. Assign roles to each family member; you may even play a role, asking one of the family members to observe. Review with the family the specific behavioral steps of the communication skills you will use in the role-play. Be sure to set up a role-play situation that the family is likely to encounter in real life. This will make it more effective and the family members will find it easier to carry out their roles.

**2. Incorporate humor.** Most people feel some awkwardness practicing new skills and often are afraid they'll make mistakes. Humor can ease some of the awkwardness and tension of the practice.

Find ways to make the role-play fun. Make jokes about the scenario, exaggerate certain role responses, and laugh at your own mistakes. You set the tone for having fun with the role-plays. One great way you can break the ice and set the stage for humor is to play the child's role first. Seeing you act like a tantrumming or defiant child can help put the adults more at ease and make them more willing to participate.

When setting up the role-play scene, you may want to avoid emotionally loaded scenarios at first. The role-plays can be realistic and still avoid scenes that might embarrass, anger, or belittle a family member.

**3. Practice the skills through the role-play to the family's limits.** This skill component means role-playing the situation repeatedly until the family has reached its limit of understanding the new skill. Sometimes, the first role-play scenario involves asking the family to use the skill incorrectly or not at all. Then in subsequent role-play practices, you can gradually remove yourself from the main role of demonstrating the skill, and eventually let the family members practice the skills while you observe. These role-play practices may occur during one session or be done over several sessions with the family.

You probably have reached the family's limits when members are no longer showing interest, not participating, repeating the same mistakes after being given feedback, or generalizing the skills correctly during a couple of role-play scenes.

**4. Provide feedback to family members about how they implemented the skills during the role-play.** Throughout the role-play scenes the family acts out, give each person specific feedback regarding his or her use of the skills. Remember to use humor when suggesting how the person could use the skill differently. Encourage family members to practice the role-play using your feedback until everyone demonstrates that they understand the skill.

Feedback also can include comments about how their use of the new skill seems to change the responses of the other family members participating in the role-play. Let's go back to the earlier example with the family that is practicing communication skills. In a role-play, family members are incorporating the skill of stopping the conversation to take a five-minute break, but are not taking time to think about what they want to say using "I" statements. In your feedback, you could suggest that in the next role-play, they set a timer and spend five minutes writing down what they want to say with "I" statements. Feedback also can include praise for the steps of the skill the family is implementing correctly and suggestions for improving other steps. You can even provide feedback by demonstrating through role-play how the skill steps can be altered.

**5. Praise family members for their efforts at incorporating the skills in the role-play.** This component is critical for motivating the family to use the practiced skills in real-life situations. Praise the family's attempts and successes at incorporating the new skills in the role-play scenes. Be specific when you describe what family members have done correctly. You may point out that it is difficult to learn new responses to deal with problems, and tell family members how well they have demonstrated the ability to use these new skills. Help the family members feel good about their ability to use the new skills in the future by praising the progress they demonstrated in the role-plays.

## Summary

The role-play technique can be an effective teaching tool when the five skill components are used correctly. Remember that you can assess and evaluate your own teaching as well as the family's abilities by paying attention to how family members perform in the role-plays. If a family member does not seem to understand the skill, make adjustments in the role-play by breaking the steps down into smaller, more specific, concrete steps. If the family has difficulty understanding that the role-play is only a pretend, practice situation,

the role-play technique may not be the best tool for teaching the skill with that family. Do not try to cajole or force a family member to participate in a role-play. If someone is too shy, thinks the exercise is silly, or does not comprehend the purpose of the role-play, try another teaching technique and forego the role-play.

When using the role-play technique, you will know that you have been successful if the family members enjoy themselves while demonstrating their understanding of and ability to use the new skill. In fact, families have told Boys Town Consultants that they remember the skills practiced through role-plays because of the fun they had seeing the Consultant act out in the role-plays. The role-play technique is an effective teaching tool that enhances the Consultant's relationship with the family.

# Confrontation

When most people hear the word "confrontation," they think of its negative connotations. The most common definition of confrontation is coming face to face with someone, especially with defiance or hostility. Society perceives confrontation as something that usually is difficult, a clash between two people who don't like each other or can't agree.

But in the Boys Town Family Preservation program, confrontation is a positive intervention technique where a Consultant expresses a concern that behavior needs to change or that feedback should be implemented. By having family members use self-exploration and accept mutual ownership of the problem, the Consultant can create a situation that allows the family members to change.

This chapter will focus on confrontation as a means to create change, especially where change is difficult for family members.

## Components of Confrontation

The confrontation technique consists of these seven components:

1. **Be empathetic.**
2. **Define the problem in family-goal terms.**

3. **Describe the behaviors that need to be changed.**
4. **Ask for input through exploration of the situation.**
5. **Listen.**
6. **Make a plan for implementation.**
7. **Praise family members.**

Let's look at the components of the confrontation technique to identify and describe a definite set of behaviors that can help you use confrontation most effectively with your families.

**1. Be empathetic.** As we have discussed in other chapters on intervention techniques, empathy is important in establishing your relationship and concern for the family. Letting family members know you realize how difficult change is and how much you appreciate their efforts to make changes will begin any confrontation on a note of concern for the family.

**2. Define the problem in family-goal terms.** Defining the problem you want to address by referring to it in the context of the family's goals — not yours or the caseworker's — and addressing how this problem is interfering in achieving those goals keeps the focus on the family and the changes family members want to see occur. Point out how their actions or failure to act is incongruent with making progress toward achieving their goals.

**3. Describe the behaviors that need to be changed.** Specifically describe the behaviors that are creating the problem. Tell the family, clearly and without being judgmental, what

you perceive is happening. This allows the family and you to understand what needs to be changed with as little interpretation as possible.

**4. Ask for input through exploration of the situation.** Find out from family members how you can help make this situation easier. Ask them if your suggestions were too complicated, too much to handle, not on target, or just confusing.

**5. Listen.** Listen to what family members tell you. Most families will let you know why they feel something didn't work or give reasons for why they didn't use a skill or engage in a certain behavior.

**6. Make a plan for implementation.** Working with family members, make a plan to change anything they didn't understand, clarify behaviors that are needed to bring about changes, and explain how and when you want them to use the skill again.

**7. Praise family members.** Make sure you let them know how well they are doing and tell them you believe in their ability to make changes in their home. Everyone needs to be encouraged and given hope.

# Factors to Consider in Using Confrontation

Now that we have looked at the components of the confrontation skill, let's discuss some factors that determine its use and effectiveness.

First, as stated earlier, society often perceives confrontation as something that is uncomfortable and distasteful; for example, an argument or a yelling match that leaves the people involved feeling depressed or angry. In order to use confrontation in an intervention, you must overcome this negative perception and demonstrate it as a positive way to change behavior.

At Boys Town, confrontation is viewed as an opportunity to challenge family members while trying to determine why they are not using the skills necessary to make changes in their situation. Confrontation also provides an opportunity to teach. By confronting the family, you are trying to uncover what it is about a skill you taught that is making the family hesitant to use it. The information you obtain allows you to teach the family more productively. Change is difficult for anyone, and we see confrontation as an opportunity to join with family members to move toward their goals and address their agendas.

Second, confrontation usually does not take place during Phase I of the intervention. Phase I should be used for identifying and increasing the family's strengths as well as assessing the situation that is endangering the child. Unless the child's safety is an immediate concern, this is not an appropriate time to confront family members about something they are not doing.

Confrontation usually takes place in two situations. The first is when a family member fails to follow through with a suggestion you have made repeatedly. For example, you are two weeks into the intervention and have been working with a grandmother on setting age-appropriate boundaries for her 12-year-old granddaughter. The grandmother has agreed to talk with her granddaughter about these boundaries and you have even role-played

how to do this. But for the third day in a row she has allowed her granddaughter to stay out until 1 a.m. and have boys spend the night. After assessing the situation and your behavior, you may decide to confront the grandmother during your next visit. The second situation is when a family member engages in a behavior that could have serious repercussions, such as the child being removed from the home. For example, you are working with a family that has been referred because the stepfather and teenage son do not get along and often come to physical blows. After observing these interactions and attempting to teach alternative behaviors to both the stepfather and the son, you discover these fights are still occurring. This also would be an appropriate time to confront the family members about these behaviors.

In both situations, it is important to assess your own natural biases and motivations concerning the welfare of the child in the home and the behaviors that you think need to be addressed. As discussed in previous chapters, you must avoid imposing your morals and values on the family. Being aware of your values will keep you focused on the family and what must be done to change the endangering situation so the child can remain at home.

A third factor to consider in using confrontation is maintaining the relationship you have built with a family. Be careful not to damage or abuse this relationship by demanding change or becoming angry. When you recognize the family's strengths and attempts at using the skills you are teaching, family members will be more likely to listen to you. They also will be less likely to become defensive while being confronted. Staying focused will help you remain calm so that you are not angry when you confront the family. Staying focused and continually assessing your behavior, as well as the family's agenda through active listening and exploring, is just as important at this stage as it is during the initial phases of the intervention. Confrontation should always be done in the context of caring about a family.

Fourth, be sure to assess how the confrontation will affect the family members and how they will respond to you. First and foremost, assess your own behavior. Ask yourself what you might have done to cause the family to not follow a suggestion or try a skill? Do you have a strong working relationship with this family? Did you teach too much too fast? Were the steps too big? Are you on the right agenda/goal? Have you correctly identified the endangering situation? Are you imposing your morals and values?

Examining these areas may cause you to take another approach with the family and may help you determine why the family is not being successful with the skills being taught.

Confronting a family inappropriately (e.g. arguing, blaming family members, telling them what they have to do, and not listening to them) could result in family members "tuning" you out. When this happens, they are no longer benefiting from your teaching and your time with the family is not being used effectively. This may create friction in your relationship with the family, which could lead to visits being canceled and assignments not being completed. In extreme cases, the family might ask you to leave. If this occurs, it may be time to back off, assess your behaviors and your relationship with the family, and determine a new course. Even if family members listen attentively, nod their heads, and agree with everything you say, it doesn't mean the situation will change.

A fifth factor to look at is the outcome of your teaching through confrontation. Did the situation change? Are family members now using the skill you were teaching, or have they stopped engaging in an inappropriate behavior you discussed with them? If change has occurred, pat the family on the back and use some of the Effective Praise techniques we talked about earlier. If not, begin over by assessing the Consultant behaviors we have discussed.

Example 1 at the end of this chapter shows how confrontation can be used.

## Summary

As you can see, confronting a family can be a very positive and supportive time for both you and the family. Confrontation can often be a turning point in your work with a family. When done effectively, confrontation can help you recognize how your behavior affects the family and help you identify the most efficient way the family learns new skills. There doesn't need to be accusations, recriminations, or hostility to make confrontation effective. In fact, confronting a family member with concern, specificity, and support is more effective. Using the steps described in this chapter will help make a difficult and often frustrating situation easier while helping a family make changes.

# Example 1

The family has been referred due to neglect charges against the father (Rico). These involve monitoring issues and failure to provide basic needs (food and proper clothing).

You have been working with Rico on the problem of his 12-year-old daughter (Amy) staying out all night and Rico's goal of establishing curfew times. The father has set 10 p.m. as the curfew time and you have worked with him on giving the daughter a consequence when she violates the curfew. Rico has decided that Amy will lose one minute off her curfew the following night for every minute she is late. However, Amy has been late every night for the past week and Rico has not followed through with the consequences.

You have thoroughly assessed the situation and your behaviors. You have discussed the situation with the father after each incident and have decided to try confrontation to address why he has not given Amy a consequence for being late.

*Consultant: "Rico, I noticed Amy was late again last night. Did you take time off her curfew for tonight?"*

*Rico: "No. I planned to but she was not in a good mood today so I didn't want to mess with her."*

*Consultant: "I can sure understand that trying to talk to Amy when she's angry is really hard and knowing you plan to give her a consequence sure makes it seem harder." (Empathy)*

*Rico: "It sure does."*

*Consultant: "I'm wondering if you still feel curfew is a problem? You did say your goal was to set a curfew so Amy would be home at night and you wouldn't get any more neglect charges against you. Is that still how you feel?" (Define the problem)*

*Rico: "Oh, yes. I don't like Amy running the streets at night but I just don't think I can do this."*

*Consultant: "Well, you have already set a curfew and have told Amy what would happen if she came home late. The only thing that needs to be done now is to make sure that when you say she will lose time, you follow through with it. If Amy is threatened but there never is a follow through, she will quit listening and keep staying out late. Is there anything I can do to make this easier for you?" (Describe behaviors/Ask for input)*

*Rico: "I don't know."*

*Consultant: "Are you comfortable with Amy losing one minute for each minute she's late?" (Ask for input/Listen)*

*Rico: "Oh yeah. That's not the problem."*

*Consultant: "Are you nervous about how Amy will react when she loses time?" (Ask for input/Listen)*

*Rico: "Yes! I just know she's going to blow up and I just don't want to deal with that."*

*Consultant: "Would it help if I was here the next time you gave the consequence and then again when Amy is supposed to be home early? We also can talk about what to do when Amy gets angry." (Make a plan)*

*Rico: "Yes, would you? It would be easier if I had someone here until I got used to this."*

*Consultant: "Sure. How about if I come back tonight around 10, which is Amy's cur-*

*few, and if she's late I'll stay until you give her the consequence and then return tomorrow night when you need to make sure she comes home earlier? Let's also take a few minutes now to talk about what you want to do if Amy gets angry." (Make a plan)*

*Rico: "That would be great. I really appreciate this. I know I should be able to do this on my own but Amy can really get angry sometimes."*

*Consultant: "That's okay. You will be doing this on your own before you know it. Sometimes we all need a little support at first when trying something new. You are very good at setting curfews and you are doing a wonderful job of making sure Amy knows what to expect. You just need to let her know you are serious. You'll do fine. (Praise) Now that we have a plan to deal with Amy staying out late let's talk some more about a plan to deal with her anger."*

# 17

# Mediation and Contracting

*Webster's Dictionary* defines mediation as an intervention between conflicting parties to promote reconciliation, settlement, or compromise. For our purposes, a more generic definition might fit; that is, a process in which individuals or groups ask a neutral third party, with no power to make a decision, to help settle disputes. In this chapter we will discuss the Boys Town Family Preservation Services mediation process, mediator behaviors and goals, the different roles a mediator plays, and how a mediation session is conducted. We also will explain how to develop a written contract, the outcome of most mediation sessions.

## The Process of Mediation

The process of mediation involves a discussion of issues or options in response to a problem. It helps individuals to arrive at a mutually agreeable decision.

Typically when one thinks of mediation, labor contract talks or labor strikes come to mind. When two sides of an issue reach an impasse, they call in a mediator to help negotiate a settlement. In the Boys Town Family Preservation program, the parties who need mediation usually are parents or guardians, and children. As a Consultant, you are the mediator when disputes arise. You help settle disputes between family members who cannot agree on an issue.

This process has been beneficial during treatment when there is frequent arguing between family members, when there is little or no communication or compromise, and when family members are not listening to each other's views. Mediation provides an avenue for the Consultant to begin negotiations, compromise, and communication among family members. Often it can be a valuable tool when unresolved conflicts or important issues arise and create an impasse to treatment. The Consultant can use the process of mediation to help the family move beyond a singular, all-consuming issue and on to learning skills.

When a settlement or agreement is reached, it often is necessary to develop a mediation contract that spells out and clarifies what each individual agrees to do. When working with families, this contract can sometimes be a verbal agreement.

## Mediator Behaviors

In order to successfully mediate a family's disputes, Consultants must adapt a certain set of behaviors.

The first set is called trust-building behaviors. These behaviors allow the Consultant to build trust between the parties who are dueling with each other. The first behavior is active listening, which is discussed in Chapter 8. It is important to remember that in working out a mediation between family members you must be able to listen, to sometimes be a silent participant. Demonstrate interest with head nods, smiles, and facial expressions of concern. As both a Consultant and a mediator,

you must be able to be comfortable with silence. By not interjecting your opinions, you will encourage family members to talk, an important step toward helping them arrive at an agreement on their own. At the same time, though, you must be able to describe and repeat back to the parties what their concerns are, and know when it is appropriate to do so. Be careful not to evaluate whether or not you agree or disagree with their concerns; just be able to describe them.

A second trust-building behavior is promoting equality. This means that during this process, you are going to be an equal with the family members while promoting equality between the family members involved in the disagreement. Be sure to show empathy and concern about what the family members are going through. Concentrate on praising input and the fact that the family members are cooperating to fix the problem, rather than on the content of what they want changed. Equality should be promoted even when working through child/parent mediation. In order to conduct mediation, the children can participate only if their input and concerns are given equal consideration. It is up to you to see that all participants are given the same rights in the mediation process.

Another behavior a Consultant should engage in while mediating is note-taking. With all of the information that can come in during mediation, it's often necessary to write down what is being said and what is happening. The family is going to be expressing a lot of concerns and you need to be accurate when repeating what one party said to the other. Misinterpreting statements or inaccurately repeating something can hinder progress and sometimes push back the process.

The mediator also is responsible for making the negotiations manageable. This behavior involves preventing fighting among family members while allowing for conflict. Sometimes there is a very fine line between conflict and fighting. The difference is that fighting creates a situation where nothing is accomplished, while conflict can bring out useful information about the family and its dynamics. As the mediator, you must decide when conflict might cross over to open fighting and be prepared to redirect the session. If fighting does occur, you can do several things. You can ask the family members to talk directly to you and not to one another until they are feeling calmer. You also can ask them to separate from one another for awhile. You may need to use the crisis intervention technique described in next chapter. For mediation to work, family members must feel and be safe. Limiting the number of people involved in the mediation process also can make negotiations manageable. Working with only a few people is less time-consuming and gives everyone a chance to present his or her view. This same rationale applies to the number of issues that are being mediated. If you try to cover a large number of issues, you will become overwhelmed and little will get accomplished.

Creating and developing a problem-solving atmosphere is a crucial mediator behavior. You must get family members to focus on the future, not the past. Ask questions like, "What can you do to fix the problem?" and "What would you like to have happen to have this problem solved?" Accentuating the positive aspects of resolving conflicts can help the family think ahead to the future. Make sure you ask open-ended questions; they encourage more conversation and help family members identify their issues.

Finally, it is important for the mediator to gather all pertinent information about the problem from all of the parties involved in the dispute. Active listening, observing, note-taking, and asking open-ended questions to encourage discussion are the methods that will help achieve this goal.

While these behaviors make the mediator an active participant in the process, the family members are the ones who must come up with solutions to their problems. Your role as a mediator is to remain neutral and to lend a subtle guiding hand when necessary.

## The Mediator's Roles

The first role the mediator plays is that of a communicator. As a mediator, you set up the channels of communication between the family members who, for whatever reason, are not speaking to each other. You also intervene to transmit or translate information to those involved. This is crucial when the parties are not understanding or speaking to each other. You can model how to communicate as well as encourage and support family members to communicate more.

Your second role is that of distinguisher. This calls for you to help individuals identify their true needs. By the time families reach the point that they need a mediator, they often are feeling confused about what they really want or need. You are going to help them define exactly what must occur for the dispute to be settled. You will help modify positions as needed, ask for compromise, and try to get family members to understand and consider each other's compromise.

Your third role is that of reality agent. As an agreement is reached, the mediator works to increase each person's awareness of the needs of the others. You will help the individuals assess the risks and benefits of resolving the conflict or not resolving the conflict, and the outcome of decisions. If a person suggests an impractical or dangerous solution (e.g. a child says he will run away; a parent says she will beat her child), you must point out the negative consequences of such actions. When a person says he or she will not compromise at all, it is your job to remind that person that the conflict will continue unless a solution is found, and to suggest what he or she might have to do as part of the solution. To be a reality agent, you will need to remain nonjudgmental and be careful not to discount what family members see as important.

## The Mediation Session

The mediation session consists of five segments. This section will explain them and how each one is carried out.

- **Initial joint session**
- **Individual sessions (as many as needed to reach a compromise)**
- **Mediation contract (Agreement)**
- **Final joint session**
- **Follow-up**

### Initial Joint Session

Once you have determined that mediation is necessary, the first step will be to gather all the involved parties for a joint discussion.

Limiting the group to only the persons who are directly involved in or affected by the issue will help you remain on the topic and complete the process more quickly. To determine who should participate, you can use assessment to identify the main parties in the dispute. If this is not done before the initial joint session, it may become apparent during the session that others can contribute to resolving the conflict. These select participants can then proceed through the mediation process with your guidance as a communicator, distinguisher, and reality agent, as well as a facilitator and translator.

It is up to the Consultant to initiate and guide the discussion. This is a crucial role since family members, to this point, have not been discussing much of anything. You must be able to keep the discussion moving, handling conflict so it becomes an impetus for change rather than a reinforcer of hardened positions, and phrasing and rephrasing areas of possible agreement (Center for Dispute Settlement, 1988). During the initial joint session, identifying everyone's concerns can lead to some initial expression of related concerns.

As the neutral third party, you should begin this session by providing some information about mediation to the participants. Explaining the process to the family members is important because it is a new procedure and there are differences between it and your regular visits.

These are the main points you should share:

- Explain the mediation process and your role. You can tell family members how you will help them reach solutions by sorting through the issues without taking sides.
- Explain the different sessions, both joint and individual, and how each fam-

138

ily member will be allowed to express his or her concerns.

- Inform family members that information disclosed during individual sessions may be shared with the rest of the family, unless a family member specifically requests that certain information not be shared with everyone. Disclosures of abuse or someone's intent to harm himself or herself, or others, would not be kept confidential.

- Explain that the tangible result of this process will be a written "contract" that all of the involved parties will sign. Describe how each member will have clearly stated responsibilities in the final agreement. The "contract" will be a short-term agreement that will be reviewed at a designated time so any necessary changes can be made.

- Explain that note-taking may be necessary so that you can sort out specifics for everyone. If this has not been part of your normal routine as a Consultant, mentioning your change in behavior will be necessary.

Once the process has been explained, you are ready to begin mediating. Since you will be asking the involved family members to begin discussing a sensitive and disruptive issue, it is critical for you to remain calm and relaxed throughout the process in order to promote problem-solving. Your gestures and body posture should communicate attentiveness and neutrality. As a mediator, your goal is to begin sifting through the concerns so that you can narrow down issues into one or a few key points of disagreement and agreement. All participants need to know that their view-

point will be understood and respected so that the process can be successful.

During the first joint session, it is important for family members to begin hearing each other's concerns. Many times up to this point, no one has listened, the parties have been distracted from the real issue, or they have been too angry to reach a solution. As a mediator, you will restate their concerns and promote a solution-focused outcome. Asking questions to identify goals will convey to family members a sense of hopefulness. Questions can be phrased this way: "Tyler (son), you've stated that you want your mother to quit fighting with your dad. What would you like to see your mom and dad doing instead?"; "Rebecca (mom), your request is that Tyler stop mouthing off to his dad. What should Tyler say or do?"; "Sam (dad), you want the fighting to stop every day, all day. You also said you want to come to a quiet house after work. Is that correct?"

These kinds of questions and the discussion they evoke will help you review each family member's concerns and help identify some goals before you begin the individual sessions.

## Individual Sessions

It is essential that you meet individually with each participating family member at least once so that you can obtain detailed information about the dispute. Often, the only way to explore real positions is in private. Private sessions have at least two, and frequently three, purposes: 1) to ensure that the mediator understands the needs of each family member, unrestrained by any reluctance to speak in front of the other person; 2) to explore settlement possibilities; and sometimes, 3) to enable the family members to continue to work toward an agreement in a case in which joint hostility, intimidation by one person, or lack of assertiveness by another convinces the mediator that joint sessions are unproductive (Center for Dispute Settlement, 1988).

Finding out more specifics about an individual's concerns, areas of possible compromise, and solutions will continue throughout the individual sessions. As the mediator, you will need concise information so that you can represent each family member and promote an agreement. Again, your task is to communicate, translate, and be a reality agent for all participants. Everything you do is directed toward helping the family members share their concerns and opinions so that they can reach a solution on their own. This is important because participants are more likely to follow through with the solution if it is theirs, not yours.

As a reality agent, you will need to test each member's commitment to the agreement before the final joint session. Once you have a good understanding of what each family member wants, you can make sure that each is willing to carry out what he or she has stated in the individual sessions. Reviewing each person's compromises and solutions before writing the contract will prevent disastrous misinterpretations during the final joint session.

## The Mediation Contract

The tangible result of the mediation is a written "contract" signed by all participating family members and the Consultant (Teare, 1994). The mediation contract should first be written as a rough draft that includes specific solutions the family has agreed on. These elements must be included in the contract:

- Each family member should have equal agreements in the contract. This keeps it balanced, and everyone will view the contract as fair.
- The contract should be written in the first person: "I, Sasha, agree to...." Each family member needs to have ownership in the agreement.
- The most difficult items should be written first. Beginning with the most difficult items helps everyone see the success.
- Include only those family members who participated in the mediation. The process is more difficult to manage when you include others. If they were not there to reach an agreement, how can they carry out the agreement?
- Agreements should be as specific as possible and be written using the family's terminology. This includes time lines, who is responsible, the task or behavior, and the specifics of the task. Using specifics and family terms makes it more likely that family members will remember and stick to their commitments. Contracts should include short time lines so that they can be accomplished and the family can experience success quickly.
- If the contract involves rewards or consequences, include what they are, who will give them, and who will receive them.

After the rough draft is read to each family member, the contract is written in its final form.

Here is an example of a mediation contract that was used to help a family resolve a conflict.

# MEDIATION AGREEMENT

04-27-94

We, Bill and Dawn (parents), agree that Jamie's curfew will be 10 p.m. Sunday — Thursday and 12 midnight Friday and Saturday.

I, Jamie, agree that Sunday-Thursday I will go out two nights only, have a friend over two nights, and stay home one night without having anyone over.

For every one minute I, Jamie, am late I will lose one minute the next day.

I, Jamie, agree that prior to leaving the home or having someone over I will wait until mom comes home, report where I am going, and with whom.

We, Bill and Dawn, agree that if we are later than 6 p.m. Jamie can leave a note.

I, Jamie, understand that I must ask permission 24 hours in advance if I want someone to spend the night or if I want to stay with someone. Failure to ask beforehand will result in automatic denial of privilege.

We, Bill and Dawn, understand that Jamie can leave home for 15 minutes when angry to cool down. Any later will be considered a manipulation and result in loss of a privilege such as going out or sleeping over.

I, Jamie, understand that if I continue to argue or use foul language when prompted to stop, I will lose the privilege of going out.

We, Jamie, Bill, and Dawn, agree to review the agreement five days from today's date.

_____          _____
**Participant's Signature**                      **Participant's Signature**

_____          _____
**Participant's Signature**                      **Participant's Signature**

_____          _____
**Mediator's Signature**                          **Mediator's Signature**

### Final Joint Session

The final joint session is the time to read the final written agreement. Everyone who has participated in the mediation process should be present. Although each person has individually heard and agreed to the components of the contract, it must be read aloud to avoid any misunderstandings. If everyone still agrees with the contract's conditions after it is read, everyone signs and dates the document. A copy is given to the family.

### Follow-Up

Written contracts are not magical. We cannot assume that because family members have gone through this lengthy process, stated their willingness to resolve the issue, and written commitments on paper, that everyone will carry out the terms of the agreement.

That is why a follow-up is necessary. The follow-up is a meeting you schedule with the family to see how things are going, how the contract is holding up, and if the family needs to renegotiate any area and how it was accomplished. Follow-ups can occur during the next visit or within a few days.

Many techniques discussed in this book will be useful in the follow-up process. If the contract is not followed, you can assess the situation through these questions:

- Did you stay focused on the family's issues? It was the family's conflict that began this process; remaining on that issue is critical to success.
- Does the agreement need to be modified? Many times the family members will tell you, as early as the next day, that they've changed the contract and agreed on different terms. Great! The family has reached a solution to another dispute. You may need to help with this process, or the family may adjust the contract on its own. The important issue is that the family is not obsessed with the conflict. Members are more solution-focused.
- Is the contract no longer needed? The mediation process itself may have created enough communication to move the family forward, out of crisis and the dredges of conflict. Everyone now has gone beyond the dispute and can focus on other matters.

## Summary

Mediation is a powerful tool to use in working with families. In order for it to be successful, you must remember to stay focused on the family's issues. The issues belong to the family members and you can be most effective by helping them to solve their problem, rather than solving it for them because it seems quicker and less painful to do so. Families who can come up with their own solutions are more likely to comply and follow through with the end decision.

Obviously, you should use mediation only when it appears that other intervention techniques are not helping the family resolve an issue. There usually are indicators that will signal the need for mediation. For example, if the family is in a crisis and the members are not willing to problem-solve or speak to each other, it may be an opportune time for mediation. When this happens, some families benefit simply from developing and following a defined, written agreement that spells out each person's role.

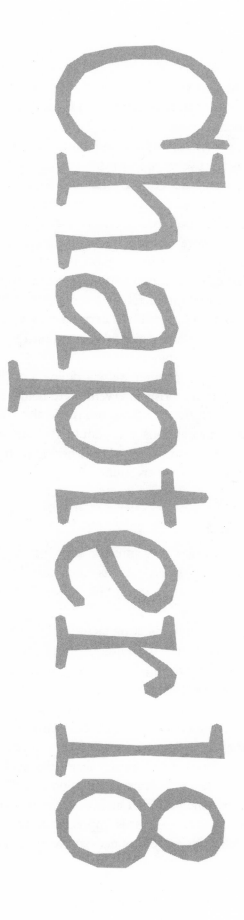

# 18

# Crisis Intervention

So far in this book we have talked a lot about identifying and developing a family's strengths. We have stressed how important it is to respect a family in whose home you are providing treatment, and how the relationship you build and the effective intervention techniques you implement will assist you in creating long-lasting changes within that home. But we would be remiss in our goal of explaining family preservation work without talking about the times when a Consultant may face a potentially explosive, dangerous situation in a home, a situation that places the family in a state of crisis. This is not the "chronic" state of crisis often associated with families that are referred to Family Preservation Services — those families that seem to have a crisis lifestyle. The situation we are referring to involves an "acute" state of crisis, where families reach such a high level of chaos and tension that they don't know how they will make it through the next day or even the next hour. These situations generally are associated with domestic violence, abuse, yelling and screaming, or family members refusing to talk to each other. Even though the family may have been referred for some of these problems, the level at which these behaviors occur during a period of acute crisis can become imminently dangerous. And even though you will remain strength-focused, understanding the reality of these critical situations and how to handle them is essential.

Working with a family during an acute crisis is a two-edged sword; there are both benefits and dangers. By helping a family sort through its crisis, you are teaching skills that can be developed later. The family also tends to be more amenable to change because of the anxiety the crisis is producing. On the other hand, the situation you are in can be frightening and unpredictable; in some cases, physical violence is possible. Learning how to recognize this danger and protect yourself is of primary importance.

In this chapter we will define a crisis and how to use crisis intervention to help a family through these difficult times. We also will discuss precautions you should take to protect yourself and others when working with families in acute crisis situations.

# Crisis

A crisis is a situation in which a family faces an obstacle to its important life goals that, for a time, cannot be overcome using the usual problem-solving methods. In other words, a precipitating factor places the family in crisis and the family's usual methods of problem-solving are not working at that time (Caplan, 1964).

It is not uncommon for a family to become upset when problems arise in everyday life. But family members usually can resolve those problems using the skills they have learned. A crisis situation occurs when those methods fail and the family is unsure what to do next. It is important to remember that a crisis does not necessarily mean that the family is confronted with a totally new situation. Rather, a crisis is more likely to arise from a situation in which a new factor is added, which makes it intolerable (Brockopp, 1973). The crisis is not the situation itself, but the family's response to the situation.

Caplan (1964) also describes the process of crisis in four stages. In Stage One, the event or situation stimulates an initial rise in tension within the family, which causes the family to respond in its usual manner because this strategy has been successful in the past. In Stage Two, the initial attempt to problem-solve the issue using old behaviors is unsuccessful and tension increases. In Stage Three, the family begins trying new behaviors (obtained internally or externally) to solve the problem. As a result the problem may decrease in intensity, and the family may use emergency problem-solving methods. Members may see the problem in a new way and solve it, or they may give up and withdraw from the situation, deciding that a solution is impossible or that the goal is unattainable. In Stage Four, if the problem remains and it cannot be solved by the techniques available to the family, or if the family cannot avoid the problem, tension increases to a breaking point, often with drastic and critical results.

It is rather obvious that a crisis is a serious situation and can have a serious effect on the family structure and the individuals within the family. However, these same features can be seen positively, and the crisis can be viewed in a potentially positive light since it is a time of opportunity during which the family may be much more amenable to and benefit more from appropriate therapeutic intervention (Schwenk & Bittle, 1979).

## Types of Crises

Most crises fall into one of two categories: situational and developmental. A situational crisis is one that results from a circumstance that the family is unprepared to handle at that time. Situational crises could develop from such occurrences as a baby being born prematurely, drug use, a drug overdose, an untimely death, or a major or terminal physical illness. Divorce within a family could cause a situational crisis, as could a change in status and family roles (loss of a job, moving to a new place, a cut in pay). These crises can overlap. In fact, many of the families we work with have two or three crises occurring at the same time; for example, a family is going through a divorce, the teenage daughter gets picked up for driving under the influence of alcohol, and the dad just took a cut in pay at work. Or a family member recently has had a major illness, which caused the person to lose his or her job, which created financial strains and possible changes in the family's status in the community.

Developmental crises are those that are expected in the normal movement of an individual from birth to death. They are predictable; we know they will arise in a family's lifetime. Many of them cannot be changed; for example, everyone goes through the crisis of adolescence. Developmental crises can be modified and made less difficult. Often, the crises associated with developmental issues seem ongoing; as soon as we get used to one stage and learn how to handle the problems that arise, another one comes along. Other examples of developmental crises include a birth, "the terrible twos," middle age, and old age.

Everyone is going to experience developmental crises. However, if situational crises occur during a time when the family is already experiencing some developmental crises, the result may overwhelm a family and create tension to the extent that the family experiences a "crisis reaction," a state of upset or disequilibrium that exists during attempts to resolve the situation (Barth, 1990). This reaction moves the family toward a state of acute crisis in which the family's customary problem-solving responses don't work.

## Crisis Intervention

With a family in crisis, crisis intervention is the treatment of choice. As mentioned earlier, a family is in a state of chaos during a crisis, and as a result, family members can experience considerable change in a relatively short period of time. Their normal pattern of behavior has been broken, their defenses are now open, and they are more susceptible to new ideas. They are motivated to solve the problem and are more open and willing to obtain assistance (Kinney, Haapala, & Booth, 1991).

Crisis intervention is an active, solution-oriented approach that focuses on the family's abilities to resolve its crisis. This intervention focuses on the immediate issues that are creating the stress and temporarily sets aside the previous issues that were being addressed. Your role as a Consultant is to help the family members divide the crisis into manageable parts they can deal with while modeling problem-solving skills that will contribute to the family's ability to address areas of difficulty. You also will continue to utilize the family members' individual strengths in order to move them toward crisis resolution, directing all of your energies to helping the family solve its problems. The ultimate goal of crisis intervention is to help the family return to the level it was functioning at before the crisis. Remember that whatever methods the family used in the past aren't working now, and members don't know how to get out of the situation they are in.

During this time, emphasis is placed on the immediate causes of the crisis, the processes necessary for regaining a precrisis level of functioning, and the family's ability to work through its problem. Crisis intervention done properly can help the family develop new and appropriate ways of approaching a crisis, new ways to problem-solve, and a better way to resolve future crisis situations. Crisis intervention views people in terms of their abilities, strengths, and potential to problem-solve. It assumes the family members will respond correctly if given information in a setting in which they can use the information, and that a family's behavior will tend to move toward desirable outcomes. It also emphasizes the active, directive role of the Consultant in the process of assisting the family to move out of a crisis situation (Brockopp, 1973).

Hausman and Rioch (1967) discuss five basic concepts for effective crisis intervention. These include immediacy, proximity, concurrence, commitment, and expectancy.

## Immediacy

Effective crisis intervention depends upon the immediacy of the treatment program. During the crisis period, the family members are open to change; the sooner you work with the family members, the more likely you will improve their functioning level. Immediacy of treatment gives value to the family because there is a sense of importance; the family is not being placed on a waiting list but rather is receiving immediate assistance.

## Proximity

When you can deal with a family's problem in the setting in which the problem occurred (i.e. the home), the solution can develop from the pertinent, positive social aspects of the environment. Therefore, it will be appropriate to that environment and it will be more likely that the family will use it.

## Commitment

One of the essential elements of working with a crisis situation and probably one of the most easily achieved is the idea of commitment. The family in crisis must be able to commit itself to working with the Consultant to solve the problem. Commitment usually is easy to obtain because the family is in a state of pain and anxiety and wants resolution to the problem. A conscious commitment on the part of family members is essential in that they need to take responsibility for their actions and their part in the crisis situation. By accepting responsibility for the crisis and the development of the solution, the family will determine the effectiveness and accuracy of the solution, not the Consultant.

## Concurrence

During crisis intervention, the Consultant must determine if the family needs additional support from relatives, friends, counseling centers, or other agencies. In some families after a crisis is over, members may still require additional services to address personal long-term therapeutic needs, such as issues that deal with suicide, marriage, rape, or abuse. In these cases, linking the family to formal or informal community resources (see Chapter 3) would be appropriate. Many families, however, simply need help getting through the acute crisis stage; then they are able to handle issues through their normal support systems and do not need additional assistance. Thorough assessment during crisis intervention will help you make this appraisal.

### Expectancy

Emphasis must be given to the family's potential, positive aspects, and skills. The family in crisis is usually aware only of its anguish and pain, and often does not view itself in positive terms. Often, family members expect a negative outcome. By showing that you, expect the family to succeed, you can cut through some of these problems and help the family see that the end can be positive. You can destroy the family's self-fulfilling negative prophesies and replace them with positive ones. The use of Effective Praise, metaphors, and reframing can enhance the sense of expectancy. (See Chapters 10, 11, and 14.) Expectancy also helps the individual family members relate to each other in a positive way because you have modeled this view of the family.

During crisis intervention the Consultant can help the family defuse the crisis and help family members ventilate and identify their feelings about the situation. This solution-oriented approach moves the family forward rather than focusing on the past. Crisis intervention is designed to be short term, offering an accurate assessment of the immediate problem; a thorough diagnostic evaluation is not necessary for an effective intervention. Remember that your goal is to bring the family back to its normal level of functioning.

Let's look at some behaviors you must engage in to make intervention with a family effective during a time of crisis. You may find it helpful to follow the "decision tree" diagram on the next page as you read the descriptions of the crisis intervention techniques.

## Consultant Behaviors

We all have crisis situations occur in our lives. The people who helped you during your crises may still feel a sense of attachment to you. Crises tend to bring people together because of the help that is provided. Often, people who are caught in a natural disaster talk long after a crisis is over about the Red Cross worker who helped them find a place to stay and food to eat. They remember neighbors who took them in and understood the fear and anxiety they were experiencing. These contacts do not necessarily last a long time, but they are significant in the degree of attachment and gratitude that remains once the crisis is over.

What are the characteristics of people who help others in need? Do they simply take over so that the person who needs help doesn't have to think or be responsible for awhile? Or do they help the person sort through the mess, assess options, and keep focused on finding a resolution to the problem?

In most cases, the second description would fit — people who come to the assistance of others provide confidence and hope, as well as help to resolve the problem and move

# Crisis Intervention Decision Tree

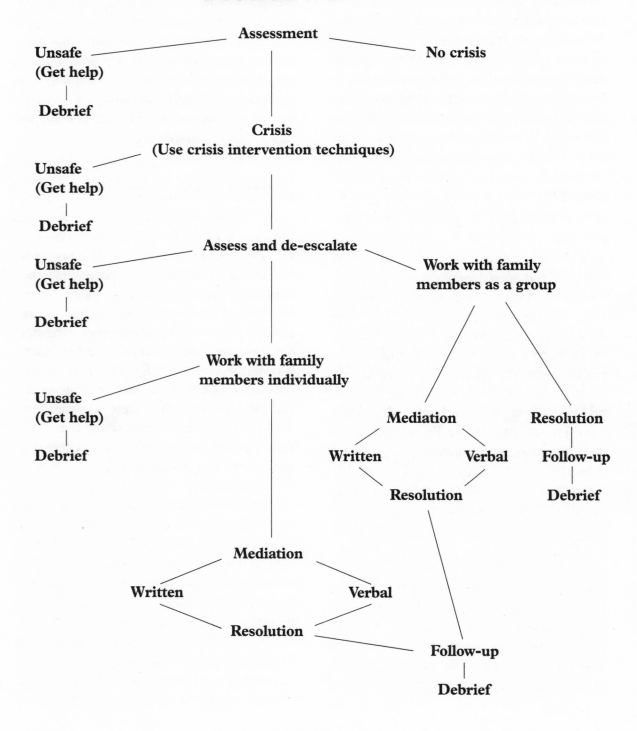

beyond the crisis. And that's exactly what a Consultant does in a family crisis situation.

One of the first things you must do as a Consultant working with a family in crisis is to determine if a crisis actually exists. It is crucial that you assess whether the family is truly in an acute crisis state or is engaging in crisis lifestyle behaviors or behaviors that are part of the family's dynamics. Members of some families often interact by yelling and screaming at each other. This does not necessarily constitute a crisis. Families that are frequently overwhelmed by issues within their environment also might consider every situation outside their normal routines a crisis, and crisis intervention is not necessary.

However, there are families that will face serious problems, and it will be important for you to assess and sort through what is real and what is perceived. Therefore, it is imperative that you assess the situation before beginning an intervention. This is a confusing and challenging time as concerns and issues continually arise. The critical areas you should assess in a crisis situation include:

• The family's perception of the problem. Understanding the family's concerns allows you to begin planning your intervention.
• The family's goals. Developing goals for resolving the crisis keeps the family focused on solutions, not problems.
• How the family has tried to solve the problem in the past. This information will provide you with a foundation upon which to build an effective solution to the crisis.
• What the outcome will look like and what you still need to do to resolve the problem.

A second behavior a Consultant should engage in is using problem-solving techniques to reach a solution within a relatively short period of time. The tension level in a home during times of acute crisis is very high and often volatile. By remaining solution-oriented, you keep the family and yourself from becoming overwhelmed and bogged down in the myriad of problems and issues that may arise. Your energies should be directed to the resolution of the crisis and the critical issues pertaining to the crisis. Your focus should be on the issues and goals that are part of the crisis. At the same time, however, the family may be trying to solve the problem in ways that are different from what you are used to using, but that are a necessary part of the family's problem-solving methods. For example, a family may engage in activities that are not related to the crisis, such as washing clothes, fixing appliances, or making beds. These activities may seem obsessive but they might help the family regain control and focus on the issues related to the problem. By allowing the family members to complete these activities, you are developing a stronger relationship with them and gaining valuable information about how they solve problems.

The Consultant also must engage in specific problem-solving techniques that work best for the family in the current crisis situation. Techniques such as **SODAS**, negotiation, compromise, and mediation are effective in dealing with crises. (Mediation is discussed in detail in Chapter 17; information on **SODAS**, negotiation, and compromise can be found in the Boys Town publication, *Teaching Social Skills to Youth*, 1992.)

Let's take a look at the problem-solving behaviors displayed by the Consultant:

- Identify the family's strengths and style in problem-solving and remain solution-oriented.
- Stay focused on resolution of the crisis and avoid getting into issues not directly related to the problem.
- Respect the family's procedures for dealing with issues. Though these procedures may seem different, they allow the family to refocus energies toward resolving the crisis.

Many crises involve more than one family member. So it's essential that you are on equal terms with everyone who is involved in the crisis and make sure that each family member is treated equally. You should remain neutral to each individual's concerns and perceptions of what is occurring. If you side with one family member, you risk getting blamed for the problem and escalating the crisis. By staying neutral you allow the family members to freely vent their frustrations and disclose their concerns and solutions to the crisis.

As always, a Consultant's verbal and nonverbal behaviors are an important part of any type of intervention. In a crisis intervention, your body language often is critical in de-escalating a situation and helping family members calm down so they can begin addressing the issues at hand. Effective verbal and nonverbal behaviors include:

- Maintaining a calm voice tone. Crisis situations often get your adrenaline flowing. This may cause you to shout or become silent, or make your voice quiver. Be aware of your reactions to various situations and consciously maintain a calm voice. This keeps you focused on remaining calm and models composure for the family.
- Maintaining nonthreatening body postures. If you are a large person, lean, sit, or sit lower in your chair. Be careful not to assume a posture that could intimidate the family. If you are a small person, be sure to assert yourself appropriately. The key is to be as neutral as possible in your posture. Your body size should not be a factor in your participation in crisis resolution.
- Being aware of your own habits. For example, if you point when you talk, try not to point; speaking that way could be perceived as lecturing.
- Above all, do not be demanding. As discussed in Chapter 2 ("Cultural and Family Differences"), you are in someone else's home and need to convey respect to the family members by not lecturing or demanding things from them.

## Crisis Intervention Components

Once you have assessed the situation and determined that the family faces an acute crisis in which two or more family members are in conflict, it is time to begin the actual crisis intervention techniques. You will now assume a very active role in the intervention. In the beginning this will mean de-escalating the situation so that problem-solving can take place. Often by simply coughing, clearing your throat, or giving other indications of your presence, you can refocus the family members' energies toward you rather than each other. If these subtle mannerisms don't interrupt the situation, use subtle body movements — leaning forward, taking a step forward or back, shifting your weight, gently swaying, or crossing your arms — to divert family members' attention from the point of conflict to you. These mannerisms may gradually become more pronounced through reality statements, statements of concern, or statements of empathy.

You should always enter a situation using the least intrusive means first in order to allow the family members to de-escalate the situation themselves and therefore remain in control. The defusing period may occur quickly or it may take some time. Usually, though, the family will be anxious for someone to come in and help, and members will gladly turn to you for that help. If emotions continue to run high, you may decide to separate the individuals involved in the conflict for a cooling-down period. This gives everyone (including the Consultant) time to get their emotions under control so they can work together on a resolution. When separation is necessary, be sure you ask, not demand, that the family separate for awhile using rationales that apply to the situation. By using Criticism by Suggestion calmly, you are letting the family members make the decision while you model calming behaviors for them.

You may determine at this time that it is necessary to work with the family members individually in separate rooms. Begin working with the person you have identified as having the most control or power in the family. Getting this person to calm down often can lead the other family members to calm down, too. In addition, remember that your safety is paramount and that the person who is in control is generally the one who is most angry and tense. By working with that person first, you are creating a safer environment in which

to continue your intervention. There may be situations where a child is the controlling member of the family; in these cases, you might want to model respect for the parents' authority in the home by talking to a parent first instead of the child. In making your decision, however, consider your safety and the safety of the other family members. Usually, working with a child first is not a point of contention with a family in which everyone is aware of the child's tension, and family members may want someone to talk to the child first.

While working with one family member, ask the others to cool down by giving them something to do. Have them read a magazine, play the piano, or work on the car. You also can give them the assignment of thinking about how things can be fixed and what needs to change. Reassure them that you will be spending individual time with each one of them so they can voice their perceptions of the problem and possible solutions.

Once the family members have been separated, allow some time for everyone to cool off. Then begin your intervention with the individual you identified as "in control."

At this point you will have determined if the situation has been defused to the point that it is safe for you to go into a room alone with a family member. Once in the room, you can begin using active listening techniques along with exploration so that the family member can vent his or her feelings and move into a solution-oriented state of mind. By directing your questions to what the person perceives to be the problem, and what needs to occur to fix the problem, you are modeling how to stay solution-oriented.

You also can use the mediation techniques discussed in Chapter 17 to talk with each family member. In these sessions, as you discuss the agenda of other family members, you will be modeling how negotiation and compromise can be used to avoid crisis situations. When individuals refuse to budge on an issue or are making unrealistic demands, the **SODAS** method of problem-solving is often useful. This method allows the family member to look at the options he or she has, as well as the advantages of each option.

Once family members, in their individual sessions, agree on what needs to occur to resolve the crisis and their roles in the resolution, they can be brought back together and a plan can be devised. This plan may be written or verbal, and should spell out each member's role in maintaining the resolution.

Whether you work with the family members individually or as a group, you will use whatever intervention techniques work to return the family to a functional state. At some point, you need to assess if the family has returned to its "normal" functioning level. Has the crisis you came into the home to address been resolved? The family may no longer be fighting and the tension may appear to have de-escalated. It may appear that the problem-solving technique you chose was effective in resolving the acute crisis, and you have considered whether or not the family needs additional services. It may appear that your job is finished. However, there's still more to do.

Once you have reached a resolution to the crisis and the family is satisfied with it, make a plan to check back with family members to see how they have maintained their resolution. Leave them with a plan on what to do if the situation begins to re-escalate. This plan could include contacting you if you feel this would be helpful to the family.

## Safety Issues

Many Consultants think that the most important element of a crisis intervention is to de-escalate the situation. But the most important element is really your safety. You cannot help anyone if you are injured. If emergency help is needed, someone must be able to make the call. If you are hurt, you will not be able to make that call. Throughout this book we have talked about being sensitive to family needs. Now it's time to talk about the reality of working in other people's homes and the situations that can arise under crisis circumstances.

Since the Boys Town Family Preservation program began in 1989, there have been several instances where Consultants faced dangerous circumstances. One Consultant was working with a family that had a history of domestic violence when the husband began a fight with the wife that escalated to dangerous proportions. In another incident, a child brought a rattlesnake into the house and said he was going to let it go. Once, a girl pulled a butcher knife on her brother and threatened to kill him. There also was a guardian who threw the 15-year-old son on the ground and began to hit him. All of these situations bring home the reality of dealing with families in crisis. You must monitor and assess your own safety because no one else is going to.

With that thought in mind, there are several things you must do when you first enter a family's home to begin an intervention. First, locate the doorways and exits. That way if you find yourself between people as they begin to fight, you know where your escape route is. You also should look around for weapons or objects that could be used as weapons. Never try to intervene in a confrontation involving weapons or physical assault. It's better to leave and get help rather than try to stop a child who is threatening someone with a knife or a caretaker who is beating a 15-year-old.

Be alert and watchful for any potentially dangerous situations that my threaten your or the family's safety. One of the most difficult times to leave a family is when a child is being hurt or a victim is being victimized. But you must remember that in acute crisis situations, a family member's adrenaline is pumping and the individual often is not aware of who he or she is hurting. If you try to interfere, you are likely to be hurt and no one will be able to help you or the family. If you see that a situation is escalating, leave and go get help.

In listening to child-protection workers and Consultants from around the country, it seems that the most experienced workers are always aware of what could happen and what objects are present in the environment that could be dangerous. Then when a situation begins to escalate, only a quick assessment is needed to determine where you are in relation to danger. This is not the time to be naive about serving families. It is the time to protect yourself by respecting the potential dangers to you within the environment.

Part of taking care of yourself includes winding down after the crisis is over. It is difficult to pull a family through a crisis and not have emotional baggage left over. After dealing with the intensity of a crisis, it is important for you to take some time to debrief. Be sure to seek support and validation from both your supervisor and peers concerning how the crisis was handled. We often are too critical of our own work and we need fellow workers to bring us back to the reality of working with needy families. Avoid becoming overly involved with what occurred in the family. As you debrief, don't look at a crisis as a step backward in your intervention or as a sign of a failed intervention. Keep focused on the opportunities crises provide for teaching a family and creating progress and change. Analyze the incident when it is over to determine which intervention techniques worked and which ones didn't, and assess what good came out of the crisis. Then discuss it with your supervisor so he or she is aware of the situations you faced and can provide you with an objective point of view on the situation. By looking at the situation from the perspective of an objective observer, you can separate yourself from the flood of emotions that were unleashed during the visit. You can understand what your limits are and respect them.

And remember that your task during the crisis was to return the family to its normal state of functioning. No one is expected to be perfect in crisis situations. But the more you talk to someone and analyze the incident, the better you will manage your own stress level, and the more prepared you will be for the next visit with this or another family crisis.

## Summary

Crisis intervention is a specialized approach that Family Consultants can use when a family faces an acute crisis. This systematic method of assessing and intervening can help a Consultant assist families with their problems in a fashion that is constructive for both the family and the Consultant.

Consultants need to be secure in themselves to do crisis intervention. They must be able to put themselves wholeheartedly and unflinchingly into the relationship with the family. They must be able to give of themselves to satisfy the family's needs. However, they must be careful not to get so involved that they lose their own perspective or jeopardize their safety. Finally, they must be able to walk away once a resolution is found, assess all that has occurred, and use what they learn to make their next crisis intervention successful.

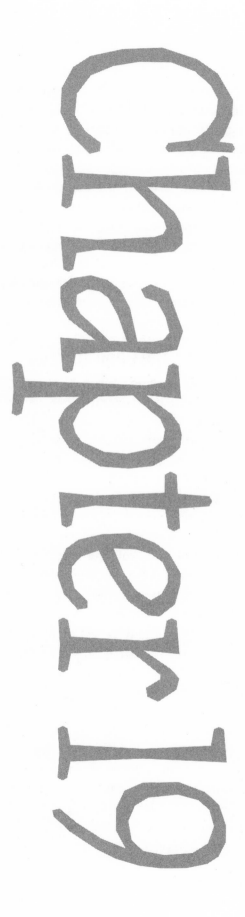

# 19

# Perceiving Opportunities to Teach

A common question asked about the effectiveness of family preservation programs concerns how much a family can learn in such a short amount of time. This question has merit since the average length of a Boys Town intervention with a family is between six and eight weeks. The challenge to the Consultant is to make the most of the time that is spent with the family. The Boys Town Family Preservation program recognizes this challenge and emphasizes having a Consultant make every moment spent with a family purposeful. We've found that an intensive, focused, competency-based intervention can be extremely effective in keeping families together and teaching skills that a family can use for years to come. The focus of this chapter is how Consultants can perceive opportunities to teach during the intervention so that time spent with families is as productive as possible.

An opportunity to teach is defined as anytime the Consultant is with the family. This can be at the family's home, at the store, or at a restaurant. It also can be while the Consultant is helping the family do laundry, cooking dinner, or taking the children to the park. In all of these situations, the skilled Consultant can find an opportunity to teach a family. Why? Because a family is always engaging in some type of behavior, interaction, or discussion while a Consultant is with them. An opportunity may be a situation in which family members fail to recognize a skill they could use or use a skill inappropriately. Or it could be when a family uses a skill or part of a skill effectively.

The key to successful teaching is the ability to recognize or perceive an opportunity to teach. And the Consultant must know the different ways he or she can teach skills to the family when these opportunities arise.

## Perceiving the Opportunities

Imagine sending your child to school and finding out that 10 percent of her day is spent in lectures about reading, writing, and arithmetic, and the rest of the day is spent in recess. You probably would be infuriated that your child is not receiving an adequate education. You might even argue that your child's teacher is wasting valuable time and failing to provide the best education possible. If this scenario was true, you would not hesitate to transfer your child to another school because her current school is wasting, overlooking, and ignoring opportunities to teach.

Most people fully expect their children to be educated in a variety of ways throughout the entire school day. A Consultant who is providing intensive services to prevent the out-of-home placement of a family's children is held to these same high expectations. Every moment a Consultant works with a family provides opportunities to teach skills. A Consultant must recognize and capitalize on these moments with a teaching effort referring agencies expect and families who want to stay together deserve.

From the moment you begin working with a family, you are going to be assessing strengths and problem areas. You also will be assessing the opportunities for teaching this family. Some opportunities to teach will be obvious. For example, there may be visits where you observe a lot of activity going on — the nine-month-old eating feces from the cat's litter box while a parent and teenager yell at each other in another room and the parent grounds the teenager "for life." These two opportunities would offer ample chances for teaching. On the other hand, there will be visits where there is little activity, such as when you are meeting with only one family member, or a family tells you there are no problems. During these visits, opportunities may be less obvious. But whether the opportunities are obvious or subtle, you should be teaching all the time. A visit where there is little going on simply challenges the novice Consultant to work hard to discover what, when, and where to teach.

Opportunities to teach are most easily perceived when the Consultant has a strong foundation of knowledge in child management, child development, issues of abuse and neglect, communication, and other problem areas families commonly encounter. Knowing the theory and skills that make for a successful therapeutic intervention is key to being able to assess and perceive opportunities to teach. Also, opportunities to teach become more evident as you spend more time with each family and are able to assess strengths and weaknesses. Your initial visits with a family will provide countless opportunities but you may not be able to easily recognize some of them until you notice patterns as the opportunities are repeated.

# Teaching to Opportunities

In this section, we will highlight several ways to teach that have not been described in Chapters 7 through 18. As each method is explained, you will find they are often subtle, but very effective because they can be used frequently and strategically. Many of these methods are nonverbal. That is, they can be carried out without talking. They provide more avenues to influence family behaviors and bring about change more quickly, especially if used whenever opportunities are perceived.

## *Modeling*

Modeling is effective because imitation repeatedly has proven to be a powerful learning process. This method can be easily used throughout the intervention and is especially useful during the first phases.

Modeling is based on the principles of Social Learning Theory. It is one of the most effective ways to teach new skills (Baldwin & Baldwin, 1986). We know that one person's actions can serve as a model for others. Common examples of the effects of modeling are when children imitate their parents' discipline styles by putting their dolls or stuffed animals in "time-out," or when a family member charged with physical abuse says, "That's the way my parents raised me!" Another example is when a teenager wears a bandanna, leather jacket, and baggy pants after seeing his peers wear the same kind of clothing.

Teaching through modeling can be a deliberate or an unconscious act. By talking with a teenager about an upcoming date, you may be deliberately modeling to the parents how to communicate with their child.

Unconsciously, you are teaching stylistically by conveying mannerisms and other quality components of interacting. Whether deliberate or not, you are constantly teaching through modeling. Good Consultants are very deliberate, taking care to model what they want people to learn in every interaction (Father Flanagan's Boys' Home, 1991).

Without talking about what is being taught, a Consultant can demonstrate a variety of skills. Instead of trying to explain a new skill to a family member, you can simply model the skill and the family member can observe what happens. For example, as part of your treatment plan, you can model to parents how they can maintain their household and meet their children's basic needs, even during bouts of depression. You can preplan some meals so they just have to be taken out of the freezer and heated, and get into the routine of doing one load of laundry each day, and giving the kids baths daily, or placing money in envelopes to pay bills as soon as the money comes in. By you doing these things every day during your visits, you are showing the parents that even though they may not feel like going through these routines, they have to in order to take care of the family.

You also can model for a parent how praising a child for engaging in appropriate behaviors can motivate the child to respond with more appropriate behaviors. For example, you can model the effectiveness of praise by telling the four-year-old what a good helper she is when she clears the dishes off the table. Then when the child asks if she can do another chore to help, you can continue to model giving praise to the child for asking what other things she can do.

Modeling is a good method for teaching alternative ways to manage behaviors that family members may never have considered. You can demonstrate through modeling how using negotiation or anger control can affect behaviors instead of trying to convince the family to try these skills simply because you say "they work." If you effectively model how a new skill works, you won't need to convince the family members that it does. They will be more eager to learn and try these skills if they have observed their effectiveness.

Because modeling is such a powerful method for teaching new skills to families, it is very important to understand that you are modeling behaviors every moment you are with a family. Given this, your actions should be thought through and be consistent with the concepts you want the family to learn. How is the following scenario an example of inappropriate modeling?

## Example 1

*The Consultant is talking with the grandfather in the kitchen about problems he has been having with high blood pressure and headaches. The seven-year-old grandson comes into the room and demands that someone help him finish his math homework. The grandfather yells that when he is done talking and making some coffee he'll help him. The grandson continues to whine and starts shouting out questions like "What's 22 minus 9?" His questions get louder and he approaches the Consultant with his worksheet and says, "How do I do this problem?" The Consultant explains to the child how to work the problem and praises the child for asking for help.*

It is possible to inadvertently model inappropriate skills if you are not careful. For example, if you were to engage in a debate with a youth about whether she has the right to stay out as long as she wants, you may be modeling to the youth that arguing with adults is acceptable.

The Consultant in the example modeled inappropriate discipline skills for the grandfather. First, the Consultant modeled that it is okay to answer the demands of an interrupting, shouting, whining child. Second, the Consultant modeled how one adult can undermine the limits set for a child by another adult. The Consultant may have been trying to reinforce "asking for help" behaviors in the grandson, but probably reinforced "demanding and interrupting" behaviors instead because those behaviors got the grandson the immediate attention he wanted.

In what ways could the Consultant have modeled appropriate behaviors in this same scenario? The Consultant could have repeated to the child what the grandfather said about helping him when he was finished talking and making coffee. The Consultant also could have ignored the whining behavior while praising any "waiting" behaviors the child demonstrated.

When using modeling, there are several factors that will increase the likelihood that the family will learn from watching the Consultant (Baldwin & Baldwin, 1986). For one, when you demonstrate a behavior that produces rewarding consequences, family members are more likely to want to imitate that behavior. If you model how simply redirecting a toddler away from the TV controls to his own toys gets the child to stop messing up the TV reception, the observing parent is likely to imitate this behavior because it produces rewarding consequences for the parent. Second, modeling provides the most information when it is done in full view of the family. It only makes sense that the more visible your behavior is for the observing family members, the more the family can learn from watching. Third, modeling is most effective if the family respects and likes the Consultant. Therefore, you will have to use caution in using modeling if a therapeutic relationship has not been established with the family. If modeling is done carefully and not presumptuously, then it can foster a stronger relationship. Also, family members are more likely to imitate the modeled behaviors if they are not too far beyond the family's present skill level. You can perfectly model setting up an elaborate contract with the teenager several times to motivate her to attend school regularly, but if the observing father is illiterate, there's little chance that he will imitate the behavior and use contracts with his daughter. It would be like asking someone who could barely pick through "Chopsticks" on the piano to imitate a concert pianist after watching the pianist perform in a concert. Your heart may be in it, but it's too difficult to learn complex skills merely by observing.

Another advantage of modeling is that it allows you to teach several new skills without wasting time with lengthy explanations. For example, you may not want to take the time to explain how to be assertive when calling a utility company to question an error on a bill. But you can demonstrate with ease through modeling how to be assertive over the telephone by calling the utility company yourself in the presence of the family and asking about the error. Not all the skills you model will neces-

sarily be imitated by the family members, but you should be aware of the skills they do begin to imitate. Are they imitating you correctly? You can use this information to refine how you model and teach skills to the family. Modeling is a powerful tool and, used correctly, can be an extremely effective way to convey information about skills that are beneficial to the family and the family's situation.

## Prompting

Prompting is another method that can easily be used throughout the intervention without verbal explanations. Prompting helps remind family members to use a new skill that they have already learned at the appropriate times. It helps them discriminate when or how often to use a skill. The use of prompts generally is faded out as the family gets used to knowing when to use the new skill. Prompts can be "physical, verbal, or other assists that help a person perform a behavior that would have been unlikely without assistance" (Baldwin & Baldwin, 1986, p. 198).

Prompting is used when the Consultant sees an opportunity for the family to use a skill the members are learning. As a Consultant, you will become aware of when certain skills are best used and can communicate this sense of timing to a family member through prompts. Prompts can be used to teach when skills should be used as well as how family members can generalize the skill in a variety of situations. Often a family will begin to recognize opportunities to use skills after only a few prompts.

Prompts can come in a variety of forms. Verbal prompts might be a question, like "Is this a time that time-out might work?" or "Is this a behavior you want to praise?" Verbal prompts can be a brief statement ("Try it"), or a simple sound (clearing your throat). Nonverbal prompts can be well-timed winks or nods, or other gestures. Giving a thumbs-up signal to a youth to remind her that now is a time she can demonstrate anger control by going to her room, or winking at a parent who is hesitating about confronting his son are other examples of prompts.

Prompts can be part of your treatment plan or you can model them to family members. For example, you are working on having a teenager in the family ask permission before going out. You have worked with the teenager to make sure he is doing this and have prompted him to do so. As a result of your modeling, the parents are now prompting the youth to remember to ask permission before he leaves the house.

In the later phases of the intervention, after a few skills have been taught to the family, prompts are used with more frequency. In fact, you may feel like an orchestra conductor, giving small cues to different family members to try skills at various times during a visit. As the family members begin to feel more comfortable using the skills and show they know when to use the skills, you can fade out the prompts.

## Ignoring

There will be times when ignoring will be an effective strategy to decrease unwanted or disruptive behaviors. Ignoring means not giving attention to inappropriate behaviors so that the behaviors are not reinforced. Usually, you ignore a behavior because it is irrelevant or disruptive and you want other behavior to occur. Oftentimes, we do not realize that attending to a behavior actually provides reinforcement, which increases the behavior. There are a number of behaviors you could choose to ignore; they include tantrumming, yelling, arguing, complaining, burping, or watching TV during a visit. Even though these disruptive behaviors may be difficult to ignore, you can be most effective at decreasing them by not paying any attention to them. Ignoring is a way to decrease the frequency of a behavior by taking away the reinforcement provided by attention.

Ignoring can be used when you perceive an opportunity to decrease an inappropriate behavior or skill the family is using. Consider this example. You have a parent who is always complaining about his in-laws. After two weeks of exploration, you have determined that the in-laws have little to do with the family's situation or agenda, and that the parent is complaining to apparently divert you away from the issues you are working on. As part of your treatment plan, you decide to use ignoring to decrease the amount of complaining. When the parent complains about his in-laws, you avert your attention to the children and their activities, or get up to play with the dog. However, when the parent begins discussing the topic you were previously addressing and is back on task, you return your attention to him.

Ignoring would work the same way in a situation where a whining child disrupts your conversation with the child's parents. You can talk louder, take the parents into another room, or pretend that the whining child isn't there. When the child begins using an appropriate voice tone, you then can pay attention to him. In many cases, you can ignore inappropriate behaviors in such a way that the person who is engaging in the inappropriate behavior will not be aware that you are averting your attention on purpose.

There are several precautions you should consider when using ignoring. First, it is not safe to ignore some inappropriate behaviors. A tantrumming child who is kicking at a bedroom window cannot be ignored. In this situation, discipline techniques such as giving consequences should be used. Another precaution to consider is that using ignoring is likely to create a temporary increase (or burst) in the inappropriate behavior before the behavior decreases.

Behavior bursts happen when reinforcers are withdrawn after a behavior occurs and the person responds by increasing the behavior in an effort to regain the reinforcement. A common illustration of this concept is a situation in which a child has learned that he can get to stay up later by tantrumming at bedtime. When the parent starts ignoring the child's tantrums, the child tantrums longer and louder in an effort to get the parent to give in and let the child stay up. This increase in the inappropriate behavior is the reason you should not ignore a behavior that puts a person in danger. In the earlier example with the child kicking the window, ignoring the behavior may lead the child to kick harder. If the window breaks, the child could get cut.

Even though behavior bursts may cause an increase in the behavior you are attempting to decrease, consistent ignoring will eventually cause the behavior to decrease if your attention was reinforcing the behavior in the first place. Thus, it is important to remember that if you decide to use ignoring to decrease a family member's behavior either as part of

your treatment plan or a plan you are teaching the parents, you must do so consistently, especially when the behaviors increase. Inconsistent ignoring will eventually reinforce a higher level of inappropriate behavior. For example, your treatment plan calls for you to ignore a teenager's remarks about wanting to beat up kids and teachers at school. When the teen starts ranting and raving about fighting people at school (behavior burst), you start giving attention to the behavior. Now the teenager has learned that a higher level of the behavior (ranting and raving) will get your attention and he will begin his behavior at that level in the future.

As you can see, behavior bursts can be a painful, frustrating time for the Consultant and the family. That's why it is crucial to support the family through these bursts by being there as often as possible to reinforce the alternative behavior of the family member whose behavior you are trying to change. The advantage of an in-home intervention with a family is the direct support you can give during these bursts. Because you are in the home, you can see what these behavior bursts look like, prompt the family members when they feel like giving in, and continue to model ignoring the negative behavior and any increases.

Another important note is that anytime you are going to ignore a family's behavior or teach a family how to ignore negative behaviors, you must always reward or teach the family to reward positive or neutral behavior. This can be done by rewarding a specific behavior that is incompatible with the one you are trying to decrease. Let's say you are working with parents who talk negatively about their family. This is the behavior you are trying to decrease by ignoring. At the same time, you will give these parents your undivided attention when they make positive statements about their family. When the parents make positive statements about their family, it is incompatible with making negative statements. In other words, both behaviors cannot occur at the same time. It would be like trying to talk and remain silent at the same time; it can't be done. Your goal is to decrease the inappropriate behavior by ignoring it while simultaneously increasing the appropriate behavior through praise.

Here's another example. You are working with a family that is having difficulty with a teenager who nags his parents every time they say "No" to a request. He nags them until they change their mind. First, you could teach the parents to ignore the nagging behavior in order to decrease it. You could then teach them how to reward an incompatible behavior (the teen acknowledges the "No" with "Okay," "Fine," or "All right," in an acceptable voice tone) by praising the teenager.

Using ignoring to decrease negative or inappropriate behavior without giving rewards (i.e. verbal or tangible) to increase positive or appropriate behavior may result in a temporary suppression of the negative behavior. The family, however, is not going to learn appropriate alternatives and will eventually revert back to the old behavior (Fuoco & Christian, 1986). Anytime you are trying to teach parents to reduce negative behavior in their children, you should simultaneously teach them strategies for increasing positive behaviors. You also should teach alternative behaviors anytime you are using ignoring with a family member.

## Assignments

Assignments consist of asking the family to complete a task, engage in a different behavior, use a new skill, or monitor the frequency/occurrence of a behavior during and between visits. Assignments are used to keep the family focused on practicing the skills and learning the concepts that will bring goal attainment.

Assignments can be given to a family anytime an opportunity arises during a visit. In fact, asking a family member to complete an assignment related to the concept you are teaching is best done while you are discussing the new skill or after you have made a suggestion for the family to try. For assignments to be most effective, you need to follow up by asking family members if they worked on the assignment (if you gave them one to do between visits), or to discuss with them how they accomplished the assignment and what they liked and didn't like about the suggestion. Also ask them about the assignment's outcome. If they did not do the assignment, identify the factors that kept them from completing it. Did they understand the assignment? Is there anything you can do to help them complete assignments in the future? We have found that if you do not follow up on the assignments, the family will not take them seriously and will not work on them.

Consider this example. You are teaching a family how to manage its home budget more effectively and are teaching skills on how to gain access to utility companies to find out what outstanding balances are owed. As an assignment, you might ask family members to look up the phone numbers of the utility companies within the next 15 minutes. Or you might have them make three telephone calls to the various utilities before your next visit. You also could have them write out their projected expenses while you are there, then begin helping them develop a budget.

Depending on what skills you are teaching this family, and the size of the steps you are taking to help build these skills, your assignments will be consistent with the behavior steps you are working on with the family.

Assignments also can help you gauge where the family is in terms of understanding and implementing the skills you are teaching. If members are completing the assignments and reporting successful outcomes, you are probably on the right track. However, it is more common for a family to not complete all assignments. When this happens, it will help you determine how the treatment plan should be adjusted so that the family learns the skills you are teaching.

Finally, assignments can help the family think about using the new skills independently. Giving assignments communicates to family members that they can implement a suggestion when you are with them to support them, as well as continue to learn and practice the suggestion when you are not there. Then when you ask them about the outcomes of assignments, it will encourage them to reflect on what they did and how well it worked to fix the problem.

## Using Variety

We have discussed several methods — modeling, prompting, ignoring, and assignments — that can be used with other intervention techniques to teach families at every possible opportunity. The methods men-

tioned here and the techniques introduced in earlier chapters will provide you with a variety of approaches to help the family learn effectively and efficiently.

One of the most common pitfalls of therapy is relying on a few personally selected techniques that you know best and feel most comfortable using when teaching families. But families have different learning styles and the environment of each home setting varies. The more techniques you have to rely on, the more effective your teaching will be. Families will benefit from your interventions more if you have a lot to offer and more ways to offer it.

The Consultant who has many teaching techniques and methods will perceive more opportunities to teach. With a variety of techniques to utilize, you can do a more thorough assessment of the strengths, problems, and learning styles of the family. You can analyze the best way the family might learn the information and skills it needs to stay together. When you are aware of what teaching techniques work best with each family member, you then can tailor your intervention to use more of these techniques.

Part of the analysis process that makes teaching to opportunities so effective is the constant evaluation you do to assess how the family is progressing. When you use a teaching method or technique, watch and learn from the family members' response. You can analyze what techniques work best with each family member by asking yourself questions like these:

- Does the mom seem to understand and change her behaviors when I use metaphors?
- Does the youth stop whining when I avert my attention and ignore her?

- Does the dad respond when I praise him indirectly?
- When I model praise to the children, do the parents seem to praise the children more?
- Does the grandmother disclose more information when I actively listen to her comments?
- Do I get a clearer picture when I explore more thoroughly?
- When I use normalizing statements with a youth, does the youth appear more relaxed?
- Does the father get back on task when I use circular refocusing?
- When I reframe a situation as positive for parents, do they seem to alter their perspective also?
- When I give a suggestion to family members, do they follow through with the suggestion or do I get resistance?
- Does the family seem to catch on to an idea more quickly if I teach through role-play?
- When I confront family members, do they begin making changes or do they tune me out?
- Does the family member tell me a skill will not work, but follows through with the assignment anyway? Is the outcome successful?

These questions and others can help you assess for yourself which techniques may work best with a family and help you recognize the varied opportunities to teach that are possible when you have a variety of techniques at your disposal.

## Focused Teaching

With such a variety of techniques and methods at your disposal, and given the almost constant opportunities to teach, it is of utmost importance to remember to keep your teaching focused. There may be a big temptation to teach to all of the "problem" areas that the family presents. But unfocused teaching is confusing and often hinders the learning process. Remember how difficult it is to learn a new skill. You wouldn't ask a person who has never used a computer to learn six new computer software programs by handing her the programs and showing her to a computer. Instead, the teaching would begin with how to turn the computer on and how to get into the main frame. Instructions in how to use each program would follow.

Stay true to your treatment plan and focus on teaching to only one skill at a time. Start with the family's strengths and build from there. Direct the variety of intervention techniques you can use toward teaching one skill within one social concept area. Then once the one skill is mastered you can shift the focus to teach another skill. Staying focused in your teaching is the best way to ensure success for the family.

## Summary

As we have discussed, perceiving opportunities to teach and knowing the best way to take advantage of them will make your interventions more efficient and effective. Every moment you are with the family is an opportunity to teach.

Therefore,

- your active-listening should be strategic.
- your modeling should be all-encompassing.
- your silence should be planned.
- your suggestions should be purposeful.
- your prompts should be opportune.
- your assignments should be consistent.
- your intervention should be focused.

If you follow these guidelines, the family will be successful.

# The Boys Town Model

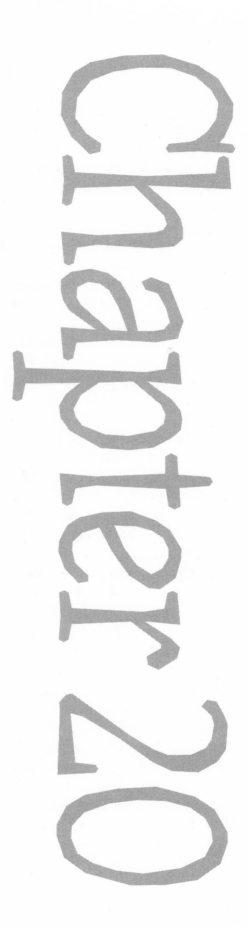

# 20

# Identifying and Building on Strengths

For quite some time, assessment and therapeutic interventions have been centered around client problems and skill deficits (Rodwell, 1987). Focusing on the client's "deficits, disease, and dysfunction" (Cowger, 1994, p. 262) has become the standard for treating clients. However, this problem-centered approach can often create problems for the therapeutic process. To highlight a person's weaknesses and dysfunctions through assessment and intervention can produce feelings of hopelessness. This can lead the client to establish a negative self-fulfilling prophecy that hinders the process of change.

Assessing only the problems in a client's life can create a climate for resistance, especially if the client senses that the Consultant views him or her in a negative light. The Consultant can come across as someone who feels superior, making it more difficult to build a strong therapeutic relationship based on understanding and respect.

When working with families, family members often do not perceive themselves as having problems; instead they feel that other family members need help. Designing a treatment plan that focuses on the "family's problems" may not fit with the family's agenda or what members think needs to be fixed. These kinds of treatment plans often start addressing a problem at a level the family members do not comprehend because they have a different perception of "the problem."

Fortunately in the last several years, there has emerged a new emphasis on assessment and intervention that takes into account the strengths of the client (Cowger, 1994; Goldstein, 1990; Hudgins, 1992; Saleeby, 1992). A strength-oriented perspective allows the Consultant to assess what a client is doing correctly and utilize those competencies to bring about change. The Consultant's emphasis should be on helping families build on skills they already have so that they can solve their own problems.

The family preservation movement greatly advanced the strength-oriented approach for working with families. Many of the earliest programs highlighted the importance of recognizing family strengths and potential resources during assessment in order to help families feel hopeful and in charge of their life situations (Kinney, Haapala, & Booth, 1991). The approach of brief family therapy and solution-focused interventions relies on finding strengths and successes and enhancing them in order to produce the quickest and most lasting changes (Berg, 1994).

There are a variety of advantages to using a strength-based perspective to assessment and treatment of families. Assessments that look to identify family strengths must be individualized so that the Consultant can understand the unique characteristics of the family's experiences. Focusing on the family's strengths keeps members from dwelling on problems and moves them toward finding solutions (Berg, 1994; Hepworth & Larsen, 1990). Also, treatment approaches that acknowledge and incorporate family strengths are likely to enhance motivation. Building on a family's positive attributes and skill abilities begins the intervention at a point the family members understand because this is where their competencies are. Recognizing and emphasizing a family's strengths minimizes the potential for resistance and enhances the therapeutic relationship, which can be particularly important with mandated or court-ordered families (Cowger, 1994).

While the aforementioned advantages for using a strength-oriented approach remain the same, the emergence of this positive perspective has resulted in a variety of differing opinions about how to define and build on strengths. The many definitions of strengths and how they should be incorporated into the assessment and treatment components of therapeutic interventions has led to much confusion. Some experts define strengths as "relationship patterns, interpersonal competencies, and social and psychological characteristics that create a sense of positive family identity" (Littlejohn-Blake & Darling, 1993, p. 461). Others indicate that strengths include interpersonal skills as well as social, resource, and environmental conditions that serve the family in a useful manner (Cowger, 1994). Many strength-oriented perspectives emphasize the importance of acknowledging family strengths as a means of building a positive therapeutic relationship and building hope (Hudgins, 1992; Trute & Hauch, 1988). In some circles, unfortunately, the process of how to use and build on a family's strength in order to help that family remains fairly vague and ill-defined.

At Boys Town, however, we have developed an effective approach to identifying and assessing a family's strengths, and using them to bring about change in therapy. Our philosophy is that the families we serve have an abundance of skills but have not quite learned how to use them effectively and to their full potential. We assess what these skills are and how they can be used to address the family's agenda and problem situation. Then we help the family refine these skills so that they are more functional and produce the best long-term results.

These behaviors are conceptually defined as "social concepts." A social concept is defined as the ability to interact with others in a given social context in specific ways that are socially acceptable or valued and, at the same time, personally beneficial (Dowd & Tierney, 1992). Social concepts, then, are sets of skills that do not necessarily remain constant, but may vary with the social context and particular situational demands.

The use of appropriate social concepts represents a complex chain. Each social concept can be broken down into separate skills that can be further broken down into separate behaviors, as in the following diagram.

## Social Concept

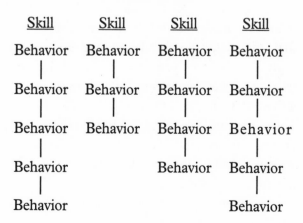

The philosophy of the Boys Town Family Preservation program is that all families demonstrate strengths within these social concepts or some aspect of them, even though the families may have learned to use them incorrectly or incompletely. Instead of concentrating on the deficits a family may have in a social concept area, we look for skills the family already has but has not completely

## Example 1

*You have determined during your assessment that a family's agenda is for the son, Reuben, and his stepfather to stop getting into physical fights. Through exploration and observation you have determined that these fights usually occur when Reuben is told he cannot go out with his friends, especially if he hasn't completed a task his stepfather has given him. An argument begins and the result is a physical confrontation. You determine that the family needs to learn the social concept of "anger management." In order to learn this social concept, the stepfather and son need to learn the skills of "calming down" when an argument begins to escalate, "problem-solving" a situation prior to its occurrence, and possibly "how to negotiate" so that they both get what they want. Each of these skills then can be broken down into their individual behaviors. The skill of "calming down" may consist of these five behaviors: 1) recognizing physical signs of anger; 2) calmly walking away from the other person; 3) going to another room or outside; 4) doing something to cool down; and 5) reconvening to discuss the issue calmly.*

developed. Our job is to help the family hone its skills in order to develop a finished product. This can be done using the intervention techniques described throughout this book. Once learned, these "finished" skills become viable alternatives for the family in situations that previously resulted in trouble.

As mentioned earlier, social concepts are made up of many separate skills. These skills can further be broken down into separate behaviors. In a behavioral program, it is important to distinguish between these skills and the behaviors that are a part of them. Behaviors are individual, discrete, observable acts demonstrated as part of a larger measure of activity. Skills are sets of related behaviors or components that are designed to produce positive results for the family in defined situations. It is the consistent and generalized use of such skills that constitute the social concept (Dowd & Tierney, 1992).

Boys Town defines a family strength as a behavior that a family member already possesses and uses with some degree of competency. For clarification purposes, we will refer to this strength behavior as **BAS (Behavior As a Strength)** throughout the rest of the chapter. With Reuben and his stepfather, Reuben's strength may be his ability to calm down by going outside and shooting baskets once he walks away from a possible confrontation. The stepfather may be very good at remembering to discuss the issue once everyone has cooled off. Reuben's and his stepfather's strengths lie in different behaviors, and this helps the Consultant determine where treatment should begin with each person. Let's look at the skill of "calming down" and the behaviors that make up that skill using the model in the diagram presented earlier.

## Anger Management
(social concept)

*Calming down* (skill)

**Recognize signs of anger**
|
**Calmly walk away**
|
**Go to separate locations**
|
**Engage in cooling-down activity**
(Reuben's BAS)
|
**Deal with issue once cooled off**
(Stepfather's BAS)

Family members can have more than one behavioral strength for each skill area. The remainder of this chapter will focus on how family strengths are identified and built on.

# Success in Starting with Strengths

When you begin working with a family, you are likely to be overwhelmed by the many problems the members present. You face the great challenge of sifting through mounds of information in order to make a useful assessment and design an effective treatment plan that can help the family change and stay together. The way you start this challenging task will determine your effectiveness and influence your chances of success. The Boys Town Family Preservation Model prescribes that identifying and building on the family's strengths will be the most efficient and effective means of bringing about change.

The reasons for starting with the family's strengths are numerous. First, when you set out to identify the strengths in the family, you can establish a partnership with the family. After all, family members are the experts on each others' behaviors and their own responses to those behaviors. As the Consultant, your expertise lies in teaching skills to influence behavior patterns. You must rely on the family members' expertise to learn how their behavior patterns play themselves out. It is impossible to develop a skill that is based on the family's strengths without an assessment of the family's expertise. Therefore, when identifying what social concepts to address and the behaviors in which the family's strengths lie, it is important that the family begins to see the value of the skills you will teach. If the family perceives that these skills are meaningful only to the Consultant, it is much less likely that the family will internalize and generalize these skills. It is therefore critical that the treatment process includes rationales that explain the personal benefits of learning such skills (Dowd & Tierney, 1992).

Second, families often engage in behavior patterns that may be creating or fueling the problems. They may be trying to get their needs met in inappropriate ways because they don't know any alternative ways. A family member who doesn't know or is unable to correctly use critical social concept areas may have grown up in an environment where positive social behavior was not taught. Appropriate styles of interacting with others may not have been modeled by the adults present or valued by the local peer culture or neighborhood. The family member possibly didn't receive any direct instruction in how to get his or her immediate needs fulfilled appropriately. The lack of reinforcement for important social concepts may be a particularly critical feature in learning histories of families

with serious behavioral and emotional problems. For example, Patterson (1982) found that parents of children who were later described as having aggressive behavior problems were more likely to: 1) use harsh commands and demands with their children; 2) reward negative behaviors with attention or compliance; and 3) ignore, or even punish, prosocial behaviors that their children demonstrated at home. These families, then, are more likely to have little expertise in critical social concept areas such as problem-solving strategies, refraining from drug or alcohol abuse, preventing domestic violence, communication, controlling abusive impulses, and meeting children's basic needs.

While one task of the Consultant may be addressing inappropriate behaviors, another simultaneous task is to encourage and motivate families to replace those behaviors with more socially adaptive responses. It is important to remember, however, that families are doing the best they can with the skills they have. Some family members may have tried to change but found that their problems got worse. They might think change is too painful. Or perhaps family members received no support in their efforts to change their behaviors. Oftentimes, families get confused about what approach they should take to fix a problem and they get tired of being told so many different things. Consider how many different ways tantrumming behaviors can be addressed. Choosing the "right way" to stop tantrumming can be a confusing and exhausting process for any family. As a Consultant, you must acknowledge and respect the family members' reasons for their behaviors. Strengths are then easier to identify and motivations for behaviors are understood.

Another reason to begin with the strengths of family members is that you are in their home, on their turf, and must convey respect to their way of life. To establish an environment of respect while in the family's home, you should identify strengths and not point out weaknesses and inadequacies. If a stranger entered your home and started suggesting how you should decorate, or told you that you were parenting your children wrong, you would probably feel offended and defensive. In a similar sense, you are the "stranger" entering the family's home. Recognizing and complimenting the family's strengths will help foster a strong relationship and will minimize the potential for resistance; offending the family by criticizing will only hinder your intervention.

You will have to work to earn the respect of family members by thoroughly listening and exploring their agenda. You must understand the family's ideas and values, or your ideas will not be welcomed. To blindly suggest changes that you think the family should make to solve problems may impose your values and unnecessary pain on the family. By starting your intervention with what the family does well within the skills you want to teach, you are ultimately telling members that they do have skills and that the skills they possess are going to help fix their problem.

In our earlier example, Reuben's strength (BAS) was his ability to engage in a cooling-down activity and his stepfather's strength (BAS) was dealing with the issue once everyone had cooled off. In this situation, if the first thing you decided was that Reuben needed to learn the behavior of walking away without arguing and that the stepfather needed to learn how to go to a separate location to calm down when he started getting angry, they may feel uncomfortable with behaviors they are not accustomed to using. As a result, Reuben and his stepfather probably would not follow through with your suggestion. If you identify and build on strengths, or those behaviors that come naturally, you can prepare family members to accept and implement suggestions that tie into their strengths later on in the intervention.

Finally, given that most family preservation programs are time-limited, lasting anywhere from four weeks to six months, you will want to use an approach that will produce the quickest, and yet, most enduring change. A strength-oriented approach allows you to help the family members make changes by further developing skills they already have rather than starting from scratch to teach new skills the family has no prior experience using. It makes sense to start the intervention with something the family already knows and does well. If you build on the skills the family already uses to some degree, you may find that only a few refinements to the skills are needed in order to bring about the desired change. This will limit the amount of skills that have to be taught, reduce confusion by simplifying the intervention, and bring about change more quickly.

## The Boys Town Approach

The Boys Town approach to using strengths to bring about change uses this three-step process:

**Identifying the strengths**
**Increasing the strengths**
**Building on the strengths**

## Identifying the Strengths

The process of identifying the family's strengths begins the moment you begin working with the family. As discussed in Chapter 4, assessment is one way to identify strengths. You must start by assessing the family's agenda in order to understand the family's perceptions of the problems. What does the family want to fix first? Having the family prioritize the problems demonstrates respect for what family members feel is most important to them. Once you understand the family's agenda, you can start to look for the family's skills within that agenda. The time it takes to assess the agenda and the skills the family members have will vary for each family. You may be able to assess part of a family's agenda and identify skills members have within that social concept area during the first 15 minutes of your initial visit. With other families, it may take two or three visits to accomplish this.

Family members are likely to display several skills that may or may not relate to the problem areas they describe. Identify as many skill areas as you can. You might not build on all of them, but you definitely should identify the skills each family member displays. Sometimes you will be able to identify skills within the family's agenda that will overlap with the problem areas that endanger the child or children. There will be differences in what family members perceive as the problem (their agenda) and what the caseworker or you perceive as the problem (situation endangering the child). This should not affect your search for the family's strengths or your priority to identify a strength within the family's agenda. Beginning with the family's agenda will enhance your ability to help the family members generalize the skills they have.

There are several ways to assess the family's behaviors or skills within its agenda. Look for any descriptions or demonstrations that indicate that the family members can do some behavior correctly within the problem areas they identify or within areas that endanger the child. Anytime you observe a family member demonstrating a behavior that seems to fix the problem or any part of the problem, even temporarily, you might ask how he or she fixed the problem, why that particular solution was used, and how well it worked. This will allow you to determine if family members understand what they have just done, and open up the conversation so the family can elaborate on a possible strength. Through active listening and exploring, you are uncovering what the family members do correctly within the social concept you have identified as being the most beneficial to them. Keep focused on the present. If you have difficulties, ask about skills family members have used in past similar situations.

For example, you are working with a youth (Mia) who has been shoplifting with her friends. You determine that she needs to learn the social concept of "not breaking the law," which may include the skills of "resisting peer pressure," "choosing appropriate friends," and "controlling the impulse to steal." Mia doesn't seem to have any behaviors that make up these skills that you can build on. In this case you may need to begin exploring the past and asking questions to determine if Mia ever engaged in behaviors such as saying "No" to a friend; leaving her friends because she didn't like what they were doing; avoiding peers who were involved in drugs, gangs, or breaking the law; or stopping herself from stealing. (For a more complete listing of skills and behaviors, refer to the Boys Town publication, *Teaching*

*Social Skills to Youth*, 1992.) This may reveal a behavior you can use as a starting point.

Other ways to identify a family's strengths include observation, formal assessment tools, and input from the referring worker. You also can watch how family members handle such situations like conflicts, child misbehaviors, communication, and safety issues. This observation will provide you with clues about the skills they have in handling a variety of problems. With assessment tools, you can determine what skills the family members believe they have in different areas and then look for signs of these strengths. Also, the referring worker may be able to tell you how the family has managed crises in the past and what the pattern of resolving problems has been.

It is important to remember that it is your responsibility to stay focused on what the family is doing correctly within the problem areas, not on what they are doing wrong. Family members may not recognize or believe they have any skills that will help them solve their problems. If this is true, they will likely stay focused on the negative and will not be able to answer a question such as, "What are your strengths?" or "What do you do right?" Do not expect the family members to have the insight to tell you what their skills are, but listen and look for evidence of these strengths through your assessment and observation.

The behaviors and skills a family possesses are not always easily and readily identified. You must be aware of how behaviors that are displayed during problem times also can be interpreted as strengths. To better understand the process of identifying behavioral strengths (BAS) when so much seems to be going wrong, consider the following example.

## Example 2

*A father and his two teenage daughters are referred to Boys Town Family Preservation Services because the girls are repeatedly skipping school and staying out all night without permission. Both girls have been placed in shelter care in the past. During your assessment, the father tells you that his main agenda is to get his daughters to obey him and to respect his authority. He says he feels like he is not in control. And he doesn't know why his daughters turned on him, since he provides them with everything they ever ask for. His goals are to have the girls go to school every day and to do their daily chores. From what you observe and what the referring worker has reported, this father does not know how to discipline his girls effectively. This gives you an idea that the father would benefit from improving the social concept of "child management." He gets angry when the girls skip school, but he seldom uses consequences. This provides you with a skill area the father needs to develop — "using consequences." As you further explore the problem, you begin to assess the father's strengths. He can get his daughters to fix supper every night without being reminded. The girls also pay for any long-distance phone calls they make. When you further explore, you discover a strength: He will not give the girls rides to their friends' homes until after supper and he hides the phone from the girls until they pay their bill. This provides you with a behavior strength (BAS) within the skill area that needs to be addressed. The father has a strength in withholding privileges to manage some of the girls' behaviors. Withholding privileges is what this parent sometimes does correctly within the skill area. You now have a place to begin treatment.*

Let's look at this example using the model discussed earlier in the chapter.

## Child Management
(social concept)

### *Using consequences* (skill)

**Withholding privileges**
(Father's BAS)

Notice in the example that the strength that was identified was one of the behaviors that can make up the skill "using consequences." The father probably does not use this type of consequence with the problem behaviors he wants changed (i.e. the girls skip school), but he has shown you a strength within the skill that you can begin developing.

The following is a list of several common social concept areas and a few possible associated skills as well as behaviors that may make up some of these skills. For a more extensive list of social concepts, see the Boys Town publication, *Teaching Social Skills to Youth* (Dowd & Tierney, 1992). This book has social concepts that are designed primarily for use in working with youth, but they can easily be used in your work with families.

## Preventing Neglect of Young Children
(social concept)

### *Meets children's basic needs* (skill)

**Child is fed or has access to nutritious food**
|
**Child has adequate clothing for outdoors**
|
**Child has adequate shelter and place to sleep**
|
**Child receives necessary medical treatment**

### *Recognizes potential safety risks* (skill)

**Monitor child's whereabouts regularly**
|
**Poisonous items are out of child's reach**
|
**Exposed wires are covered**
|
**No animal feces for a child to pick up**
|
**Sharp objects (knives, nails) are out of reach**

## Anger Management
(social concept)

### *Recognizes when getting angry* (skill)

**Able to recognize physical indicators of anger**
|
**Knows what pushes his/her anger buttons**
|
**Understands what anger is**

### *Engages in stress-reducing activities* (skill)

**What activities calm him/her down quickly**
|
**Understands when to engage in these activities**
|
**Uses activities when feeling stressed**
|
**Continues to engage in activities until calm**

## Communication
(social concept)

### *States wants and disagrees appropriately*
(skill)

**Uses a pleasant or neutral voice tone**
|
**Plans what he or she will say ahead of time**
|
**Has a rationale for his or her viewpoint**

**Respects others' views** (skill)

**Looks at the person who is talking**
|
**Does not interrupt the person who is talking**
|
**Indicates that he or she heard the other person by saying "Okay," or by nodding head**
|
**Asks questions to obtain more information**

## Increasing the Strengths

Once you have identified a skill the family has shown some competency with, you will need to identify the behavior or behaviors within that skill that are the family's strengths. When that behavior or set of behaviors has been identified, you can begin working with family members on having them use the behavior more often. Providing praise is an effective way of increasing this frequency. As discussed in Chapter 10, Effective Praise is the process of providing a reward after a behavior occurs to increase the probability that the behavior will occur again. Verbal praise alone often can reinforce (or increase) a behavior. When verbal praise by itself is not reinforcing (does not increase the probability that the behavior will occur again), you may need to provide a tangible reinforcer (also discussed in Chapter 10).

Hepworth and Larsen (1990) describe the power positive reinforcement has on clients this way: "When positive feedback is utilized to document the cause-effect relationship between their efforts and positive outcomes, clients experience satisfaction, accomplishment, and control over their situation" (p. 125). Not only do the family members feel good about the behavior they are utilizing, but they are more likely to use that behavior again and again. The goal is to make the family members' skills sounder by developing the behaviors within a skill. Often, our natural instinct is to tell a family what it is doing wrong. But in Family Preservation Services we have to identify what behavior the family members are using correctly and ask them to use it more often.

The following components address how to increase an identified strength through verbal praise. You will notice that these components are similar to those for Effective Praise.

1. **Acknowledge the behavior specifically and tie in a rationale for how that behavior relates to the family's agenda.**
2. **Verbally praise the person's competence in using the behavior to affect change.**
3. **Give assignments that encourage the person to continue to engage in the behavior.**

**1. Acknowledge the behavior specifically and tie in a rationale for how that behavior relates to the family's agenda.** Let's go back to the example involving Mia and her problem with shoplifting. Mia describes being able to walk away from her friends when they use drugs and has told them she will not use drugs. Whatever her motivation is for saying "No" and leaving her friends when they use drugs, and not saying "No" when they shoplift, she is describing a behavioral strength (BAS) that can help her achieve her goal of staying in her home. You can point out to Mia that walking away and refusing to use drugs are sensible ways of preventing her placement outside the home. You have specifically acknowledged the behavior and tied-in a rationale for how that behavior fits with her goal of remaining at home.

**2. Verbally praise the person's competence in using the behavior to affect change.** Verbal praise should be tactfully stated and carefully toned so that it is sincere. Praise should be stated in a way that credits the family member's accomplishments and not the Consultant's. Avoid using "I" statements in reference to what the family member is doing right. In the example of Mia leaving her friends when they use drugs and not participating, you can praise her competence in being able to prevent her placement outside the home with a statement like this: "Boy, it's great how you keep yourself from getting into trouble and possibly being placed by not using drugs and leaving your friends when they do. You probably stop a lot of nagging and pressure from your friends by letting them know up front that you will not use drugs and by leaving when they do." Every time the person describes using the BAS or actually engages in the behavior during one of your visits, provide verbal praise. The more opportunities you can find to praise, the more quickly the BAS will be increased and used more often.

**3. Give assignments that encourage the person to continue to engage in the behavior.** Finally, you can use assignments to further reinforce the family member's BAS to bring about an increase in the frequency of those behaviors. Assignments are a way of asking and encouraging the family to keep engaging in a behavior, which in itself can be reinforcing. Assignments that are commonly used include asking the family member to "keep doing" the BAS that you praised or to "keep track" of how many times he or she does the BAS. In our example with Mia, you might give her this assignment: "Let me know when I come back for my next visit how many times you walked away or said 'No' to your friends when you didn't like what they were doing."

Assignments impress upon the person that the behavior he or she is using is important and effective in bringing about change in some way.

When you are using these three components to try to increase the frequency of a family member's BAS, be sure to observe the person's response and evaluate your attempts to reinforce (increase) the strength. You will know that your praise has been effective only if you observe family members engaging in a BAS more often than before you started praising it. Do not rely on what family members tell you about how often they are using the BAS when you are not there; instead, observe and count during visits to determine if the person is using the BAS more frequently. If you observe the family member "doing" the BAS more often, than you have been successful at increasing the strength. This is your behavioral cue to begin adding on to or building the BAS.

If you do not observe the BAS increasing, several factors may be hindering the process. You may have identified and tried to increase the wrong behavior. This sometimes occurs when a Consultant observes a behavior that the family member rarely uses. Sometimes, family members might describe a behavior or skill that they have not actually used. For example, a parent may tell you that she uses time-out when her toddler does not mind. But you may never see the parent use a time-out or any of the behaviors that make up a time-out when the toddler is not minding.

Perhaps the skill you have identified does not fit within the family's perception of the problem, so your attempts to praise and tie in rationales do not match the family's agenda. As Consultants, we often can look at a situation and assess what skill the family needs to "fix things." Then we search and search for some indication that the family member has a strength in that skill area, and many times we will take even the smallest indication, even if it occurs only once. It is not until we run into resistance and roadblocks that we sit back and realize that the strength we attributed to the individual was not the individual's true strength.

Sometimes the behavior or skill that was identified is not reinforced through verbal praise; therefore it is not likely to increase. If you find there is no change after several attempts to increase a BAS, you will need to assess your behaviors and the possibility that more observation, active listening, and exploring is necessary to identify another behavior the family uses. You may even have to find another skill area that fits in with the family's agenda and goals. Once you have found a skill within the social concept and have identified the behaviors within the skill that the family does right, it is time to begin building on the strength.

## Building on the Strengths

When you have identified a behavior within the skill area and successfully increased the family member's use of the behavior through verbal praise, the family is ready to begin building on the behavior. But before you begin that process, you must determine whether increasing the family member's use of the BAS will be enough to fix the problem. Sometimes, if the family member engages in the BAS more frequently, the change the family wants will occur. For example, the father who begins taking privileges away from his two daughters more often when they engage in inappropriate behaviors may find that he is generalizing this behavior to the areas of school truancy and they are obeying him. The father no longer sits back while his daughters skip school and disobey him, and the problem is fixed to a point that the family is satisfied. In a case like this, you may not need to build further on the BAS. Usually, however, getting a family member to use a behavior more often doesn't fix the problem. It does prepare the family to refine the BAS in order to develop the skills that are necessary to fix the problem.

Building on a behavior to achieve a desired skill is a method that has been defined and used by behaviorists for years. (See L.K. Miller's, *Principles of Everyday Behavior Analysis*, 1980, for a more thorough explanation of behavior analysis.) For our purposes, building on a behavior is defined as the process of making a series of small suggestions that a family member can add to his or her BAS to gradually learn the whole desired skill that is being taught. Each time a suggestion is made, the Consultant continuously reinforces this new approximation until the family member has consistently incorporated the suggestion with the behavior. Consider the earlier example of Reuben and his stepfather. Reuben, whose strength is in the behavior of doing something to calm down once he walks away from a possible confrontation, may be asked to try coming back into the room where his stepfather is after he calms down. Each time Reuben engages in a such a behavior and comes back into the room, he should be reinforced with some form of Effective Praise. After Reuben uses these two behaviors together, you can begin adding a third behavior. This formula helps you stay focused on teaching only one behavior within one skill until the family member demonstrates the ability to use it before moving on.

You might think of the behavior as the separate links in a chain. Each one needs to be molded into a certain shape. Once one is finished (Reuben calms down), you begin molding the next link, or behavior (Reuben returns to the room). Once all the links are completed, you put them together to create a chain, or skill (Calming Down). These skills or chains (Calming Down, Problem-Solving, and Negotiation) join together to form a necklace, or social concept (Anger Management).

Building on a strength occurs gradually through this process. The technique that is most often used to mold a behavior into a new skill is Criticism by Suggestion (discussed in Chapter 13). You will need to make suggestions that the family members understand and are able to try. One good way to begin molding the behavior is to ask the family members what ways they think they could improve their skills. If family members can generate reasonable options that they could incorporate with their behavior, suggest that they try them out.

Many times, a family member cannot think of any ways to improve a behavior. That's when you can ask him or her to try one of your suggestions. Be sure you are not asking the family member to take too big of a behavioral step. If you ask a parent who typically argues and yells with her teenager for 30 minutes before grounding the teen for a month to not argue and calmly give the youth a small consequence in 20 words or less, your suggestion may be too difficult. The parent will not be able to incorporate the suggested changes. By taking smaller steps, a family member will show you through increased use of a new step that it is time to add more. An example of a smaller step would be asking the parent to argue for only 20 minutes before grounding the teenager for two weeks.

Once you have made a suggestion, you will want to do as much teaching as possible to show the family members why this suggestion should be incorporated with their existing behavior. (This teaching is done using the techniques discussed in Chapters 7 through 18.) Model for the family how to use behaviors with the suggested changes. Role-play, give rationales, use metaphors, and give prompts to get family members to use the suggested changes whenever possible. Give assignments that motivate the family to use the suggestion during visits and between them. And when the family members use the behavior incorporating the suggestion, praise them every time they do it.

When they have incorporated the suggestion with their behavior successfully several times, then give the next suggestion. Repeat the teaching and praise for this new suggestion.

The following case example is provided to illustrate the process of identifying the strength behavior and building the behavior into a skill.

## Example 3

Kysa Jones and her 20-month-old son, Terrance, were referred to Family Preservation Services due to several confirmed child neglect charges. The referring worker's main concerns were that Kysa was not providing for her son's basic needs.

During the first two visits with Kysa, the Consultant explored the family's agenda, perception of the problem, and goals. Kysa explained that her biggest problem was getting her money to last until the end of the month. She said Terrance always ran out of milk and cereal before she could get more from the local program she utilized. Kysa also reported that Terrance bugged her a lot throughout the day and she got exhausted trying to keep up with him. Kysa disclosed that she did not feel like she knew how to parent Terrance, and that she was concerned that there might be something wrong with him because he cried a lot. One of her goals was to get Terrance to play by himself and stay in his room so she could relax. Another goal was to make her money last until the end of the month. During the first visits, the Consultant explored and identified behaviors that would help Kysa achieve these goals. Whenever Kysa got low on food she would pull out a list of churches and local food pantries and call them for help. Kysa also was able to pay her cable bill every month because she felt she "had to have her HBO." Whenever Kysa heard Terrance in the kitchen, she usually got up to check on him.

Kysa's strengths were in supervising some of Terrance's activities, paying some of her bills on a regular basis, and generating options when she ran out of money. These BASes could be a part of several skill areas, including "budgeting," "problem-solving," and "comparison shopping."

At this point the Consultant decided that the first social concept area to be developed would be "money management" because Kysa's strengths of being able to generate options and pay some bills would address her main agenda of running out of money before the end of the month. During the next two visits, Kysa's BAS of generating income and resource options was increased. Every time Kysa came up with options she could use to help meet her family's needs, she was verbally praised. The Consultant used the rationale that Kysa used some great money management skills and was always looking for ways to take care of her family and get her bills paid. She was assigned to keep track of how many times over the next day she looked at the different financial options she had to help pay for something her family needed. By the fourth visit, Kysa had located and used two more programs to help her get food and pay a late bill; these two options Kysa tapped into indicated an increase in her strength of generating resource options. Kysa's strength had been increased through Effective Praise, which in turn made her more aware of what her strengths were.

Kysa's BAS was developed into the skill of "budgeting" because she was so good at looking at different options that were available to her and could pay some bills on time. The behaviors for "budgeting" are: 1) Listing monthly expenses and income; 2) Listing all resource options that can supplement her income or provide things the family needs; 3) Dividing the expenses, income, and resource options equally for each week; 4) Making out an envelope for each week of the month and depositing an equal share of the income in each envelope; 5) Paying bills and shopping weekly, spending only what's available in that envelope; and 6) If the money is gone at the end of the week, generating options from known resources for help that week.

The Consultant made suggestions to Kysa to begin developing and building on her BAS. The first suggestion was to generate a list of resource options she could use throughout the month to supplement her income. The Consultant used rationales, metaphors, modeling, role-plays, prompts, and assignments to make sure Kysa understood when, why, and how she could implement this suggestion. During two visits, Kysa worked on developing this list. Every time Kysa came up with a new option, she was rewarded with praise or an offer from the Consultant to help her with housework, which was rewarding to Kysa.

The next suggestions for helping Kysa build her behaviors toward the skill of "budgeting" were gradually added. Each time Kysa demonstrated an ability to incorporate one suggested behavior along with her BAS, she was praised. Then another suggestion for trying another behavioral step would be made. Each time Kysa was able to incorporate the suggested behavior with what she was already doing, she would be praised.

The suggestions that were made to help Kysa improve her use of "budgeting" came in this order: After being asked to generate options for resources that could supplement her income, Kysa was asked to list her monthly expenses and income. The next suggestion was for Kysa to divide her list of expenses, income, and resource options into four equal portions for each week of the month. The Consultant suggested that Kysa deposit the four equal portions of expenses (bills), income, and resource options into four envelopes, one for each week. Then Kysa was asked to try to pay only that week's expenses and bills with the money she had designated for that week only. If Kysa found that she needed more money to meet that week's expenses, the Consultant suggested that she use one of her resource options, such as the food bank, to make it through the week. The Consultant reminded Kysa that it would be a challenge to try to stick to a weekly budget, but used the rationale that she could then make her money last throughout the month and meet her family's needs. Kysa demonstrated an ability to incorporate these suggested behavioral components with her strength behavior over an eight-visit period.

Over that two-week period, Kysa had more money than she had at the same time last month. She was able to keep food in the home and begin a payment plan on some of the bills she was behind on. Kysa also had begun spontaneously planning weekly activities for Terrance that did not cost much and utilized some of the local resource options that she had discovered. She found a church that provided free child care two mornings a week. This allowed Kysa to take care of basic household chores and have time to herself, something she had wanted.

Kysa's BAS of generating options had gradually been developed into the skill of "budgeting," which she felt was useful in reaching her goal of paying her bills and having her money last until the end of the month. By having her money last through the first two weeks of working on "budgeting," Kysa was able to achieve the referring worker's goal, too. She had provided for Terrance's basic needs by having food in the home consistently. Now Kysa was ready to learn additional skills in the social concept area of "money management" and perhaps build more skills that would help her with other agenda items.

Using the social concept-skill-behavior model, the skills and behaviors described in Example 3 would look like this:

## Money Management
(social concept)

### *Budgeting* (skill)

**List monthly expenses and income**

|

**List resource options that can supplement family income**
(Kysa's BAS)

|

**Divide income, expenses, and resources into four equal weekly portions**

|

**Divide and deposit money in weekly envelopes**

|

**Pay bills and expenses with weekly allowance from envelope**

|

**If weekly allowance does not cover expenses, use resource options for that week's expenses**

Linked together, these behaviors make up the skill of "budgeting." The skill of "budgeting," linked with the skill of "problem-solving," linked with the skill of "comparison shopping," make up the social concept of "Money Management."

# Summary

At Boys Town we believe that identifying the strengths family members have within the skill areas that are most beneficial to them is critical in developing effective treatment plans. Getting family members to increase their use of these behaviors and then develop them through intervention techniques will help the family and the Consultant to see success quickly and over a long period of time.

Social concepts consist of several skills that can be further broken down into behaviors. These behaviors are where we begin looking for and identifying a family member's strengths. These behaviors are ones that are already being used by the family and are both concrete and measurable. They also pertain to the skill and ultimately the social concept being developed.

If you remember to start where the family is by identifying its competencies and then building from there, your intervention will be quicker, more effective, and longer lasting. Families who are made to feel like they have the ability to fix their problems, will.

# 21

# Phases

Families that are referred to family preservation programs are facing many challenges and problems in their day-to-day lives. They are dealing with routine events as well as the possibility that the family will be separated because one or more of the children could be placed outside the home. These situations create a multitude of daily, if not hourly, crises and problems for a family. This can overwhelm not only the family but also the Consultant who is trying to remain focused and solution-oriented. Problems keep arising from all directions and soon a Consultant begins to feel ineffective as numerous crises surface.

In the Boys Town Family Preservation Model, however, there is a process that guides Consultants as they build on a family's strengths and confidence. This process is called **Phases**, and it is designed to individualize treatment and help a Consultant remain focused on treatment issues. This specific Model provides Consultants with an effective road map for treatment planning that compels them to move forward with a family. Because the Model directs them to focus on a few key issues, Consultants are not easily distracted by the many peripheral issues that may arise in the course of treatment.

Consultants report that the Model is not so structured that the family must be made to "fit" into it; instead, the Model can be made to "fit" the family by emphasizing the family's unique needs, goals, and strengths. The Phases Model also allows room for a Consultant's individuality. One Consultant said, "At first I was skeptical about how the Model would constrict my interventions with families. I was afraid it would keep me from being creative and wouldn't allow me to meet the family's individual needs. But I found the opposite is true. It helps me individualize my treatment by working on skills they (family members) need, which are based on their own strengths."

One of the most exciting aspects of working with families is watching a family develop its skills and confidence. Consultants cite the Model's emphasis on self-reliance as another important component that facilitates the maintenance of treatment gains. Strengthening a family's self-confidence can be a major accomplishment in any time frame. The Boys Town Family Preservation program is short term in length and intensive in hours, but the Phases Model is designed to be effective in any long- or short-term program. And it is the foundation of teaching a family enough skills to create a safe, nurturing environment in the home while encouraging self-reliance.

The Model is composed of six Phases that the Consultant uses to guide his or her work with the family. The Phases are used to assess treatment strategies, remain focused, and delineate appropriate outcomes. Moreover, the criteria established for ending services promotes success, makes outcomes more measurable, and, as noted by one administrator, helps in providing the "best quality services to children and families."

You might think of Phases as six rooms in a house that is being built. There is much work to be done. You will be working with the family on what needs to be done in each room, how the work can be accomplished, and the work each member will do to finish all six rooms. In the first three rooms, you will give the family members all the answers and help them develop a better working knowledge of the skills they already possess. In the fourth room, you'll hand off the blueprints and encourage the family members to direct the work in the remaining rooms while continuing to inspire them to achieve greater architectural perfection. When the family members reach the fifth room, you'll help them survey all they have done, monitor how well they continue to use their skills, and help them realize that they have the answers to their own questions. By the time the family has reached the sixth room, members will have learned all the skills necessary to build additions to their home or even build a new house without your assistance.

Each Phase is slightly different from the one before it. But like rooms in a house, they all are under the same roof and there are similarities, too. If you apply the ideas and techniques in this chapter, you'll be able to recognize each Phase, know what to do when you reach each one, and learn when the family is ready to be guided into the next one. You also will be able to determine when to disengage and end services with a family based on the level of competency that is achieved and measured in the last Phase.

Everything you have learned in the previous chapters is drawn together in the Phases structure. This is where you put all of your intervention techniques together and begin working with a family within a specified framework. The remainder of this chapter will discuss each Phase, including each one's focus, assignments, intensity, and requirements for moving from one Phase to the next.

# Phase I

Phase I is probably the most crucial Phase because this is where you begin developing the foundation for your house. You could build a house without a foundation, but over time, as you begin adding new rooms and increasing the weight of the structure, it eventually will collapse. Similarly, if you don't build a strong foundation with the family, you will meet resistance as you begin to make suggestions and later push members to achieve more. Family members will quit working with you, and your treatment eventually will collapse.

Phase I is essential to identifying the family's strengths, and assessing the family's agenda, values, roles, and structure. All of these factors are critical to making your work with the family effective and efficient. In this Phase, you begin to develop a picture of the family you are working with. It's a time to observe what activities the family engages in, and how members interact with each other, with you, and with outside agencies. It's the place to begin your work, not by telling family members what to do, but by finding out who they are and what they are already capable of doing. By praising family members for what they are doing right and not immediately making suggestions, you are telling them that you respect them and their abilities as well as honor their way of doing things. Family members need to know that you view

them as the experts on their family and the family's situation. If you simply go into a home, tell the family what the referring agency said is wrong, and begin making suggestions, you are setting up the family and your treatment for failure.

When Boys Town first developed Phases, it looked at the differences between two kinds of Consultants: those who work at developing a relationship with the family up front, recognize the family's strengths, and spend time getting to know family members as individuals, and those who begin services by telling the family their perception or the referring agency's perception of the family's problem and how they are going to help the family fix its problems. We found that with the second kind of Consultants, it wasn't long before the family began resisting the intervention by not showing up for visits, canceling visits, not following through with the Consultant's suggestions, and in some cases, even firing the Consultant. Since we've started using Phase I, no family has fired a Boys Town Consultant. We believe Phase I leads to reduced resistance in families and sets the theme for treatment — that we are in partnership with the family in fixing its problems. Many families we work with have built up defense walls and are leery of service providers. Phase I is designed to break down those walls so effective change that is beneficial to the family can occur.

With all of its positive points, however, Phase I often is hardest on Consultants. As Consultants in a helping profession, our first instinct is to go in and "help" by fixing the family's problem ourselves, or by telling family members how to fix it themselves. We know we have a lot to offer the family and can often see, from an objective viewpoint, that the problem has "simple" solutions. However, experience has told us that trying to move through this Phase too quickly and giving the family suggestions too soon can later hinder the progress of therapy.

Let's look more closely at the different areas you will be addressing and how they fit into Phase I.

## Focus

The focus of Phase I is on family assessment, identifying and building on family members' strengths, and building relationships. All three areas are essential as you begin working with a family and designing the treatment plan.

Family assessment gives a clear picture of the dynamics within the family and what problem the family perceives it wants fixed. With an accurate assessment, you are beginning your intervention at a place that almost guarantees that the family will work with you. By focusing on understanding the family and helping the family fix what it wants fixed first, you are showing family members that you understand their situation and conveying respect for their ability to handle situations within their home.

Assessment in Phase I also includes identifying the situations that endanger the child, the family's goals for services, the family's strengths and capabilities, and the ABC's of the problems the family identifies. (See Chapter 9 on exploration.) Without this focus, treatment stumbles, becomes confusing, and accomplishes little.

You also must focus on identifying what the family does right — the Behavior As a Strength (BAS) — within the agenda the family has identified. (See Chapter 20.) Many times the families we work with have multiple problems and it is easy to get overwhelmed trying to fix all of them. By focusing in Phase I on what the family wants to fix and what members are already doing right within that area, you are providing yourself with a blueprint for services. By assessing a family's agenda, identifying what members are doing right within that agenda, and building on that strength (BAS) through praise, you will begin building a relationship with the family.

Building a strong relationship with a family creates an atmosphere that will foster cooperation and help you determine how best to enhance this cooperation. This is critical in Phase I because in order to even begin effective treatment you must first have a good relationship with the family. (See Chapter 5.) We believe your relationship with the family is the foundation upon which change is made, and without a solid foundation, effective and long-lasting change will not occur.

Let's summarize the focus in Phase I. The numbers assigned to each listed item correspond with numbers that are used in the case example that will be presented throughout this chapter.

### Assess
- family's agenda-1
- family's strengths (BAS)-2
- situation endangering the child-3
- family's and referring agency's goals-4
- family's dynamics-5
- ABC's of problem areas-6
- family's capabilities-7

### Identify and build on a strength
- identify family's behavioral strengths-8
- increase one BAS through praise, modeling, and assignments-9

- do not critique or give suggestions for changing the BAS-10

### Build relationships
- explore family's agenda-11
- focus on family's strengths within the family's agenda-12
- communicate respect-13
- treat family members as experts-14
- praise strengths-15
- discuss family's interests and hobbies-16
- provide concrete services-17

## Assignments

As mentioned in Chapter 20, assignments are a way to teach the family skills. Assignments in Phase I are structured around the BAS within the agenda of each family member. Because you have already done a thorough assessment to identify the BAS, the first few assignments you give will simply be to ask the child, parent, grandparent, aunt, foster parent, etc., to continue using his or her strength (BAS). This increases the BAS and assists you in developing a strong foundation. Inadvertently focusing on a behavior where a strength does not exist or is not within the family's agenda may create resistance later in therapy and delay, if not halt, treatment.

By staying focused on what the family members are already doing, you convey your respect for their expertise and abilities, as well as develop a stronger relationship with them. Telling family members to continue using a skill they are already using tells them you believe they know what they are doing and that you are not going to come in and begin demanding changes.

Some common examples of Phase I assignments that can help you and the family stay focused on the BAS include asking a family member to "keep doing" the BAS and "keep track" of how many times he or she does it, and having the family member tell you what happens when he or she does the BAS again. You might even ask family members to try the BAS a certain number of times before your next visit.

Assignments also keep you focused on the family's agenda, which helps you develop a more thorough treatment plan. These assignments keep the family members focused on using their strengths more often, making them more comfortable with the behavior as well as more aware of how using it affects others.

You also will have the opportunity to see how the family reacts to praise and how you need to individualize this intervention technique to each family. Praise is a potent intervention technique and when used effectively will increase not only the family's use of its BAS but also keep the family moving toward its goals.

Let's summarize assignments in Phase I:

- focus only on the BAS within the family's agenda
- set a goal of increasing use of BAS
- follow up

## Intensity

Our general rule of thumb is that a Consultant puts in as many hours as necessary to increase a strength in order to build a relationship with a family. The Boys Town Family Preservation program is an intensive program and therefore invests more hours a week during treatment than many longer-term programs. In Phase I and the following Phases, the amount of time suggested is based on the Phase a family is in and not necessarily the length of the intervention. A Consultant may be in Phase I one to two days or as long as eight or ten days, depending on the family and the Consultant. Generally, however, our Consultants spend from six to nine face-to-face hours with a family during the course of Phase I. On average, the visits last two to three hours a day. Since Phase I is so critical to developing the foundation of treatment with families, considerable time should be given to beginning assessment and identifying the family's strength (BAS), thereby establishing therapeutic relationships.

Let's summarize the intensity of hours spent with a family while in Phase I:

- hours based on Phase, not week of treatment
- approximately six to nine face-to-face hours
- spend as much time as necessary

## Moving to the Next Phase

In moving from Phase I to Phase II, the Consultant needs to make sure he or she has properly identified the family's agenda and a strength within that agenda. When that strength is developed, it will help the family solve its problems.

Identifying and staying focused on the family's agenda sets precedence for the remainder of your treatment. Moving to Phase II without understanding what the family wants fixed will result in unfocused teaching, confused family members, and a failed intervention. In Phase II you will begin devel-

oping or building on the family's BAS using the intervention techniques discussed in this book. Before doing that, it is imperative that you have accurately assessed the BAS and have begun to see the family use it more often. Observing a family using the BAS more frequently is one indication that your assessment is accurate.

Your relationship with the family also needs to be strong prior to moving to Phase II. You want a strong relationship with the family so that you can make suggestions and motivate members to higher and more refined levels of skill usage later in the intervention. You will have established a strong relationship by the end of Phase I if you have followed the guidelines listed in Chapter 5, including focusing on the family's agenda and increasing the family's BAS. A strong relationship often is evident when a family is completing assignments and looking to you for help.

Let's summarize how to move from Phase I to Phase II:

- agenda identified
- increase in BAS is identified and observed
- relationship with family established

Throughout the remainder of this chapter, we will illustrate the Phases process with a case example of how a Consultant advances the family through all six Phases and how treatment differs and flows in each one. We have labeled this text **Example**, and it will follow the explanation of each Phase. The numbers in parentheses (1) refer to the elements discussed in each Phase.

The case example will focus primarily on the mother in the family to simplify our description of how Phases works. Please realize that frequent interactions and much skill development work occurs with the children throughout the Consultant's intervention. Days are numbered from the start of the intervention.

## Example: Phase I

*This information was provided at referral: The family consists of a single mother, Molly, and four children: Micah, 6, Alex, 8, Kurt, 9, and Macy, 12. The referring agency is concerned that Molly is depressed, which keeps her from meeting the basic needs of her children (3). The children all have been in some sort of placement at varying times, and Kurt currently is in a psychiatric placement for setting fire to a local convenience store and stealing. This information came out during a child protective agency's investigation that started when Molly neglected to have a doctor check stitches in Kurt's leg and the leg became infected (3).*

**Day 1:** When the Consultant arrives for his first visit, he takes time to make sure Molly understands the program and begins exploring with her what things are occurring in the home that she considers problems (1). While the Consultant is listening to Molly, he is assessing family interactions (5) that are taking place around him. Molly discloses that each of her children has been in about two or three formal placements, and that she is frustrated with having neglect charges continually brought against her (1). She also says

she is frustrated because her children engage in inappropriate behaviors such as skipping school, setting fires, staying out all night, and not helping around the house (1). Molly says she feels overwhelmed (3), and though she is willing to try, she is not sure if she can keep her kids at home with her. Through exploration the Consultant and Molly discuss what she thinks needs to occur for her to be less overwhelmed and for the children to stay in the home (4). Molly wants all of her children to help around the house, wants Alex and Macy to attend school every day, wants the children to return home when they are supposed to, and wants all of the children to stop setting fires.

The Consultant asks Molly which problem she would pick to fix first. He explains that beginning with one goal and problem area will enable him to help her fix that problem more quickly and move on to another if necessary. Molly decides that the children staying out late is her biggest problem and the one that gets her in trouble most often (1,3). Molly feels that fixing this problem first would help stop the neglect charges (4). This information provides the Consultant with areas to explore with Molly concerning what she does when the children don't come home until late, how the children respond, and what current rules she has for when the children go out (6).

*The Consultant also explores the children's perspectives of the problems occurring within the home and what they would like to see change (1,4,11). This is done throughout Phase I and will continue as change occurs.*

While the Consultant is discussing Molly's perceptions of what is going on in the home (1,5,11), he observes Macy sweeping the living room floor. Macy says this is one of her chores. The Consultant also watches Alex throw a temper tantrum when Molly says he can't have a snack. Molly "sticks to her guns" (mother's lingo) and does not give Alex a snack during this tantrum. Molly receives praise from the Consultant for "sticking to her guns" and following through with a limit she set by not giving in to Alex's tantrum (7,8,12,15). Molly is asked to continue this behavior (9). While further exploring Molly's agenda of the children staying out late, Molly says she has set some rules; one is that when the children come home from school and she is taking a nap, they are to stay in the house and not have any company until she wakes up (12). Molly also says the children are supposed to be home before she goes to bed (2,12). The Consultant asks Molly what she does when the children are late and she replies that there is nothing she can do (6). Molly believes the children return home when they are tired or when another family finally kicks them out (6). The Consultant praises Molly for her ability to get her children to do chores, for "sticking to her guns" by not giving into Alex's tantrum, and for telling the children when they should be home (8,9,10,12,15).

*Molly has presented several potential behavioral strengths. Each is identified and praised by the Consultant, who will assess them to determine which one will best assist Molly in meeting her goals. In order to do that, Molly's agenda must first be fully identified so that the strength Molly has within that agenda can be identified and increased as the BAS.*

The Consultant also continues to explore these situations to uncover more of Molly's strengths. Over the course of the visit, while Molly and the Consultant are washing dishes (17), Molly discloses that she is a recovering alcoholic and drug addict and that she hasn't used drugs in more than 18 months. She says she did attend a party the previous weekend but didn't drink or use drugs. She says she enjoys the adult company and needs to get out of the house every once in a while. Molly said that Macy had confronted her about going to the party (5,6). Molly also said that she left the party every 45 minutes to check on her kids (2,6,7). On one check, she discovered that Macy had boys at the house; Molly reprimanded Macy and made the boys leave. The Consultant saw this behavior as an opportunity to teach Molly, through praise, how well she checks on her children (8,9,12,15). The Consultant has begun to identify several strengths (2,8) Molly has and begins praising these behaviors (15) while asking her to continue using them.

*This will allow the Consultant to assess which of Molly's strengths will serve her best in fixing her agenda of the children staying out late (1,12).*

Prior to leaving the first visit, the Consultant again asks Molly to continue checking on her children (9,10). Molly reports that she is going to another party that night and will check on them during the party.

**Day 2:** On the next visit, the Consultant follows up with Molly to see if she checked on her children during the party she attended the night before. Molly reports that she came home every hour, and that all the children were home and everything was okay (2,3,5,6,7). After praising Molly for checking on her children, the Consultant explores what Molly is having problems with that day (1). Molly still has the same agenda items: the children skipping school, not helping around the house, staying out all night, and setting fires (1,11). Molly is asked which of the problem areas she would like to work on. Molly states she would like to continue addressing the problems of the children staying out late (1). Molly says she is concerned about Macy being "boy crazy," though she does not believe Macy is sexually active. Macy is present during the visit and confirms this while continually interrupting Molly and the Consultant (5). The Consultant uses this opportunity to model for Molly how to have Macy wait until Molly is finished talking before giving Macy attention.

Macy's interruptions occur frequently during the visit as Molly talks about how all of her children have set fires at one time and stayed out late at night (3). Macy also is given an opportunity to discuss these issues, since Molly doesn't seem concerned about discussing them in front of her. But Macy tends to use this time to gain attention through negative talk and inappropriate behaviors. This provides an opportunity for the Consultant to model expectations for having an appropriate conversation. Molly attempts to distract Macy by telling her to check on Micah and find out where he is. As Macy leaves, the Consultant praises Molly for checking on the children by having Macy see where Micah is (2,8,9, 10,15). He asks Molly to let him know how many times she gets the children to help her by checking on each other when she is busy.

*From all the behavioral strengths Molly has demonstrated in the first two visits, the Consultant chooses the strength that will best help Molly address her agenda of the children staying out late. The Consultant has identified Molly's BAS as checking on her children (9). Molly checked on her children quite frequently, and this was observed to be a rather natural behavior for her. Also, this strength was increased fairly quickly by praise. The Consultant, however, continues to assess other behaviors the mother engages in that may be strengths to build upon later.*

*The Consultant also used the exploration technique to help Molly define her agenda as a measurable goal that could be achieved. The agenda of getting the children to not stay out late was phrased as the goal, "To have all children in the home by their designated curfew times six out of seven days of the week." Throughout the Phases, the Consultant will continue to explore and make Molly's goals specific and measurable so that progress can be gauged more easily.*

**Day 3:** During the next visit, the Consultant takes Molly to a local food pantry to get groceries, which Molly indicated was her agenda for the day (1,17). While taking care of this, the Consultant explores the assignment from the previous visit. Molly reports that she asked Macy to find either Micah or Alex twice, and Macy did (8,9). The Consultant asked how Molly got Macy to check on Alex and Micah for her. Molly said Macy knows that if she doesn't, she will get punished. This was explored further and Molly reported using positive consequences, such as giving the children more free time with their friends, and negative consequences, such as taking away privileges. However, Molly said she didn't like to use consequences because it often created a hassle. Usually the children tantrummed when she took away privileges and this made her feel like a "mean mom" (5,6).

Later at home, however, the Consultant observes Molly ignoring Alex when he begins to pester her for money to go to the store. Molly even uses redirection to get Alex involved in another activity. This does not last long and Alex begins poking and tickling Molly to get her attention. Molly initially tells Alex to stop but then begins engaging in the same behaviors. This interaction begins to escalate into shoving, pinching, slapping, and biting. Molly again appears to be engaging in the same behaviors as Alex. The Consultant uses this opportunity to observe the family's dynamics (5) and gain some information regarding Molly's tolerances and boundaries (6). The wrestling ends when a glass of water gets spilled. The Consultant then explored Molly's comfort level with this type of interaction with Alex. Molly was comfortable with the wrestling but admitted Alex tends to become aggressive sometimes (1).

A short time later, Alex begins to pester Molly again for money and when she says "No," he begins shouting, crying, stomping his feet, and throwing things. The Consultant and Molly went out to sit in his car and talk so that he could model how to walk away from arguments. Alex followed them a short time later, and banged on the windows and jumped on the car, demanding that Molly return to the house. This provided an opportunity to model and praise Molly for ignoring Alex's negative behavior (15). Alex continued his behaviors and the Consultant modeled offering a reward as positive reinforcement to Alex. The Consultant told him that if he got off the car by the time the Consultant counted to 10, his mother would return to the house shortly. But if he continued to yell and kick the car, his mother would stay in the car for a longer period of time. Alex initially ignored the Consultant but eventually got off the car and went inside. A short time later, the Consultant and Molly walked back into the house to model following through with his agreement. Alex was playing in his room (5,7).

During this time, Molly made several statements of a depressive nature (3,6,7). The Consultant explored these statements further and discussed them by phone with his supervisor and with Molly's psychiatrist. The psychiatrist explained the family's history to the Consultant and agreed to accept responsibility for closely monitoring Molly's depression. Because the Consultant recognized these statements as indicators of imminent endangerment issues, he addressed the crisis to ensure the safety of the family members. The Consultant became more directive and asked Molly to stick to a plan for taking care of herself and to set up an appointment with her psychiatrist the next day. While the Consultant and Molly were discussing her plan for the night, Molly got up to make sure Alex was still in his room playing (2). Molly was praised for checking on Alex and was asked to continue checking on all her children.

*Despite the crisis situation, assignments remain focused on increasing Molly's strength, which is checking on her children.*

**Day 5:** During the next visit with the family, the Consultant explored if Molly had any opportunities to check on her children since he last saw her. Molly reported that she had checked to make sure Micah was outside in the front yard the day before, and had called outdoors for Macy once (9). The Consultant then explored Molly's agenda for the day and found that she had made an appointment with her psychiatrist and was to see him in two hours (1). Since she needed a ride, the Consultant agreed to provide one (17) and asked Molly how she was feeling. Molly said she felt depressed (7) but was better able to handle things. However, her affect during the entire visit appeared flat (3). Several times during the visit, Micah engaged in inappropriate behaviors such as cussing, hitting his brother, and not cleaning up soda pop he spilled, but Molly did nothing (3,5,6,7). When the Consultant explored these situations with Molly, she simply shrugged them off. This was further explored and Molly disclosed that there often are times when she doesn't feel like doing anything and sleeps a lot (3,5,6,7). During these times she expects the children to take care of themselves and not get into trouble.

The Consultant assessed that another imminent endangerment issue needed to be addressed (3). He needed to make sure the children were safe and that their needs were being met, so he asked Molly if the children could stay with friends for the day or until Molly felt capable of parenting them. Molly agreed with little emotion, and the Consultant spent the remainder of the visit making arrangements for the children to stay elsewhere, at least until Molly returned from her appointment. During Molly's appointment, her psychiatrist told her she should leave the children at their friends' houses and take care of herself, which was arranged.

**Day 5 (evening):** When the Consultant visited later that evening, Molly looked very different. She was dressed nicely and smiling, and had a very positive attitude. She said she felt better after therapy and had received food stamps and support money in the mail that day. She reported still feeling depressed but not enough to ruin her day. Molly had called the houses where her children were to make sure they went to school and had already called the school so the children would know they were to come home after school the next day (2). The Consultant provided several concrete services (17) so that Molly could take care of errands she needed to run, such as getting food and paying bills. During this time, the Consultant continued exploring Molly's depressive moods and what she did to come out of them. Molly was not very good at recognizing these times or when the moods came and went (3,6,7).

*There appears to be many problems going on in this family's home. The Consultant has assessed Molly's agenda,*

*identifying long-range problems that need to be fixed, as well as immediate endangerment problems that need to be addressed. The Consultant assessed one problem area as Molly's inability to recognize when she is becoming depressed and how she can to take care of her children during these times so that the children can remain at home (3,4,6). Despite all of the problem areas that the Consultant has identified, he still strives to stay focused on increasing a behavioral strength rather than suggesting many solutions to fix all the problems. The Consultant determines that Molly's BAS of checking on her children can be built into skills that will effectively address these endangerment issues (12).*

*The Consultant determined that teaching the social concept of "child management" (24,28) would be appropriate and that Molly's strength (25) of checking on her children could be developed into the skill of "monitoring" (27) within this social concept. The social concept of "child management" was chosen because it addresses Molly's agenda (24) of the children staying out late and the Consultant's concerns about making sure Molly knows where her kids are and what they are doing. By accomplishing this, she can keep them safe and meet their needs, which are the referring worker's goals. The skill of "monitoring" will focus on addressing these concerns.*

During this time, Molly asks the Consultant how he is going to fix the problems she is having with her children. The Consultant explains to Molly that she knows her children better than anyone, and that he can't fix the problems. But he tells her that she has the abilities to do so (13,14), and offers to help her find ways to use what she knows to accomplish that. Through his exploration and active listening, the Consultant is demonstrating to Molly that he considers her the expert on her children (14) and recognizes that she already has some skills that will help her solve her problems (12).

*Exploration is an ongoing technique used by the Consultant to determine the family's dynamics (5), assess the family's capabilities (7), and specify the family's goals (4).*

At this point, the Consultant assesses whether or not the family is ready to move to Phase II. Molly's agenda of the children staying out late at night has been identified and the BAS related to this agenda has been identified and strengthened. Molly is checking on her children (8,9,10) more often, and has even checked to make sure that Macy was at a friend's house (9). Molly also has followed through on assignments that focus on her strength. There also are indicators that a therapeutic relationship has been established. Molly has begun to look to the Consultant for support as the children resist her and appears open to his suggestions.

*Because all of the Phase transition criteria are in place, the Consultant decides to move to Phase II and begin developing the social concept of "child management" and Molly's skill of "monitoring" through her BAS of checking on her kids.*

*Throughout Phase I the Consultant has not given any suggestions other than to address immediate endangerment and safety issues (i.e. suggesting the children stay with friends while Molly is depressed), after which he immediately returned to Consultant behaviors typical of Phase I (10). The Consultant spent 16 hours with the family during Phase I.*

# Phase II

Now that you have developed a strong relationship with the family, identified the family's agenda, observed a strength within the agenda, and seen family members use their strength more often, it is time to begin further developing that strength. This will be possible because you first spent considerable time with the family members developing their trust and setting them up as partners in change. This trust now gives you an opportunity to give more direction to the family members and refine the skills necessary to keep the family together.

Phase II is where the action begins. Here you pull together all your strategies and intervention techniques to begin creating skillful families. You won't start by teaching family members new, foreign skills, but by showing them how the skills they possess can be taken to new levels and used in different ways to create change that is longer lasting and more enduring. Like an artist teaching new students, you have become familiar with the family members, learned their personalities, assessed their abilities by watching them on their own, and devised a place to start teaching. Now is the time to put the canvas on the easel and teach the students different ways to use the paint, or how to highlight their painting by using the strokes they already know in different, more refined ways. In Phase II, it is time to put the family's canvas on the easel and begin teaching the family members ways to improve their skills.

Phase II focuses on building on strengths and teaching skills within one particular area, called a "social concept." (See Chapter 19.) Because the program is intended to be short term, you will focus on a limited number of skills that are consolidated into one social concept in Phase II. This social concept has been tailored to the family's needs and consolidates the family's agenda, the situation that is endangering the child, and those strengths identified in Phase I.

Social concepts span a range of family functioning areas, including child management, prevention of abuse and/or neglect, problem-solving, communication, and household management. Within a social concept area, several key skills can be taught that will enhance the BAS identified in Phase I. Remember that it is important to strengthen those skills already in the family's repertoire and to work toward the family's objectives. This strategy is more effective than relying only on teaching techniques that the Consultant may prefer but which may be foreign to the family.

Let's look at the areas of focus for Phase II, as well as the types of assignments given, the intensity, and the factors that determine when to move to Phase III.

## Focus

One area you will be focusing on in Phase II is continuing to increase the BAS in order to develop the skills of a social concept that can achieve the family's goals. Staying focused on developing one skill at a time allows you to make the most of the family's potential. This keeps family members from feeling overwhelmed by trying to learn several new skills at one time.

During Phase II you will begin developing skills within the first identified social concept area by making suggestions to family members. These suggestions will build their BAS into skills that are beneficial to them. These skills are developed by using the various techniques described in Chapters 7 through 18. Intervention techniques such as Effective Praise and the use of tangible reinforcers are used in Phase II everytime the family applies the skill behaviors and implements suggestions you have made to refine that skill. Modeling also can be used to move the family members on to trying the next behavioral step in developing the skill.

One of your goals in Phase II is to refine the BAS into a skill that is functionally sound. To become functionally sound, a strength behavior (BAS) must develop into a skill that is effective and works as intended. For example, you might identify a young mother's habit of "calling others for help" when she can't make her baby stop crying as her unrefined BAS. However, the "calling for help" behaviors aren't always effective because she sometimes calls a girlfriend who gives poor advice or calls the hospital when the baby just needs to be fed. You can refine this BAS of "calling for help" into the skill of "asking for help appropriately." To do this, the mother will need to learn who and when to ask for help by learning additional behavioral steps, such as determining the baby's needs, consulting a list of possible helpers she can contact, and stating her concerns so others will know how they can help her. If the mother learns all these behaviors and uses them appropriately, she will have developed a functionally sound skill ("asking for help appropriately") that works to meet her needs.

Another goal of Phase II is to develop more skills toward social concept acquisition. Once the family's use of a skill becomes more successful, you may decide to begin developing another skill within that social concept based on the same refining-the-BAS strategy that has been discussed. For example, the young mother's skill of "asking for help appropriately" fits under the social concept of "preventing neglect" of her infant child. Another skill that you may want to teach within this social concept area is "meeting nutritional needs." This skill can be refined from another one of the mother's BASes you have identified and increased, such as "having baby's proper formula available." You could then teach the additional behavioral steps that make up the skill of "meeting nutritional needs." These additional behavioral steps might be scheduling feedings, recording the intake of food, and reporting the baby's food intake to the doctor. Each skill taught during Phase II should be made functionally sound and should fit under one social concept area.

The number of skills that can be taught within the social concept and the amount of time spent on each one is determined by the information you gain while developing the first skill. This information provides clues on the family members' abilities, such as the pace at which they learn and the amount of information they can process at a given time.

By consolidating your teaching within one social concept in Phase II, you are able to stay focused when concerns not related to the family's agenda arise during treatment. For example, a father who has a bipolar disorder had identified his agenda as taking care of his family during his manic and depressive cycles. You have identified the father's BAS as his ability to take his medicine every day; the BAS has increased so that the father takes the medicine on time every day no matter what. Through your teaching, you help the father refine his BAS to the skill of "establishing routines" by helping him learn additional behavioral steps, such as scheduling daily activities, organizing household chores, and assigning tasks to various family members. You have solidified one skill — "establishing routines" — and have identified the social concept as "household management"; your treatment is structured around these. However, five days into Phase II the father tells you that the bill collectors are calling and threatening to take away his car. Instead of stopping the current focus of your treatment, you could first determine if the skill of "establishing routines" can be used to address his problem with the bill collectors. If not, see if there is another related skill (e.g. "problem-solving," "budgeting") within the social concept that can be taught to address this issue. By staying focused and teaching within this social concept area, you prevent confusion in your intervention and have an opportunity to strengthen the social concept.

These types of presenting problems will arise continually as you work with families. Dealing with these concerns by remaining focused within the social concept and the skill you are currently teaching will assist you in returning to the issues you were previously addressing. This will make your teaching more effective and less confusing.

Continually assessing goals will help the family keep track of its progress and will help you plan changes in emphasis or direction. In Phase II, however, you should have established the family's goals in terms that are specific enough so that you can measure success. This can be done by asking the family members how they will know when they have achieved a goal. Getting this input from the family members involves them in the treatment by showing that you are working to help them gain success. Having goals in which success can be measured helps the family and the Consultant recognize when success has occurred.

Phase II is where the family begins to learn how skills work to change behavior and why using skills a certain way produces the most effective change. It is important that you begin to teach the family members the reasons why these skills work so that they can internalize their use. Knowing why something works or doesn't work makes it easier for them to see how their own behaviors influence the behaviors of others. It is not uncommon for families to have superstitions about why certain inappropriate behaviors occur; they might blame the full moon or the fact that it's a leap year. By teaching families why certain skills affect the behavior of others, you are placing the responsibility for change with them. This understanding and responsibility helps produce long-lasting changes in the family.

In Phase II, you also continue to assess if you are sticking to the family's agenda by exploring and actively listening to the family to determine if change is occurring (the family's agenda can change daily); to determine what kind of success members are feeling; and to determine what they think still needs to

change. By making assessment an ongoing process, you will be aware of any changes that occur in family dynamics, situations, and goals.

It is essential during Phase II that you assess what dangers still exist within the family environment that could cause the children to be removed from the home. By making assessment part of your ritual for every visit, you keep focused on identifying any unsafe situations and therefore accomplish one of the referring agency's goals — preventing placement while assuring the children's safety.

You may discover that the family needs to learn more skills within a different social concept area to ensure that the children remain safe. In Phase II you will want to identify any strengths that will further help the family address these unsafe or endangering issues. Focus your teaching on the skills within the first social concept as you look for strengths (BASes) within another social concept area. Then, using praise, begin to increase the frequency of these newly identified BASes in much the same way as you did in Phase I. This provides you with a foundation on which to build new skills in Phase III.

Ongoing assessment allows treatment to flow smoothly enough so that if changes occur within the home, your treatment plan can adapt to these changes. It is important that you also continue to assess the ABC's of problem situations that arise (see Chapter 4), as these provide clues as to how your suggestions are being perceived and implemented by the family.

Often, the trust you developed in Phase I creates in the family a confidence that you have all the answers. In Phase II this confidence is encouraged because it provides the

Consultant with more opportunities to teach and encourage the family to use its skills. To further sustain this trust, you must be available to the family to provide support and answers when necessary. The answers you give need to be grouped around the family members' strengths and skills within their agenda. This tells the family members that you will be there to support them as they try new behaviors and refined skills.

Part of the trust the family has developed in your ability to answer questions comes from the concrete services you provide. By helping the family acquire food, clothing, and housing, providing rides, setting up appointments, etc., you create a bond with the family. Providing concrete services is part of a treatment plan that builds relationships and meets the family's basic needs. Also, you can begin to teach family members how to obtain services so that you can begin directing them toward independence.

By solving problems quickly at the beginning of therapy, you will give family members hope, build better relationships, break down resistance to therapy, and establish your own credibility.

Let's summarize our focus in Phase II.

### Build the strength
- move toward the desired goal-18
- refine BAS by teaching additional behavioral steps-19
- identify and increase other BASes within first social concept-20
- build additional skills by refining other BASes-21
- vary intervention techniques-22
- simultaneously praise strengths within second social concept area-23

### First social concept
- based on family's agenda-24
- based on strengths-25
- teach how skills affect behavior-26
- limited number of skills taught-27
- only one social concept-28

### Assess
- family's agenda-29
- continue to assess issues endangering children-30
- ABC's of problem situations-31
- family's and referring agency's goals-32
- family's dynamics-33
- strengths in areas that endanger children-34

## Assignments

In Phase II you are looking for different outcomes to your assignments besides simply increasing the BAS, as in Phase I. Assignments are designed to provide you with information about your treatment and the family's capabilities within your treatment. This information will let you know if the steps you are teaching the family are unclear or too large, if the pace you have set in teaching skills is too slow or too fast, if you are on the right family agenda and strength, and what the family's limits may be in using skills. The outcomes of assignments will help you adjust your intervention, if necessary, so that it is effective in meeting family goals and preventing placement of a child. This in turn will benefit the family by individualizing your teaching to fit the needs and aptitude of the family.

The outcome of assignments lets you know if you can continue refining the BAS or if you need to allow more time for the family to practice the behavior at its current level. If the family is not following through on assignments, this could be an indication that your treatment should be adjusted. The family may not understand the assignments or the skill steps you are trying to teach. If the family is completing assignments accurately and effectively, this usually indicates that your teaching is on target and the family understands what changes it can make.

By assigning the family to try your suggestions, change can occur at a greater pace than if you tried to teach the family members new skills but never asked them to try the skills. Examples of assignments you might have the family complete include trying suggested skills whenever specific problem behaviors arise, making lists of how trying the skills worked, and practicing skills prior to encountering problem situations. Always follow up on the assignments you give the family. This is a way to gauge how well the family is implementing the skills. If you give assignments but never follow up on them, you are only giving busy work and wasting valuable information that could assist you in developing your treatment plan and staying focused on it.

In summary, assignments in Phase II are:

- developing the BASes into skills
- teaching new behaviors and skills
- given during and between visits
- followed up

## Intensity

Typically, the number of hours a Consultant spends with the family increases in Phase II. This is because the Consultant is beginning to teach members how to use skills at a new level and they may be initially nervous about trying them. By supporting the family members during this process, you are encouraging them to not give up. If necessary, you should be with a family to provide support every time a new behavior or skill is used. Family members need to feel that you are truly their partner and know that if you are going to ask them to try skills that will create problems, that you will be there to support them. Lending this support helps the family members feel that you are interested in really helping them and makes them more open to further suggestions you may make. A family that knows you will be there to lend support is more likely to try suggested skills.

Many of the families we have served have commented positively about the support they felt they were getting while trying different behaviors or skills. Many parents said they felt overwhelmed by the behavior bursts their children exhibited when they incorporated a Consultant's suggestions, and felt they could not have gotten through those times without their Consultant's support.

Intensity in Phase II also increases because you are teaching a lot. As situations present themselves, you are faced with opportunities to teach. Being in the home frequently creates more opportunities to teach, which provides more practice for the family, which in turn provides more information to you on the progress of therapy. Oftentimes, families initially feel overwhelmed by the amount of time we say we will be in their homes. After they begin to see success, however, they report that the time spent teaching them how to refine their skills and why they should be refined helped them feel more confident to handle situations when the Consultant was not present.

Intensity also is high because you need to be in a home to assess what is occurring. The more time you can spend with the family in a variety of situations, the more information you will obtain. For instance, seeing how a parent handles a tantrum at a laundry mat may give you information on how he or she handles one at home. Spending time with individual family members also can provide you with perspectives on the family and the family situation that are different from those you might obtain when you see the members together.

Providing or helping the family obtain concrete services to gain a greater understanding of the family dynamics and use of skills also takes time. Encouraging the family to maintain its daily routine while you are in the home may make for longer visits, but the trade off in information is well worth the time spent. As discussed in Chapter 5 on relationship-building, concrete services strengthen relationships, make visits with the family seem less intrusive, and provide insight into the family's lifestyle.

Generally, Consultants spend 10 to 15 hours with a family each week in Phase II.

High intensity in Phase II is necessary to:

• support the family
• teach to many opportunities
• make accurate assessments
• observe family dynamics

## Moving to the Next Phase

When deciding to move to Phase III, you must assess the family's competency in using the skills taught in Phase II. Are family members using them fairly consistently without prompting from you? Is the family verbalizing some degree of satisfaction from working with you and is there an observable outcome of goals?

The family's competency in using skills is measured by the degree to which the family is creating change within the home. Are the skills functionally sound and is the family using them consistently enough to fix its problems? In Phase III you may decide to teach the family a new social concept in order to prevent placement of the children. If this is done, the skills taught in Phase II must be sufficient to allow the family to meet its agenda needs. Therefore, before moving on, you must be sure that the family understands how to use the skills and is using them fairly effectively.

Consistency also is important because the skills taught in Phase II will be reinforced only on an intermittent basis in Phase III; this is so the focus can primarily be on the new social concept and skills.

In order to keep the family motivated to continue moving toward its goals, members must feel some degree of success from having worked with you so far. Assessing the satisfaction level of the family throughout your intervention and addressing any issues of concern is necessary to keep the family open to suggestions you will make in later Phases.

Family members need to feel that the efforts they have put into changing the way they normally respond to situations have been beneficial. Being able to see some form of progress toward their goals provides them with encouragement to continue the process of change.

In summary, you are ready to advance from Phase II to Phase III when the family members:

- demonstrate a degree of competency in using skills
- use skills fairly consistently
- see progress toward goals

## Example: Phase II

*The Consultant has moved to Phase II and started building on the strength of checking on the children (25). The social concept of "child management" (28) was chosen because it incorporates Molly's strength (25) and focuses on her agenda of the children staying out late (24). The skill developed now is "monitoring" (27).*

*The skill of "monitoring" is broken down into these behavioral steps:*

- *parent has specific rules regarding curfews, boundaries, etc.*
- *parent asks where children are going before they leave the house*
- *parent teaches children to report where they are going*
- *parent checks regularly to make sure the children are where they're supposed to be*
- *parent requires child to check back on a regular basis*

**Day 6:** The Consultant begins developing Molly's BAS using a variety of intervention techniques (22). Molly is asked to define what staying out late means to her (291). Molly believes the children should be home before she goes to bed, which can be between 8 p.m. and midnight. The Consultant uses Criticism by Suggestion (19) to suggest to Molly that setting a specific curfew would let the children know exactly when she expects them home. This would make checking on them (25) easier because she would know where they were supposed to be at that time every night. This is the first behavioral component the Consultant suggests toward building the skill of "monitoring." Molly was given the assignment of deciding what time she felt the children should be in the house at night. She decides Macy can stay out until 10 p.m. because she is older but the two younger ones need to be in by 8 p.m. (32). The Consultant asks Molly if she would be able to stay up until 10 p.m. to make sure Macy is in. He gives the rationale that Molly has to be awake to make sure the children (18,26) come in on time. Molly believes she can do this because she is up late with her own friends on nights Macy is out.

The Consultant also explored with Molly what she does with the children when she goes out. Molly says she has Macy watch the younger children and Molly returns home several times to check on them. If they are not home, however, Molly goes back out and returns later to check (30,32,33). The Consultant explores what Molly does if she finds that Macy is gone and has left Micah and Alex at home alone. Molly reports that she'll usually stay home until Macy returns, or she'll take the children with her sometimes.

Molly admits that neglect allegations have been made against her in the past when Macy was supposed to be baby-sitting but left the younger children at home alone (30,32,33). The Consultant uses this opportunity to teach the next behavioral step of the "monitoring" skill by suggesting that Molly find out where her children are going before they leave the house (18,19). He explained to Molly that knowing where her children are planning to go before they leave the house will make checking on them easier (25,26). The Consultant ties in the benefit that having Macy report where she is going will let Molly know if she needs to make other baby-sitting arrangements for Alex and Micah.

The Consultant then set up a role-play to practice the suggested behavior of having the children tell Molly where they are going before they leave (22) to make certain she understood what the Consultant was suggesting. At one point, the Consultant modeled (22) asking the children where they were going as Micah was getting ready to go outside. The Consultant asked Micah where he was going and Micah said he was going to a friend's. The Consultant modeled getting specifics by asking which friend and asking Molly what time she wanted Micah to check in with her. The Consultant used this opportunity to point out to Molly that she now knew where Micah was going in case she needed to get him. He used the rationale that Micah was more likely to stay at his friend's house now that Molly knew where he was (26). Molly was given the assignment of finding out where her children were going before they left the house (22).

At 3 a.m. the next morning, the Consultant received a crisis call from Molly regarding a problem she was having with Macy. When the Consultant arrived at Molly's home with the police (the Consultant didn't know how dangerous the situation might be), Molly said Macy had been running around all night and would not stay home (29,30,31,33). Molly was upset and was afraid she would hit Macy. The Consultant praised Molly for calling him before she hit Macy (34), and began exploring both Molly's and Macy's perception of what was occurring and what the problem was (31). Macy admitted that she had disobeyed her mom because Molly was asleep when Macy came home and Macy figured her mom wouldn't know if she left again. Molly said she woke up at midnight to find Macy gone and stayed awake until she returned at 1 a.m.

The Consultant modeled (22) problem-solving techniques for Molly and used this opportunity to continue developing the skill of "monitoring" (19). Molly was asked if she felt that the 10 p.m. curfew was too late for Macy because Molly had said she could stay awake until Macy came in. Molly agreed she did not always stay up until 10 p.m. but that this was the first time she woke up to find that Macy wasn't home yet.

The Consultant used this opportunity to teach Molly how asking Macy where she was going before she left (18,19) and checking to make sure she was home when she was supposed to be

(18,19) may have kept Macy from disobeying her. He explained that if Molly did this, Macy would know Molly was waiting up for her and knew where to find her if she wasn't home on time. Molly decided to change Macy's curfew to 8 p.m. and handled Macy's screaming and yelling by ignoring her. Molly received incidental praise from the Consultant for ignoring Macy's inappropriate behavior (20). However, when Macy continued to yell, Molly relented (33) some and said that if there was a special occasion and she knew exactly where Macy was, she might let her stay out longer. Molly felt changing the curfew was a large enough consequence and decided not to give another. After this plan was set up, both Molly and Macy agreed to go to sleep and talk again later in the day. However, the Consultant left Molly with a plan to call Macy in as a runaway if she left before they got up the next morning.

**Days 7 and 8:** *The Consultant has already worked with Molly and developed her BAS (checking on her children) through establishing curfews, and finding out where her children are going before they leave the house. He will now add the behaviors of having the children tell her where they are going and checking back with her periodically (19). Teaching also will occur with Macy, Alex, and Micah on telling their mother where they are going before leaving the house and checking back with her occasionally while they are out.*

*The Consultant also is beginning to identify BASes in other skill areas within the social concept of "child management" (20). While the Consultant stays focused on teaching the behavioral steps to "monitoring," he begins to intermittently praise Molly's strengths of setting limits and levying consequences (20). These strengths are behavioral components of the skill "corrective teaching," another skill area the Consultant believes Molly would benefit from as she tries to address her agenda.*

Molly began using monitoring behaviors more frequently and was becoming more consistent in making sure she knew where her kids were, either by asking them or them telling her where they would be. They also set up a plan for the children to check back with their mom throughout the day or evening, and for Molly to call the places where they said they would be to check on them (18,19).

During a visit, the Consultant asked Molly where the children were in order to check on how well she was monitoring their whereabouts. She replied that Macy was at Jessica's, Alex was at Tyler's, and Micah was in the house. When the Consultant did not see or hear Micah, he modeled (22) for Molly how to check on him by getting up and looking around the house. Molly wasn't sure where Micah was. The Consultant went outside with Molly and found Micah in the garage with a friend playing with matches. There was a burning smell in the garage but no flames or fire could be seen. As a precaution, the fire department was contacted to make sure the area was safe (30). Firefighters arrived and determined there was no danger. By this time, Molly was frustrated and crying, and the Consultant modeled (22) remaining calm and dealing with the situation. The other child was asked to go home and Micah was brought inside. Micah began yelling, screaming, calling Molly names, and crying. Molly was becoming overwhelmed and the Consultant prompted her to send Micah to his room (22). Molly did this.

*Sending the children to their rooms was identified earlier in Phase I as a behavior Molly had used in the past.*

The Consultant modeled (22) remaining calm by sitting down with Molly and talking about calming down, and developing a plan for dealing with the situation. Molly picked up on the modeling and followed along with the conversation. When Micah calmed down and stopped yelling and throwing things for three minutes, the Consultant modeled praising Micah and letting him come out of his room. Anytime he began to re-escalate his inappropriate behaviors, the Consultant modeled sending him back to his room (22). Molly followed this and engaged in the behaviors the Consultant modeled throughout the visit.

Molly was asked how she was going to handle the situation regarding Micah not being where he was supposed to be and setting the fire (31,33). When she could not think of what to do, the Consultant explored how she handled

other instances where the children set fires or were not where they were supposed to be. Molly described a few instances where she would levy some form of consequence such as grounding or spanking to discipline the younger children (31,34). The Consultant praised Molly's past efforts to discipline the children in order to let them know that setting fires and not being where they were supposed to be is unacceptable (20). In order to strengthen this BAS, the Consultant assigned Molly to continue to discipline the children when they did something unacceptable. Molly gave Micah a consequence (20, 25) of staying in the house for two days. The Consultant praised Molly.

*Even though the problem behavior of setting fires needed to be addressed, the Consultant maintained the focus of teaching around the skill of "monitoring." The Consultant provided reasons why monitoring the children is important in preventing them from having opportunities to start fires. The Consultant modeled many other skills during the visit, but focused on the skill of "monitoring" and incidentally increased another of Molly's strengths (BAS) — disciplining by levying consequences (20,28).*

**Days 9 and 12:** Using various intervention techniques, the Consultant focused his teaching on developing Molly's skill of "monitoring." Modeling (22) proved very effective with Molly as she picked up on behaviors more often when the Consultant modeled them for her. Therefore, extensive modeling as well as role-play (22), which utilizes a form of modeling, was used frequently to teach Molly. Her assignments over the next several visits also were designed to help further develop the skill to make it more functional (19,26). These assignments included telling the Consultant how many times she checked on the children and whether they were where they said they would be, counting the number of times she needed to remind the children to tell her where they were going, and keeping track of how often she checked on the children rather than them checking in with her.

During these visits, the family's agenda (29) — getting the children to not stay out late — was continually explored and remained the same. The Consultant also continued to explore Molly's feelings of depression (30), as well as assess safety issues (30) that may be endangering the children. During one visit, Molly told the Consultant that she and the children had gone to the store and stocked up enough meat and food for several meals. The Consultant gave Molly incidental praise for making sure there was food in the house and planning several meals ahead of time (34).

*The Consultant spent these visits talking with the children individually to begin working on their issues and developing their strengths. The children were very independent and had developed skills to meet many of their own physical needs, such as finding food, getting their own clothes ready, taking their own baths, and putting themselves to bed (34). Though it was reported many times that the children were dirty, smelly, and out late, their ability to take care of themselves was assessed as a strength (children's BASes) and the Consultant began developing it through praise (23).*

**Day 13:** Molly entered another episode of depression. The Consultant used this opportunity to work with her on how to monitor the children and make sure she is meeting their needs during these episodes, how to obtain respite care if she felt she needed it, and how to make sure meals were pre-planned (22,30). Because Molly had developed her monitoring skill and the children had developed reporting their whereabouts, it was not surprising that she was able to have her children tell her where they were going, and check back with her periodically (18,19,25). During this time, Molly did not get up and check on the children herself. The Consultant worked with the children on following through with Molly's plan for them to help her get through her episodes of depression. Since Molly was unable to self-reflect earlier on how she behaved differently during depressive episodes, the Consultant recorded her behavior and her abilities to handle her children and meet their needs (30,31,33). This helped Molly become aware of how her behaviors changed and the physical indicators that might help her recognize the onset of a period of depression before it occurs.

*This also provided the Consultant with an opportunity to work with the children on taking care of themselves, knowing who to contact in case of emergency, how to obtain or prepare food, and being responsible for some of their own behaviors (26).*

*When Molly went into her depressive episode, the Consultant again had to deal with the presenting crisis in order to address the endangerment issues that arise during these episodes (22,30). The Consultant tried to tie in as much teaching to the skill of "monitoring" as possible, but again had to be more directive in helping to make sure the children's basic needs were being met. The Consultant assessed that a second concept area will probably need to be introduced to deal with Molly's depression and how she meets her children's needs.*

Molly was able to contact her mother (34), who took Micah and Alex to her house. She also called a respite care agency that found a place for Macy for the three days Molly thought she would need help. After three days, Molly was able to resume her parental responsibilities to the point where the children could return home. Though Molly's depressive episode lasted longer than three days, she felt that was all the time she needed help with taking care of her children. Molly and the children were praised (34) for their accomplishments and the Consultant cooked them a big dinner for their efforts.

*Molly's skill of "taking care of the children's basic needs" was intermittently reinforced throughout Phase II because this is a strength area that may serve as a BAS when the Consultant moves to Phase III (23). The Consultant has assessed that Molly's ability to meet her children's basic needs is an issue that will have to be resolved in order to keep the children safe and at home (30).*

**Days 14, 15, 17, and 18:** Molly reported that she was having a problem getting the children to do what she asked, and the Consultant continued to explore the problem with her (29,31,33). Through observation, active listening, and exploration, the Consultant assessed that Molly had become very good at monitoring (18,19) her children's whereabouts and began teaching her how to use this same skill to get her children to do what she wanted them to do. The Consultant explained to Molly that monitoring her children also could include monitoring their chores, school attendance, school work, and various other situations in which she had reported problems (26). The Consultant assessed that Molly's BAS of giving negative consequences had increased as Molly had twice more grounded the children for not being home when they said they would be (20). The Consultant pointed out to Molly how good she had become at verbalizing consequences and levying specific and appropriate consequences, and how these also could be used to address the problems she was reporting.

*The Consultant assessed that Molly's agendas of getting the children to come home at night, obey curfews, attend school regularly, and consistently help with chores would be best met by helping Molly to develop another skill under the social concept of "child management" (27,28). Because the Consultant has taught Molly the behavioral components of "monitoring," and Molly is using most of the components when she uses that skill, the Consultant will now begin to build on Molly's BAS of giving negative consequences to build the skill of "corrective teaching" (21).*

*The skill of "corrective teaching" can be broken down to include these behavioral steps:*

- *describe to the child his or her inappropriate behavior*
- *give the child a negative consequence (Molly's BAS)*
- *describe to the child the appropriate behavior that is expected*
- *check to assure that the consequence is carried out*

(Adapted from *Common Sense Parenting*, Burke & Herron, 1992.)

During these next few visits, the Consultant builds on Molly's strengths of levying negative consequences (20), and checking on her children in order to build the skill of "corrective teaching." He uses a variety of intervention techniques to introduce and teach each of the skill's behavioral components (22). Molly follows through with the Consultant's suggestions of giving Macy negative consequences when she disregards curfew or does not tell Molly where she is going. Molly still reports some hesitancy with giving consequences to Micah and Alex when they argue with her even though she has clearly established a rule about this (31). Metaphors and rationales were used with Molly to get her to understand the importance of following through with consequences every time the children break a rule (22,26).

Over these four visits, assignments were given to encourage Molly to use the skill of "corrective teaching" with each of its behavioral components as she learned them (20). Molly and the Consultant began to see some positive outcomes from Molly's use of the skill. The children haven't skipped school since Molly established this as a rule and no fires have been set (18). Molly even had started giving positive consequences every other day when the children attended school and obeyed curfew, something the Consultant had previously modeled.

The Consultant continued to praise Molly's use of the "monitoring" skill. During one visit, however, Molly did not know where Macy was. The Consultant explored with Molly what had happened and Molly was able to reflect that she forgot to ask Macy where she was going and when she would be back (31). The Consultant used metaphors and gave Molly reasons why it is important to be consistent in monitoring the children by knowing where they are going every time they leave the house (26). Although Molly forgot this time to find out where Macy was going, the Consultant had observed and recorded that Molly was monitoring her children's whereabouts and activities with increasing consistency. He pointed out her progress and she reported that she felt the children were being more respectful of curfew and house rules. Molly also reported that the children were starting to do chores more readily since she had begun using "corrective teaching."

*The Consultant assesses that Molly has demonstrated competency in using the skills of "monitoring" and "corrective teaching." She has correctly used these skills on many occasions to bring about change in her children's behaviors. Molly is even recognizing some progress in meeting the goals identified within her agenda (18). Although Molly still needs to learn more about the opportunities to use these skills, she understands the basic behavioral steps needed to make each skill work. As the Consultant moves into the next Phases, Molly's understanding and use of these two skills will be further developed and refined.*

*The Consultant believes Molly still needs to meet her children's basic needs, especially when experiencing a depressive episode. Molly has demonstrated some strengths in this area, such as in Phase II when she had her children stay with other people until she felt able to resume her parenting responsibilities and developed a plan to meet the children's needs while continuing to deal with her depression (23,34).*

*These strengths were incidentally praised. Molly also demonstrated a strength in buying food in advance so the children would have enough to eat (23,34).*

*Because Molly demonstrated an ability to use "monitoring" and "corrective teaching," and the problems Molly has with taking care of her children when she is feeling depressed continued, the Consultant decided to move into Phase III. The Consultant incidentally praised the strengths Molly displayed during her depressive episodes, such as feeding her family with available food and setting up respite care for the children. Molly seemed to have food available for the children fairly consistently, so this behavior was identified as a BAS to be built on in Phase III (35). The Consultant had 26 hours of face-to-face contact with the family during Phase II.*

# Phase III

In Phase II the social concept being taught focused on the family's agenda. In Phase III, you can do one of the following:

1. **Keep the same social concept and refine the skills addressed in Phase II.**
2. **Keep the same social concept and develop more skills within the concept.**
3. **Develop a different social concept.**

Your assessment throughout Phase II should help you make this decision, a decision based on the safety of the children as well as the family's and referring agency's goals. Frequently, the social concept that is developed to address the family's agenda also addresses the situation that is endangering the children. In these cases, the social concept stated in Phase II remains the focus throughout Phase III. The decision then becomes whether to finely tune the skills the family began developing in Phase II or to develop different skills within this same social concept that will benefit the family.

In other instances, a second social concept needs to be considered in order to prevent the placement of the children. This concept may need to address issues that are very sensitive with the family, such as sexual abuse, substance abuse, or mental illness. By addressing the family's agenda first and working on building a strong relationship with the family, the family's reluctance to approach these subjects will be reduced. Phases II and III differ simply because of the concepts you are teaching to. They are not designed to require two separate social concepts or a limited number of skills. It may be necessary to lengthen this Phase for some families in order to address skills that are needed to keep the family together. Keeping families together and ensuring the children's safety is your ultimate goal. Determining whether one social concept or two social concepts will achieve these goals is a decision you must make while continually assessing the family's situation.

Let's look at Phase III's focus, assignments, intensity, and conditions for moving from Phase III to Phase IV.

## Focus

In Phase III your focus is on the new social concepts being developed through building new strengths and new skills.

Like Phase II, Phase III's emphasis is on teaching the family members skills that will help them accomplish their goals and keep the family together. Your choice of a social concept or skills within that concept area that you will teach in Phase III is determined by the additional skills the family needs to learn in order to address any remaining endangerment issues. As you move into a new social concept area of teaching skills, you shift your focus to these particular skills.

The way these skills are developed is very similar to how skills were developed in Phase II. Remember that in Phase II you only incidentally praised the family members' strengths in the second concept area in order to prepare for Phase III. Now you will take one of those strengths (another BAS) and increase it through consistent praise. You will use the same intervention techniques and the same process of building on the family members' behavioral strengths (BAS) to develop skills to accomplish this. The areas being assessed in this Phase also are the same. You begin with one skill within the new social concept area and reinforce it continually to encourage the family and assist members in gaining the confidence they need to utilize the skill. Teaching continues around why and how skills change behavior and the family's responsibility in that change.

Your goal in Phase III is to choose and teach skills within a social concept area that will help the family address issues that endanger the children. If you find in Phase III that you have several areas that might need to be addressed to reduce the risk to the children, you should choose the social concept area that will have the most impact in bringing about for change, fits with any remaining goals the family or referring worker may have, and will yield the most useful skills. Then you will look to build on behavioral strengths within the skill areas you plan to teach. For example, you find in Phase III that a family has not dealt with substance abuse, truancy, and unemployment issues. You will need to determine which of these issues put the child in danger of placement and what skills family members must learn in order to deal with them. You must determine what additional skills the family needs so that the children can continue living safely in the home and then teach these skills one at a time in Phase III.

In Phase III you also want to maintain the skills acquired in Phase II by reinforcing them on an intermittent basis. By continuing to reinforce these skills, you are creating change that will last longer over time and is more easily maintained. If you stop reinforcing the skills from Phase II or cut back the reinforcement too quickly, the skills will gradually decrease in frequency and stop. It's like working at a job; you may not receive a paycheck every day, but if you don't receive one occasionally, you lose your motivation to work. Though your focus is on the new social concept and the skills being developed, you continue using some of your intervention techniques with the Phase II skills. When family members learn that they can fix problems through consistent use of the refined skills, continual reinforcement is no longer necessary. The family members are reinforced by the success they achieve in dealing with their own problems.

Goal achievement should be observed at this point in your intervention. Family members need to see that the work they have done is getting them something they want. Continually updating the family's goals and progress toward those goals is essential. This means regularly asking the family members if they feel successful in meeting their goals and what other goals they want to achieve. For example, a family may have given you at the beginning of services several goals it wanted to accomplish. These may have included having the 12-year-old daughter stop telling lies; having the parents work as a team with the children by having one parent not negate the discipline handed out by the other; and having the 12-year-old not report her parents for abuse whenever they appropriately discipline her. In Phase III you have explored with the family its progress toward these goals. The parents now report that the 12-year-old is no longer reporting them as abusive, but is still telling lies several times a week. The parents also report that they are communicating more about discipline but continue to negate each other's chosen discipline if they disagree. By updating the family's goals through exploration, you assess information that is pertinent to your treatment and can adapt your intervention plans to use this information.

As you can see, several of the family's goals may already have been accomplished and the family may be feeling successful by Phase III. By focusing on the new social concept and intermittently reinforcing the skills learned in Phase II, you are helping the family achieve these goals. Being able to give family members clear indicators of goal attainment provides them with hope, confidence, and feelings of success.

Let's summarize the focus of Phase III:

### Strengths

- build on new BAS within new skill area-35
- focus teaching in new social concept/skill areas-36

- intermittent praise of family's use of Phase II skills-37
- teach family why skills work-38
- vary intervention techniques -39
- only teach within first and second social concepts-40

## Assess

- issues endangering the children-41
- parents' and referring agency's goals-42
- family dynamics-43
- family's identification of success-44
- family's limits-45
- identify ongoing problems-46

## Social Concept

- may be same social concept with refinement of skills from Phase II-47
- may be same social concept with new skills-48
- may be different social concept-49

## *Assignments*

The assignments for Phase III should be focused on the new skill you are teaching. As in Phase II, you will want to give assignments that encourage the family to try new behavioral steps that you are teaching in order to build a functionally sound skill. The assignments should be progressive, requiring family members to incorporate more and more of the behavioral components you introduce so that they learn how to use the skill more effectively with each completed assignment. The family needs to gain proficiency in using the new skill areas being developed. Through the use of assignments, you are providing opportunities for the family to practice these behavioral components and skills, as well as gaining information about what the family still needs to learn in order to meet its goals.

Assignments should remain focused on the second social concept. As a general guideline, you should give during every visit of Phase III at least one assignment that focuses on the new concept and associated skills that are being developed.

Occasionally, you can assign additional tasks that help maintain Phase II skills. These assignments provide opportunities for the family to maintain skills they have already learned while further refining them. The more the family practices a skill, the more ingrained that skill becomes and the greater the chance is that the family will continue using the skill after you are gone.

In summary, the assignments for Phase III focus on:

- new skills being developed within the second social concept
- maintaining Phase II skills

## *Intensity*

As in Phase II, you are continuing to teach the family to build skills that will help achieve its goals. It is going to take some time to teach the behavioral components to the skills so that the family learns to use the skills effectively. You also will want to spend time observing the family using the skills, assessing change within the home, and supporting the family members as they continue to develop their skills. The level of intensity in Phase III will depend on the family's capabilities and the extent to which you have previously taught skills. By Phase III, family members usually have already built a trust in you and have confidence in your ability to help them. For this reason, they are more likely to use skills as you suggest them.

The family members also have developed skills in Phase II that may assist them in quickly acquiring Phase III skills. For that reason, intensity is individualized to the family's needs. Due to the teaching you will be doing in Phase III, however, intensity needs to be maintained at a fairly high level. You will now be looking for opportunities to teach the family within the new social concept area while continuing to address skills from the previous social concept. This will require you to meet with the family when you know there will be teaching opportunities. Skills must be observed in order for you to get a clear picture of the level of the family's capabilities and what changes still need to occur within the home to keep the children there. The level of intensity could be the same as in Phase II — approximately 10 to 15 hours a week — depending on the family's circumstances.

Let's summarize the level of intensity for Phase III:

- fairly high intensity
- approximately 10-15 hours a week for each week in Phase III
- individualized for each family

## Moving to the Next Phase

Moving from Phase III to Phase IV requires some serious assessment on your part. The family must know the skills it needs to keep the children in the home. This doesn't mean that family members have the skills down to a science or even that they are using them to the fullest extent you believe they can. However, you must be sure that you have taught the family enough skills to keep the children safe and at home, built on the right strengths to maintain the skills over time, and

addressed what the family and referring agency requested in order to reduce the risk of the children being taken out of the home. Observing members actually using the skills rather than having them say they used them provides a solid base for moving to Phase IV. You can continue to fine-tune members' skills, but they should be at a point where the initial issues are no longer occurring.

If the family has been observed using the skills consistently and fairly independently, and the risk of placement has been assessed as low, it's time to move on to Phase IV.

Here's a summary of what needs to occur prior to moving to Phase IV:

- reduced risks to children and minimized endangering issues
- family members have been taught enough skills
- family members' appropriate strengths have been built on
- all skills are being used somewhat consistently
- skills are effective and functionally sound
- goals are identified and some goal attainment has been achieved

Let's continue with our example of intervention during Phase III.

### Example: Phase III

*During Phases I and II, the Consultant explored and assessed when the children's needs were most often neglected to the point of endangering the children (30). During Molly's depressive episodes, she had the most difficulty in meeting their needs. Through observation, the Consultant*

215

noted that Molly was able to meet the children's nutritional, medical, and clothing needs consistently when she wasn't depressed. Molly reported that most of the neglect allegations made against her came during the "worst times." She indicated that the "worst times" were when she was so down she felt sick and didn't want to get out of bed at all (41). The Consultant also spoke more with Molly's psychiatrist, who described Molly's depressive episodes as being acute and severe. But they continued to work at diminishing the impact these episodes had on her daily functioning.

The Consultant chose the social concept of "managing depression" for the focus of Phase III. This concept incorporates the referring agency's concerns of making sure the children are being cared for physically and medically when Molly is depressed (42,49). This also seems to be the remaining endangerment issue that continues to put the children at risk of placement.

The skills the Consultant will teach in this Phase, which will build on Molly's BAS, are "identifying depression," "prioritizing," and "accessing support resources."

The Consultant has assessed problems Molly has in meeting her children's needs during episodes of depression. However, these episodes appear to occur infrequently. Therefore, the Consultant will begin developing skills that will help Molly take care of her children during these times (36). The first skill to be built is "prioritizing" because Molly's strengths of providing food and arranging child care (BASes) are behavioral components of this skill. The behavioral steps to the skill of "prioritizing" are:

- List the basic daily needs of children and self
- List the needs in order of importance
- Determine which needs the children and parent can meet, and the needs others must meet when the parent is depressed (e.g. Molly or an aunt can get Micah to the doctor for allergy shots when Molly is depressed)
- Regularly review the list with the children and other support persons
- Whether happy or depressed, use the list as a daily checklist to make sure priority needs are being met
- Meet the needs of the children and self (Molly's BASes are in this behavior because she feeds the children and arranges respite care)

**Days 19, 21, and 22:** The Consultant explored Molly's agenda and discovered that Molly was fairly content with the way things were going in the home and felt she was dealing with things well (44). The Consultant reinforced Molly's abilities to handle the problems that arose with her children and discussed how important it is for her to make sure that she was meeting her children's needs (41) with regard to providing food and medical treatment when she gets depressed. The Consultant told Molly that he wanted her to feel prepared for times of depression so her children's needs can be met and so she could focus on her own needs to get through the depression as quickly as possible (42). Planning for depression, Molly could decrease her worries during her episodes and know that her children were being well cared for and able to remain in the home. Through exploration, Molly identified the goal of "taking an evening off for herself once a week without having to parent the children so I won't get so depressed" (42).

To begin building on Molly's strength, the Consultant gave Molly the assignment of listing all the daily basic needs she and the children have, such as getting food and monitoring the children (35). Over the next three visits, Molly and the Consultant worked on the behavioral steps toward developing the skill of "prioritizing" (39). Because most of these behavioral steps consisted of making lists, Molly was able to learn to do them quickly (35,36). Each time Molly incorporated one of the behavioral steps as she was learning the skill, the Consultant praised her. Molly was able to come up with a priority list and use it as a checklist two days in a row to demonstrate that she knew how to prioritize and meet her children's needs. As a reward for using the checklist, the Consultant baby-sat for Molly so she could have an evening out (17).

Molly also got excited about planning for her depressive episodes by calling several relatives and a neighbor to ask if they would provide baby-sitting or transportation for her children if she ever needed it. The Consultant also worked with the children on how to continue to meet some of their own needs every day. Micah and Alex were shown how to pick out clean and weather-appropriate clothing, and Macy was taught to cook three simple meals (40).

**Day 23:** During the visit, Molly received a call from Alex's dentist who said Molly had missed Alex's appointment to have a cavity filled. This was an opportunity to teach Molly that it is her responsibility to make sure her children receive necessary medical treatment (36,41,46); by doing so, she can prevent medical conditions from worsening (38). The Consultant explored with Molly if she felt depressed and if there were other ways she could more easily remember appointments. Molly admitted that she did not consider dental appointments priorities, but she agreed that adding all medical and dental appointments to her priority checklist could help her remember them (35).

*During this visit the Consultant also began to teach the skill of "identifying depression," which is comprised of these behavioral steps:*

- *identify common antecedents that may trigger depression (e.g. forgetting to take medication, break-up with boyfriend, placement of children)*
- *list physical and cognitive (i.e. what common thoughts are present) symptoms experienced during depression*
- *determine which symptoms appear first as key indicators that an episode of depression is coming on*
- *plan who will be contacted when symptoms first appear (e.g. psychiatrist, family, friends)*
- *list helpful things that can be done to recover from depression*
- *follow through with plan to contact support persons*
- *do helpful things when feeling depressed*

**Days 23, 24, and 26:** During these three visits, the Consultant taught Molly the behavioral steps to "identifying depression." He said that because Molly had developed a strength in being able to prioritize her needs and the needs of her children on a daily basis, she also could identify when depression was coming on by prioritizing what symptoms appear first when she gets depressed (35,36). Because Molly was in a happy and functional state of mind, she was able to incorporate the steps of "identifying depression" in these few visits. The Consultant used metaphors, role-plays, and praise to help Molly understand the importance of being able to recognize the onset of depression (38,39).

The Consultant pointed out how both Molly's and the children's needs would be best met if Molly could put her plans in action before she felt too depressed to meet anyone's needs. Molly said that she felt that if she had a way to know when the depression was coming on, she might even be able to do activities and talk with her psychiatrist to prevent herself from getting depressed at all.

During one of these visits, Macy reported that her mother had not given Alex any kind of punishment when she found him playing with a lighter in his bedroom. Macy felt this was unfair because Molly had grounded her a few days earlier for lighting a candle in her bedroom. The Consultant explored with Molly if Alex had been playing with a lighter and if Molly was moni-toring him or had used any corrective teaching (43,45). Molly said that she felt she was monitoring Alex, but that he must have snuck the lighter to his room when he went there to play. Molly did not give Alex a consequence because she caught him before he set anything on fire. She did describe Alex's inappropriate behaviors to him and the appropriate behaviors he needed to use instead.

The Consultant used confrontation to point out how not giving Alex a consequence for playing with the lighter gave him the message that playing with the lighter was an acceptable behavior. Because Molly wants Alex to not play with lighters or set fires, she needs to levy a consequence in order to stop this negative behavior (38,39,40). Molly agreed to give Alex the consequence of not letting him play alone in his room for a day. Molly self-reflected that she has trouble giving consequences because the children have been minding her so much better than before.

*Although the Consultant's focus remains on the concept of "managing depression," teaching occasionally occurs to the skills in the first concept, "child management." The Consultant is trying to help Molly use monitoring and consequence skills at every appropriate opportunity.*

*The Consultant believes that one more skill — "accessing support resources" — can easily be taught to Molly to help her better manage her depression (36). Molly has demonstrated a BAS that has been increased through her ability to contact rel-*

atives to provide respite when she is depressed. In fact, Molly has demonstrated an ability to obtain many resources for herself when she isn't depressed; she just needs to learn how to access these resources when she is depressed. The behavioral steps to this skill are:

- list resources that can assist when parent is depressed
- pre-contact resources to see how they can help
- put list of resource numbers in an easy-to-access location

**Days 27 and 28:** The Consultant uses a variety of intervention techniques (39) to teach Molly how and why she should develop the skill of "accessing support resources" (38). Molly has already contacted neighbors and relatives who agreed to provide support and respite if she is too depressed to care for the children at home for one to two days. She also identifies a need to talk about her problems with good friends, so she decides to contact her old Alcoholics Anonymous sponsor to ask if she can talk with the sponsor if necessary. Molly reports feeling good about taking control of her depression and having a plan in place to help her work through her down times (44). She thinks that just knowing that she has support available will help her from getting depressed.

*The Consultant had taught Molly all the behavioral steps to the three skills of "prioritizing," "identifying depression," and "accessing support resources." Molly seemed to understand the importance of each of these skills, talked as if she felt prepared to handle her depression with the plans she had put in place, and met her children's basic needs daily for eight days in a row. However, the Consultant realizes it will be difficult to assess how well Molly actually understands these skills and whether or not she will be able to use them correctly until Molly goes into another depressive episode. Because Molly's depression occurs at a relatively low frequency (every few weeks to every few months), the Consultant assesses whether he should move to Phase IV based on Molly's ability to verbalize and role-play her use of skills to manage her depression. Then if Molly becomes depressed in Phases IV or V, the Consultant will assess how well Molly has learned the skills and determine if more refinement of the skills is necessary to make them functional for managing Molly's depression.*

The Consultant is assessing during his last few visits whether Molly can use her child-management skills well enough so that the children are no longer in danger (41,45). He determines that she can. He continues to assess Molly's goals, as well as any ongoing problems the family might be experiencing. Molly said she was grounding Macy and Alex and taking away their phone privileges when they skipped school; she felt this had reduced the problem significantly (37,38,40,44). The Consultant explained to Molly that he had received a call from the school earlier saying Macy had missed two days of school each of the last two weeks (46). Molly immediately called Macy at her friend's house and told her to come home. Macy denied skipping school and began to cry. Molly appeared about to waver so the Consultant asked her how she could be sure that Macy had skipped school (38). Molly said she would go to the school the next day to check for herself (40) and if Macy did skip school, she would be grounded for the weekend with no friends over and no telephone. When Macy began yelling and screaming, Molly sent her to her room. The Consultant discussed with Molly how she could have kept this situation from getting as serious as it did using the skills she has learned. He helped Molly to understand that if she had monitored Macy's attendance from the beginning, she could have prevented the problem. He suggested that Molly monitor Macy's school attendance regularly, just as she monitors Macy's whereabouts after school every day. Molly said she would call the school to check on Macy's attendance.

Molly believes the fire-setting behavior is under control (41,44), and was able to self-reflect that by giving her children a consequence every time she saw them playing with matches, she stopped a lot of problems before they got started. Molly also believes the plan to talk with the school more often will help her bring the problem of skipping school under control. And though the children miss curfew occasionally, Molly states that she knows how to address the problem (44).

*By focusing on the two social concepts of "child management" and "managing depression," and developing only five skills — "monitoring," "corrective teaching," "prioritizing," "identifying depression," and "accessing support resources" — within those concepts, the Consultant was able to address all of Molly's agenda items and one of the referring agency's goals (40). At this point, the Consultant decides through assessment that Molly had learned enough skills to prevent the children from being placed outside the home and to address situations that may arise. Consequently, he decides to move into Phase IV and fine-tune both of Molly's skill areas. The Consultant spent 17 face-to-face hours with the family in Phase III.*

## Phase IV

Phase IV involves fine-tuning a family's skills. That is, taking the skills the family has developed in Phases I, II, and III, and making them more consistent, more stable, and even more functionally sound. When you leave a family, you want to make sure its members are using the skills you have helped them build. By taking these skills and fine-tuning them to make them more effective, you are assuring that the family will be able to weather normal crises as they arise.

Consider how we compared your intervention with helping the family build a house. The family is building a house with your assistance. At this point in the construction (Phase IV), family members are putting in the plumbing and wiring the house. Your job is to make sure they are installing these correctly to prevent fires or water damage. You push them to install wiring and plumbing correctly even though they may initially think it is easier to cut corners. You are there to support and strengthen family members as they stretch their installation skills to greater levels. By doing this, you are not guaranteeing that the house will withstand hurricanes or tornadoes, but that it will stand up to heavy rain, snow, or even ice storms. In fine-tuning a family's skills, you assess how well members use skills, how consistently they are using them, if the skills are being used in timely and appropriate situations, and how much of the skills members are using. This helps you assess the family's limitations in using the skills.

Determining the family's limits means finding out how much more a family can refine a skill, how much further members can take the skill, and how much more consistent they can be. As mentioned throughout this book, we do not believe in "perfect families" and are not holding our families up to the ideals of television families portrayed in *Ozzie and Harriet* or *Leave it to Beaver*. However, through assignments and intervention techniques, you are attempting to get the family to use skills consistently and with greater frequency, and to follow through with using every skill, incorporating every behavioral step that was taught. This way, the family is encouraged to use the skills accurately and can learn why the skills are so useful in bringing about changes. When a family has successfully moved through the Phases and then stops completing assignments and following through on suggestions, and expresses satisfaction with the way things are, you probably have met the family's limit. Meeting a limit simply means that the family can not or will not develop its skills any further. It may be

necessary, however, to try to stretch the family's skills so that the children can stay in the home and the family can reach its goals.

Now that you have reached this level, you will need to assess the family's skills to ensure the safety of the children. If the family's skills are not yet adequate, you may need to help the family move beyond its limits in some skill areas. You must encourage the family using rationales, Effective Praise, and confrontation to bring members to the necessary level of skill acquisition. Every family is unique, but you must create families in which children are safe and family members feel secure enough to handle their problems.

Let's look at the focus of Phase IV, as well as the assignments, intensity, and requirements for moving to Phase V.

## Focus

In Phase IV your focus is on refining the skills that you and the family have worked on. This means that you have taught the family enough skills so that the situation that endangered the children is no longer present. At Boys Town we believe it is our ethical responsibility to ensure that children are safe. Therefore, you will continue to assess family needs throughout Phase IV to develop the skills necessary to secure this safety.

In Phase III, you began determining if the skills being taught are truly reducing the endangerment risks to the children. By Phase IV, you will have to decide whether the family has made enough changes to keep the children safely in the home. If unsafe conditions still exist, you may have to consider a recommendation for placement. In this Phase, you should have enough understanding of the family's motivation, abilities, and dynamics to know if the family can keep the children safe. You will have tried to teach the family members skills based on their strengths, and will be able to determine if the skills they have learned are sufficient enough to keep the family together.

Phase IV is focused on stimulating a family to reach its full potential in using the skills that have been taught. No new concepts are introduced after this point. This is done so that the focus of intervention is on the social concepts the family already has developed rather than on trying to teach new ones. Throughout treatment, you have been assessing what social concepts the family needed to learn to prevent the placement of the children and to reach its goals. At this point in your intervention, you should have taught to all the necessary social concepts and skills.

In Phase IV, teaching becomes more conceptual and focuses on the skills and social concepts you have been addressing. By teaching conceptually while using the family's language, you are focusing the family's attention on how the skills work rather than on what behaviors to use in certain instances. You want the family to start thinking more generally (conceptually) about how and why the skills can be used in a variety of situations, and not just in one or two situations where the skills have worked. For example, a child may understand that when he does dishes like his mother asks (the behavior of completing a task), he gets more time to watch a TV program without interruption. But you will want the child to understand more generally that whenever the child follows his mother's instructions immediately (the skill of "following instructions"), he gets more privileges and freedom

to choose what he wants to do. This way, the child learns to start thinking of all the ways he can use the skill of "following instructions" to get more privileges instead of just thinking specifically about doing the dishes as a way of getting more TV time.

You can encourage families to think more conceptually about how to use the skills they have learned by talking about the skills more conceptually. For example, you would encourage grandparents who have been using grounding and taking away phone privileges when their grandson misses his curfew to talk about getting the grandson to "mind" (their conceptual lingo) because the social concept you have been working on is "discipline." Then when the grandparents use the reward of allowing the grandson to go to school ball games with friends as a way to get him to do his chores, they can see this as another way to get the grandson to "mind." As family members start to think conceptually about how they can use skills, they begin to understand better how the skills work and will be better able to think of ways to generalize the skills in a variety of situations to fix different problems that may arise. As their understanding of how skills work is enhanced, they will begin to act more independently in using the skills.

In Phase IV, additional behavioral steps may be taught in order to make a skill more functionally sound, but no new concepts or skills should be taught. This allows the Consultant to focus on refining the skills the family is already using. For example, a teenager has been developing the skill of "negotiating" to replace demanding behavior. The skill of "negotiating" consists of these behavioral components: 1) Calmly explain your viewpoint; 2) Listen to the other person's idea; 3)

Offer alternatives or compromise; 4) Give reasons for your opinion; and 5) Choose the best alternative together. (Adapted from *Teaching Social Skills to Youth*, Dowd & Tierney, 1992.)

The teenager has successfully mastered the behavioral steps of offering an alternative or compromise to the situation and giving reasons for his opinion. However, he still needs to develop being able to explain his viewpoint calmly. This is a behavioral component of the skill "negotiating" and can still be taught in Phase IV.

In Phase IV, your primary aim is to make sure the family members understand how the skills they are using work. They need to know the reasons why the skills they employ affect behavior changes in others. For example, when a person first learns to drive a car, all that he or she may know is that the oil should be changed every few months. But this understanding of car maintenance is simplistic and it is more likely that the new driver will forget or run into problems when the oil light flashes. The driver can benefit from understanding why oil is important for making the engine run, the dangers of not keeping clean oil in the engine, and how the proper weight of oil must be used. If the driver better understands how and why oil is important to making the car run, then the driver is better able to maintain the car and figure out what to do if the oil light does flash.

In Phase IV, the family needs to be given as much information as possible about how the skills that have been suggested work to bring about change so that family members become more competent in the use of the skills. The more one knows about how something works, whether it be mechanical parts or human behavior, the better able he or she will

be at identifying problems and generating solutions for fixing problems and getting things to work as they should.

Assessing goal attainment in Phase IV is imperative because the family is moving toward independence and members need to be aware of how their behaviors have helped them reach these goals. In order for the family to continue using these skills in other problem areas that may arise, members need to first see that the skills they learned have helped them reach the goals they set for treatment. Assessing the family's satisfaction with treatment through goal attainment provides an opportunity to teach the family members their part in achieving their goals.

In Phase II, you did some periodic praising to increase behavioral strengths that would be developed in Phase III. Similarly in Phase IV, you will use Effective Praise to increase the family's ability to generalize skills members have learned and to realize the part they played in goal attainment. By starting to praise the family's ability to generalize the skills, you are preparing the family to begin thinking about functioning independently. Your focus in Phase IV is not on teaching the family members how to generalize and be independent in their use of skills. Instead, it is convincing family members that they are able to generalize the skills. You accomplish this by praising them when they spontaneously generalize the use of a learned skill, setting the stage for generalization to be taught in Phase V.

Teaching begins to address the family's ability to generalize skills to different situations and environments. Any generalization the family members demonstrate by using the skills they've learned is praised and teaching focuses on why and how these skills have been beneficial in different situations. Helping family members see skills work in different situations helps them fix new problems that may arise. You also should begin assessing the family members' ability to self-reflect on how their behavior affects other people's behavior. This self-reflection is one of the keys to long-term maintenance of skills. Generalization and self-reflection will be addressed more in Phase V.

Let's summarize the focus in Phase IV:

## Attain limitations
- family understands why and how skills affect behavior-50
- fine-tune skills-51
- possibly teach new behaviors within skill areas-52
- family is using skills consistently, frequently, and completely-53
- situation endangering the children is under control-54
- assess whether to recommend placement-55

## Teaching
- conceptually-56
- no new social concepts taught-57
- no new skills taught-58
- behaviors needed to make skills more functionally sound are taught-59
- praise spontaneous generalization-60

## Assignments

In Phase IV, assignments focus on stabilizing the family's skills and fine-tuning them. Assignments used in Phase IV keep the family heading in the direction necessary to achieve goals and keep the family intact. You should give assignments that make the family's skills sounder and more consistent, and add to the family's progress toward goal achievement. These assignments also keep you focused on what the family still has to accomplish to ensure that it is going to stay together. Assignments address the additional behaviors the family members need to develop, such as adding behavioral components to make skills work better, practicing skills in various situations, and understanding how and why the skills they have been using work.

Because you are asking the family members to stretch themselves in skill areas, you will be able to see where limits are being reached and make immediate assessments to adapt your treatment. For example, you have devised your treatment with a family around the social concept of "preventing physical neglect" and have been developing the skill of "meeting medical needs" as a part of that concept. The behavioral components the parents have been building on to develop this skill include identifying health concerns that need medical attention, discussing concerns with medical professionals, scheduling regular check-ups and immunizations, and attending appointments on time. The family is very good at the first three behavioral components but continues to miss doctor appointments. You have been using various intervention techniques to stretch this behavior, and believe that the family could set up appointments and make it to them on time. Through assignments you have assessed that the family can make it to appointments but still needs the doctor's office to call the day before as a prompt; the family also is occasionally late. This information will help you adapt your treatment to either stretch this behavior to a higher level or determine if this level is adequate enough to meet the medical needs of the children. Assignments allow you to keep up with what is going on between these visits and allows the family to practice more independently.

In summary, Phase IV assignments:

- expand the family's skills
- focus on all social concepts
- focus on all skills
- focus on all behaviors
- promote conceptual understanding of why skills work

## Intensity

In Phase IV you begin to decrease the frequency and intensity of your visits so that you can assess and observe family members using their new skills more independently. As the time between visits increases, the family members will begin using the skills at a level that is comfortable for them. In the first three Phases, you taught and supported the family at a high intensity. In Phase IV, you want to see if family members are maintaining a particular level of skill use because you are there or because they have seen the skills work for them.

Because you are still fine-tuning the family's skills, the intensity of your visits remains moderately high. Generally, a Consultant spends six to ten hours a week with the family in Phase IV. The intensity with which you first begin Phase IV will be greater than the intensity toward the end of the Phase. Sometimes Phase IV will last one week; other times it will last several weeks. The length depends on how much more skill-proficient the family needs to be so that the children can remain in the home.

Phase IV intensity:

- begins to decrease
- is approximately six to ten hours a week

## Moving to the Next Phase

In deciding to move to Phase V, you will need to assess if the referral problems are under control and no longer an issue of concern. The family needs to be using the skills independently without input from you and feeling successful in doing so. The family also needs to be using the skills consistently enough so that they will be maintained after you leave. When encouraging the family members to become more consistent and functionally sound with their skills, you need to determine if there has been any resistance that may indicate that the family will stop using the skills at that level of consistency when you leave. If you feel this might happen, and this level is necessary to keep the children at home, then you still have teaching to do and are not ready to move to Phase V. However, if you are confident in the family's ability to deal with issues, and you, the family, and the referring agency are comfortable with the child remaining in the home, you are ready to move to Phase V.

When it appears that parents have stretched their skill use to the limits of their ability, Phase V begins.

Let's summarize when to move to Phase V:

- referral problems under control
- children are safe and can remain at home
- family sees success
- skills being used consistently
- skills are functionally sound

Let's continue our example with the family in Phase IV.

## Example: Phase IV

*In Phase IV the Consultant begins to fine-tune Molly's skills in both social concept areas (51). At this point in the intervention, the Consultant will focus his attention only on the two concepts of "child management" and "managing depression," and no new concepts (57) or skills (58) will be taught. The Consultant believes that fine-tuning the five skill areas within these concepts to make them more functionally sound will enable Molly to handle any situations that may arise (59).*

**Day 30:** During the first Phase IV visit, the Consultant begins encouraging Molly to be more consistent in using her skills (53). Molly reports two incidents in which Macy did not get home by her curfew; both times, Molly had to track her down to get her home. When the situation was further explored, the Consultant found that Molly did not follow through with consequences either time. The first time, Molly grounded Macy for the next night, then took her over to a friend's house to hang out. The next time Macy was late, Molly confined her to the house with no phone privileges, then let her talk to friends.

The Consultant discussed with Molly how and why the skills she is using work to manage her children's behavior (50). He also explained that "corrective teaching" works because Macy doesn't want to lose the things she likes to do, like hanging out with friends and talking on the phone. However, if Molly only tells Macy she has a consequence and doesn't follow through with it, Macy will stop following the rules because she will have figured out that Molly won't do anything when the rules are broken (56).

Molly was reminded that her goal was to be able to manage her children's behaviors (56) in different areas, and that making sure consequences are carried out will help her achieve that goal. Molly is very good at self-reflection (50) and reported that she can see how Macy would do what Molly told her to do for awhile and then not listen to her again. The Consultant suggested that Macy stopped complying with the rules possibly because Molly didn't "stick to her guns" and use "corrective teaching" consistently. He pointed out that if Molly wants Macy to keep minding her, she needs to keep managing (56) Macy's behavior using the skills she learned.

Molly also reported that she was taking Alex in for ear surgery the next week and had contacted Macy's school about her skipping behaviors. The Consultant praised Molly for making sure she was prioritizing her children's needs, and for managing (56,60) more of Macy's behaviors by monitoring her school behavior.

The Consultant again taught Molly how making sure she was monitoring her children's behavior would affect their behavior (50) because they would know mom was going to be checking on them and they needed to be where they were supposed to be.

**Day 30 (evening):** Later that evening Molly phoned the Consultant to say that Macy was having a tantrum because Molly told her she could not spend the night out with a friend. Molly was "sticking to her guns" but was beginning to feel overwhelmed. The Consultant assured Molly that she could handle this situation, and helped Molly reframe the situation. The Consultant reminded Molly that she had endured worse behaviors from Macy, and told her she could use the skills she had learned to manage this situation (51,58,59). As the Consultant continued to talk to Molly, Molly was able to say that she should use "corrective teaching" and decided to send Macy to her room for shouting and cussing.

*Since Molly had been inconsistent in using the "corrective teaching" skill, the Consultant had the opportunity to teach Molly how inconsistency causes behaviors to worsen rather than improve (50,53).*

**Day 31:** When the Consultant arrived for the next visit, he found Molly depressed and irritable. She was yelling at the children a lot but had followed through with arranging for all three of them to go to their grandparents' home the next day (54). For supper Molly had taken a casserole out of the freezer and put it in the oven. She told the children they were not to go out that night because she was not up to checking on them. When the children began to whine, Molly told them that if they stayed in, she would plan a surprise dessert for them when they returned from their grandparents'. All three children settled down and began getting their things ready.

The Consultant praised Molly for "prioritizing her children's needs," and "accessing support resources." He also explored with Molly if she had been able to identify when the depressive symptoms were first occurring. Molly said that she had a feeling the night before when she had the argument with Macy that she was feeling overwhelmed about parenting. Through exploration, the Consultant learned that Molly did not contact her psychiatrist or support sponsor like she had planned to do in order to help her through the depression. The Consultant suggested that Molly try to make these contacts and to see if it would help her work through the depression any sooner (51,59). Molly agreed to think about it and call the next morning if she wasn't starting to feel better. Molly reported feeling relieved that she had a plan for sending the children somewhere and said she was grateful for having taken the time to make a checklist to ensure that all her children's needs were met. She indicated that it was difficult to think clearly when she is in a depressed state and using the list made things easier.

The Consultant praised Molly and exclaimed at how great she was doing in meeting her children's needs and making sure they were safe. The Consultant rewarded Molly's use of the skills of "prioritizing her children's needs" and "accessing support resources" (53) by helping the children get ready, eat dinner, and clean up. He then explored what Molly planned to do to manage her depression. Molly said that if she still felt depressed, she would try her psychiatrist's suggestions of following a routine every day regardless of how miserable she felt. The Consultant left Molly with two assignments: to contact her support persons and to try her psychiatrist's recommendations for following a routine (51). Both assignments encouraged Molly to engage in behavioral steps that are necessary to make the skill of "identifying depression" more functional.

*The Consultant scheduled the next visit for sooner than he normally would in Phase IV in order to check on Molly and see how she was managing her depression. He has assessed that having Molly take care of herself is important to being able to get her children back quickly from respite care with their grandparents and move on (54).*

**Day 32:** When the Consultant returned the next day, Molly had arranged to go see some friends for the day. The Consultant praised her for "accessing support resources." Molly reported that she had called her psychiatrist and received some good advice and support (51). Molly had tried calling her support sponsor, but she was not available. Molly said she was going to follow a routine as her psychiatrist had suggested, but she felt that getting out of the house with friends would do her more good this time than staying home and following a routine. Molly was praised for coming up with more helpful ways to identify and meet her own needs during her depression (60).

**Day 34:** On his next visit, the Consultant was surprised to find that all three children had returned home. Molly reported that she felt great after two days and called to have her children come home. Molly stated she tried to keep active, like she and the Consultant had discussed, and felt that this helped her come out of her depression much faster. Molly was prioritizing her children's needs by providing meals for them, making sure they had clean clothes, and monitoring them when they were away from home. Molly was praised for managing her depression in a way that enabled her to take care of her children (53,54,55,56).

**Day 38:** During this visit, Molly reported how she had gone out with friends and had arranged to get a baby-sitter so Macy didn't have to watch Alex and Micah all evening. The Consultant praised Molly for having accomplished her goal of going out for the evening without the children. Molly said that Alex had acted up with the baby-sitter by refusing to take a bath, and leaving the yard once without telling the sitter. Molly asked if she should give Alex a consequence for this because she was not the one whom Alex disobeyed. Using metaphors, the Consultant helped Molly to generalize her skill of "corrective teaching" and understand why it would be important to give Alex a consequence for his misbehavior. Molly verbalized understanding and gave Alex a consequence.

*At this point the Consultant assesses that Molly has refined her use of skills in both social concept areas to the point that they are functionally sound. Molly is using the skill of "monitoring" to the point of knowing where her children are and whom they are with throughout the day (53). She also is using the skill of "corrective teaching" in some new situations (generalization) and with some new behaviors (generalization) to get her children to mind her better (60). By using these two skills to this extent, Molly has been able to effectively manage the referral problems and her agenda of the children skipping school, setting fires, staying out late, and not helping with the chores. Molly has used "corrective teaching" and "monitoring" with enough proficiency that she has been able to achieve her goals in these areas (54,55).*

*Even though Molly has not been completely consistent in following through with consequences, her use of the "corrective teaching" skill is sound enough to allow her to manage her children's behaviors. Likewise, Molly has demonstrated competency in managing her depression to the point of reducing the endangerment risks that her depression used to pose to the children (54). Molly is able to prioritize her children's needs when she goes into depres-*

*sion, access some support resources, and identify her depression. Although Molly could become better at contacting her support resources sooner, she is demonstrating enough skill proficiency in accessing resources that her children are no longer in danger during her depressive episodes. Molly also is reporting some feelings of success in accomplishing her goals by using her depression-managing skills. By focusing treatment on only two social concept areas (57), the Consultant was able to help the family achieve its goals and minimize the endangerment issues that put the children at risk of placement (54,55).*

Molly has expressed some concern over the Consultant's plans to end services soon. The Consultant encourages Molly, telling her that she has developed skills that will help her consistently deal with her children so she can meet her goals and that the children are no longer in danger of being removed. Molly is able to self-reflect some about how using consequences, prioritizing, and accessing support resources has helped her get the children to behave better and help her deal with her depression (50).

Self-reflection of how her use of skills affects the children's behaviors and helps her through depression has become a strength for Molly. She has begun to verbalize an understanding of the cause-and-effect relationship between using her skills and causing changes to occur in her children's behaviors (50). However, Molly does not seem to understand the cause-and-effect connection between monitoring her children consistently and how it prevents them from getting into potentially dangerous situations. The Consultant spends more time with Molly talking about how the skills of "monitoring" and "identifying depression" work to prevent the children from getting into dangerous situations and help to make sure that the children's needs are consistently being met (51).

*Because self-reflection and generalization are not the focus of teaching until Phase V, the Consultant will continue to teach self-reflection and generalization to Molly in the next Phase. However, whenever Molly spontaneously generalized a skill or verbalized an understanding of what more she could do to bring about change using the skills she has learned (self-reflection), the Consultant praised Molly. The Consultant has assessed that he is ready to advance to Phase V since Molly has met all the necessary criteria. The Consultant has spent a total of 10 face-to-face hours with the family in Phase IV.*

# Phase V

Phase V is a critical part of your intervention with families. Even though you determined at the completion of Phase IV that the child will remain in the home, that the family has the ability to deal with issues and is using the skills consistently and effectively, and that family members are seeing success, you still want to ensure that the family will act independently and confidently to maintain progress.

In the Boys Town Family Preservation program, we believe we are not being as thorough and effective as possible in our treatment, and are shortchanging the family if Phase V and VI are not accomplished. In Phase V, you direct a family toward becoming confident and capable of handling most situations that arise while keeping the family intact. By focusing this Phase on developing the abilities of the family members in areas that will help them maintain change over time and in varied situations, you are fulfilling your ethical responsibility to assure that the family has the skills necessary to keep the children in the home safe and the family together.

Phase V is a very active teaching Phase. The same variety of intervention techniques are used, but the focus of your teaching is different from the focus in previous Phases. Phase V is designed to create confidence and independence in families by teaching them that they have the abilities to fix their own problems and maintain balance within their homes. The focus of the teaching is to help the family learn how members can use their skills to fix any number of problems that may arise. Because we have set aside an entire Phase for developing a family's independence, and making sure that members know how to use skills in various situations and understand why and how they were successful, you can leave family members feeling secure that they will be able to weather most crises that come up.

No new social concepts, skills, or behaviors are taught in Phase V. The focus is on maintaining those areas from earlier Phases through emphasizing the family's abilities. One of the areas addressed in Phase V is developing the family's self-confidence and independence through stressing its abilities and achievements. The focal point of your teaching is getting the family members to generalize their use of acquired skills, self-reflect on their roles in the change that occurred, and engage in independent behaviors that are focused on fixing their own problems and answering their own questions.

Let's look at the focus for Phase V as well as the assignments, intensity, and provisions for moving to Phase VI.

## Focus

You have done tremendous work over the last four Phases building a relationship with the family and creating a partnership with its members. In Phase V you are now going to begin dissolving the partnership. This means the family members are now responsible for maintaining the changes that have occurred as a result of the skills they have developed and used, independent of you. By praising the family's ability to handle situations on its own and not giving answers to problems, you will be enhancing this independence. By using the intervention techniques to lead the family to develop its own understanding of how skills work, you will not need to make the changes, and the family members will see that they can make the changes independently.

In Phase V you will be focusing on teaching the family members how to generalize their use of the skills, and how to self-reflect about how using the skills can produce effective changes. Teaching generalization and self-reflection can be done using the intervention techniques with a different focus.

Before discussing how to use the intervention techniques with a different focus, we'll define the terms of generalization and self-

reflection, the two skills you want the family to be able to use in Phase V.

Generalization is when a person is able to take a behavior, skill, or concept learned in a specific situation, and apply it to another situation that was not specifically taught. For example, we all learn to generalize the skill of reading. We may specifically learn how to pronounce every letter or group of letters phonetically, but no one is taught how to pronounce every word in the dictionary. We learned to generalize, sounding letters out in order to pronounce new words we encountered.

In the same way, families cannot be taught how to use skills in every specific situation they may encounter; they need to learn how to generalize their use of skills. Generalization is made easier when we understand how a certain behavior, skill, or concept works. When we know something works, we are better able to analyze if the same process will work in different situations.

The family's ability to generalize the skills to various situations, people, and places is vital to maintaining these skills. When family members see that the skills they are developing are not situation-specific and can be used generally, they are more likely to continue using them. For instance, a family member who has been working on anger-control skills and has become skilled at walking away when discussions begin to escalate into arguments at home can learn to generalize anger control to other situations. If the family member realizes that these anger-control skills also will work in dealing with a neighbor who is allowing his dog to run lose in the family's yard, he will begin to see the usefulness of the anger-control skill. As the family members see success in different areas, they become more dedicated to using the skill and recognizing its usefulness for them. The family that recognizes how to generalize skills and does it is more able to act independently in solving its problems.

Self-reflection is another skill the family needs to demonstrate in order to maintain long-term change within the home. Self-reflection is the ability to understand and verbalize how one's use of a behavior or a skill affects himself or herself, others, or the environment. Many of us learn to self-reflect at an early age because parents and teachers have us relate how our behaviors affect others. Common self-reflection statements children make include, "If I talk back to the teacher, she gets mad and makes me miss recess," "If I share my toys, it makes my mommy smile," and "When I'm good at the dentist's office, the dentist gives me a toy."

Self-reflection is a cognitive process that indicates an awareness of the connection between one's actions and the effect it has on others. However, in order to know if a person is making the cognitive connection, this connection needs to be verbalized. A Consultant wants to teach family members verbalized self-reflection so that he or she can assess if they understand how their use of skills produces change in the environment or others.

By understanding how their behaviors affect those around them, family members begin to internalize the skills they are using. They must realize their roles in being able to produce change by changing their behaviors. Then they are more likely to analyze their own behaviors when things seem to be slipping back into problem states and determine what changes they can make in their own behaviors to resolve the problem. They can self-reflect about whether or not they are using the skills correctly, and if they aren't, can come up with ways they could use the skills to produce the desired effect in others or the environment.

Look at this illustration of self-reflection: A husband who has been having difficulty getting his wife to support and follow through with the punishments he gives the children learns the skill of "communication" in Phase III. He learns how to tell his wife the specifics of the punishments. His wife becomes more supportive and helps make sure the children are serving their punishments. In Phase V, the husband verbalizes his understanding of why his wife is more supportive of his discipline when he says: "I finally figured out that my wife wasn't angry with me. She just needed me to tell her more about the punishments the kids were given. I found out that when I communicate with my wife, she is supportive and even lets me know if the kids aren't doing what I asked them to do. But if I forget to tell her what kind of punishments I've given the children, she gets flustered and the kids manage to get out of being punished." In this example, the husband self-reflects the positive effect that using the "communication" skill has on his wife, and the negative effects that result when he doesn't use this skill.

A family that learns to generalize and self-reflect on the skills it has developed is more likely to use the skills long after the Consultant leaves. When a family is generalizing and self-reflecting, it is more prepared to maintain the goals that are achieved during services and fix any additional problems that may arise.

The Consultant can teach a family to generalize and self-reflect by using the intervention techniques with a different focus. The focus is not to teach specific skills in order to fix specific problems, but to teach family members how to think about these skills and why they are effective.

The focus of teaching is different in several ways. First, you will no longer provide answers to family members when they present problems. By the time you enter Phase V, you will have spent a great deal of time and energy developing the family's skills by teaching intensively. When the family had problems and requests, you were available with the suggestions. You have been reinforced for providing solutions to family problems, and in Phase V the family is getting a little nervous about the idea that you will soon be gone. It is not uncommon for some families to ask for more suggestions and claim they don't know what to do. Under these circumstances, it is easy to want to provide suggestions to just one more situation, especially if you view it as minor and not a part of the original issue. This has become natural for you and it is difficult to stop. In Phase V, however, it is time to allow the family members to stand on their own and begin moving toward independently answering those questions for themselves.

If family members ask you to help solve a problem and want you to suggest what they should do, you may lead them to the solution. You are not providing a solution, only guiding them toward one by having them use the skills they have learned. For example, a mother may admit to you that she is terrified about not having you in her home to help her deal with her hyperactive child. She might ask you what she should do if her child does not get into the special education classes that the school is considering for the child. But because the mother worked during Phases I through IV to develop her strengths and skills in the areas of advocating for her child and being assertive with professionals, you know she possesses the knowledge and know-how to deal with this potential problem. You can lead her through exploration, role-plays, metaphors, reframing, and praise to help her think through and verbalize how she might use her advocacy and assertiveness skills to fix this problem. You might set up a role-play in which you ask the mother to describe how she would present her case to school personnel by being assertive, like when she got the school to test her child for learning disabilities in Phase II.

As the mother works through the verbal role-play, you can offer praise that points out how she is able to apply her assertiveness skills to other situations, such as dealing with the school if it refuses to place her child in the special education class. Instead of providing the answers, you teach the family to find the answers using what they have already learned.

At this point in your intervention, you need to determine if the family members will be able to answer their own questions once you are gone. Providing answers at this point would send mixed messages. If you answer their questions, you are demonstrating to family members that they don't have the ability to fix their problems. At the same time, you are telling them they do have that ability to fix their problems.

If a family is unable to come up with solutions, you will need to stop and take a look at what has occurred throughout treatment. You will need to assess whether or not you have taught skills to family members in a manner that was conceptual enough for them to understand how the skills addressed their problems. Was your teaching focused on the skills that were being developed? Were they appropriate skills for the problem areas? Did the family truly demonstrate a competency in using the skills? Did you thoroughly and conceptually teach how the skills work and why? If there is any concern regarding these areas, you will need to return to Phase IV and address these issues before moving into Phase V. If you provide suggestions to the family, you will not be able to make this assessment and cannot be assured that the family can develop independence and confidence in using the skills.

Your goal in Phase V is to emphasize the family's accomplishments, abilities, and successes in treatment. Another way to promote a different focus in your teaching is by using "you can" statements. These statements allow you to model your confidence in the family's abilities and keep you focused on creating independence, not fostering dependence.

"You can" statements are responses the Consultant gives to family members to bolster their confidence and encourage them to think how they "can" handle problems independently. These statements are used to teach the family the connection between using a skill in a specific situation in the past and using the skill in a current or future situation. These statements help point out to parents that the negotiation skills they used in Phase II to resolve conflicts with their teenage son can now be used to resolve conflicts with school officials, neighbors, employers, relatives, and others.

If a family member is leery or hesitant about how to solve a problem, the Consultant uses a "you can" statement that in essence says to the family: "You can fix that problem with the skills you used to fix the problems that brought me to your home." Take a situation where a parent learned how to use rewards to motivate a six-year-old child to stay in the yard during Phase III. Now the parent seems confused about how to deal with a 12-year-old child who talks too long on the phone. A "you can" statement can be used to teach the parent that he has the abilities and knowledge to fix this "phone" problem. The Consultant in this situation might say: "Remember when you worked so hard to get Sally to stay in the yard. You used rewards to motivate her. You know how effective rewards can be. **You can** use rewards to get Tyrone to talk less on the phone and fix that problem just like you got Sally to stay in the yard." In this situation, the connection between using rewards for keeping children in the yard and getting children to stay off the phone is being pointed out so the parent learns that the outcome rewards produced in one situation can be produced in other situations.

Another way to teach families generalization and self-reflection is to have the family point out cause and effect when members use skills. If a 14-year-old boy who has been learning the skill of "complying with rules" goes outside to smoke a cigarette (one of the family's rules), you might ask him how he benefits from complying with the rule of smoking outside. You are asking the boy to verbalize the effect of compliance. If he says that he might lose privileges such as money for buying cigarettes when he doesn't comply with the rules, he is verbalizing an understanding of the cause and effect of compliance (or in this case, the cause and effect of noncompliance).

Other ways to ask the family members to describe the cause and effect of the skills they learned are to ask them to tell you what would happen if they used the skill any more or any less than they already do. Encourage them to think how the effect would be different if they used the skill differently. Questions that start with the words "What if..." are useful in encouraging the family to consider the cause and effect of skills.

The focus of Phase V teaching also is different in that you get family members to think with a future orientation. This "future" may occur tomorrow, next week, several months from now, or even several years down the road. This future orientation teaches family members what they can do in various prospective situations. By doing this, you enable them to see how the skills they have learned will help them in the future.

The future orientation can focus on everyday problems as well as crisis situations. For example, a child who was hanging out in junior high school with delinquent peers has since acquired a new group of friends after learning socialization skills in Phase II. You may ask the youth how he plans to use his skills to deal with a situation in high school if one of his new friends decides to break the law. You want to teach the youth to make a connection between choosing socially appropriate friends in junior high and choosing socially appropriate friends when he gets to high school.

An example of a crisis-oriented situation might involve parents who have learned discipline skills in the first four Phases in order to manage their teenage daughter's argumentative and drinking behaviors. You might ask the parents how they would deal with a situation where their daughter came home and said she had skipped school for a week. You would look for the parents to provide answers that indi-

cate they understand that using discipline skills to deal with the crisis of truancy is the same as using discipline skills to deal with the crisis of alcohol abuse.

By teaching family members through a future orientation, you help them see how the skills and social concepts they have learned can help them solve and generalize to other potential problem areas that may arise. Often during crises, and even with everyday problems that might seem overwhelming at the time, people have a tendency to revert back to old behaviors and ways of doing things. By focusing questions on these possible situations, you are preparing the family members to realize they already have a plan if a crisis should occur. This gives the family a sense of confidence and empowerment.

While developing the family's independence, you also continue to teach the family how to obtain services on its own. Throughout your intervention, you have been teaching the family how to connect with community resources, if needed, while simultaneously providing these services for the family. In Phase V you will no longer provide any concrete services to family members but instead will place the responsibility to meet the family's needs back on them. By supporting the family's ability to obtain these services, you are continuing to foster independence.

By changing the focus of the teaching from how to use skills to deal with specific problems to teaching the family how to use the skills independently in many situations, you will promote a sense of confidence and empowerment in the family. When a family is taught how to generalize and self-reflect, the family will know how to act independently in using the skills.

In Phase V, you will need to assess how well the family can generalize and self-reflect. Some families will be very good at generalizing skills to various situations but not at self-reflecting on their part in their goal achievement or understanding how the skills they have learned can help them in future situations. Others are good at self-reflecting but not at generalizing or answering future-oriented questions. No matter what area a family is good in, teaching must occur in all areas. Families need to see how they can use the skills they have acquired in other situations, reflect on how they made change occur, and have a plan for future problems that may arise. Without these, change is likely to be short-lived and your intervention is likely to be unsuccessful over time because the family will not continue to use the skills once you are gone. For this reason you will need to determine the family's limits in each of these areas and assess if these limits are adequate enough for the family to maintain the skills and keep the children safe.

For example, when entering Phase V you may have been working with a parent who continually said, "I don't know, he just changed," when asked why her teenager stopped lying. By the end of Phase V, the same parent may be able to say, "My child is not lying because I have been using rewards more with him when he tells me the truth and he likes these. I also use consequences with him, such as taking away things he likes to do, when he lies." Another family member might only be able to answer, "I guess maybe he didn't like having the phone taken away." This may be these family members' limits in being able to understand and verbalize self-reflection. They both are acceptable limits. The second person's answer was limited in that it was vague and not very conceptual. However, the second person did recognize that the consequence he used (taking the phone away) affected the son's behavior.

Sometimes in Phase V, family members start using skills less frequently. This is normal and often provides valuable teaching opportunities. As you begin spending less time with them and are not there to prompt and expand limits, they may begin to feel overwhelmed at having to handle things on their own and thus not use the skills as often. Generally, and predictably, the problems could begin to re-escalate if this happens. This is an opportunity to teach the family and show that its decisions to not use the skills is what caused the behavior to occur again. A family whose members are able to self-reflect on their part in the situation and understand what they need to do to fix it is the family in which changes will likely endure through crises. If family members are unable to see why things fell apart and what they need to do to fix things, you need to continue with your Phase V teaching.

In summary, the focus of Phase V includes:

## Teaching
- generalization-61
- self-reflection-62
- focus on future-oriented situations-63
- no new social concepts taught-64
- no new skills taught-65
- no new behaviors taught-66
- use conceptual terms-67

## Establishing independence
- praise family members for their solutions-68

236

- build self-confidence-69
- reinforce family's abilities in goal attainment-70
- family accessing its own resources-71

## Assignments

Assignments are designed to promote the family's independence and build confidence in its own abilities. Assignments focus on the family's use of generalization and self-reflection, as well as its handling of future-oriented issues. These types of assignments provide you with an opportunity to assess the family members' limits in these areas while relaying your confidence in their abilities. One of your goals is to have them be able to explain why they used a particular skill in a particular situation, and why it worked. The outcome of this assignment will provide you with information regarding how much more teaching needs to be done in the areas of choosing a particular skill in a particular situation, and how they understand the benefits of using the skill. This type of assignment may give you more information on the family members' abilities to self-reflect or see that they have the ability to solve problems. For example, you may ask a child who was taught to use negotiation skills with her sister in Phase II to explain why she chose the same skills with a teacher at school and why she thinks it worked.

Assignments also should focus on what a family will do in situations that may occur in the future. For example, parents who learned the skill of "giving consequences" to deal with their son's problem of stealing could be asked what they would do if the police called one evening and said their son had been picked up while vandalizing a local business. The parents should be able to relate that they would use consequences to address the vandalism behaviors just as they had used consequences to address stealing behaviors.

Also, assignments should be directed toward the family's ability to generalize skills to other situations or circumstances. An example of this may be asking the parents how the skill of "establishing a routine" they developed to keep their house clean in Phase II could be used to help them get the children to bed every night.

Assignments in Phase V are not focused on increasing the family's skills. By this time you have already taught family members what they need to know, skillwise. Now assignments are focused on how the family can maintain its use of the skills. Will the family be able to use the skills at the same level of competency after services end? The assignments in Phase V should help you assess this.

In summary, assignments in Phase V focus on:

- self-reflection
- generalization
- future orientation
- family's abilities

## Intensity

In Phase V you continue to decrease the frequency and intensity of visits. By doing this, you are getting the family members ready for a time when you are no longer working with them. The intensity level doesn't decrease so quickly that the family feels like it is being "dropped off a cliff," but is gradually faded so that the family moves from reliance on you toward independence. The family will have more time alone to try to use its skills to address everyday problems and can assess how well it is able to function without your assistance. This time away from you allows the family members to realize that they can act independently in using the skills they have. Family members need time to adjust to the reality that you won't be in the home much longer and that they will be on their own.

The gradual reduction in intensity during Phase V conveys to the family members that you truly believe in their abilities and that you are proving that by not being in their home as often. If you were to continue to visit fairly often and stay longer than necessary, you again would be sending a mixed message — you're telling family members to be independent while still spending a lot of time in the home. Making your visits shorter and further apart continues to develop the independence the family needs. This is vital in assuring long-term maintenance of skills.

As families test their independence by decreasing their use of skills, you should continue to teach self-reflection, promote generalization, and provide support while continuing to build their confidence. This sets the stage for you to be able to assess at what level the family will maintain skill use when you are not there. Intensity is generally two to five hours a week in Phase V.

Phase V intensity:
- decreases in frequency
- decreases in intensity
- generally two to five hours a week

## Moving to the Next Phase

The move from Phase V to VI can be made when you have seen great changes in the fam-ily members' abilities to generalize their skills to different situations, self-reflect on their roles in goal attainment, and act independently in using the skills. The work you have done in Phase V has produced better responses from the family in these areas, and though you determined in Phase IV that the child was no longer in danger of being removed, this becomes more apparent as the family is able to generalize, self-reflect, and use skills independently. The family's skills are still functionally sound and the child is no longer in danger at this point. Family members recognize goal attainment and are continuing to set more goals in which their responsibility for achieving them is understood.

In order to move from Phase V to Phase VI, the family should be able to:

- generalize skills
- answer future-oriented questions
- self-reflect
- independently use functionally sound skills
- maintain the safety of children

## Example: Phase V

*In Phase V the Consultant will focus his teaching on the areas of self-reflection (62) and generalization (61) by discussing future-oriented situations (63). The Consultant has assessed in Phase IV that Molly is very good at reflecting on how her behaviors affect her children's behaviors. On several occasions, she has demonstrated the ability to change her behavior based on her understanding of how using "corrective teaching" gets the children to behave as she would like. The Consultant will continue to teach self-reflection to "corrective teach-*

*ing," as well as teach Molly to generalize and self-reflect about the other skills she has developed.*

**Day 41:** During this visit, Molly brings up several concerns she has about Micah entering first grade in the fall and what she should do if he begins setting fires. The Consultant asked Molly how she had managed to get Micah to stop setting fires over the last few weeks. Molly indicated that she did not let Micah play with matches or lighters. The Consultant further explored with Molly what she had done to make sure Micah did not get matches and how she had dealt with Micah when he was caught with matches or lighting fires. Molly was able to self-reflect that she would use "corrective teaching" if Micah ever sets fires (62,67). The Consultant prompted Molly to remember what she had done to keep matches away from Micah. She was able to remember that she was more careful about monitoring where her matches were and she checked on Micah more often.

The Consultant then helped Molly generalize by making the connection with a "you can" statement about her ability to use "monitoring" and "corrective teaching" to fix any problems she might encounter with Micah setting fires at school (61,67). Molly was able to verbalize a tentative plan for checking Micah's backpack and pockets before he left for school to make sure he didn't have any matches. She also talked about consequences she could use with Micah during the school year (64,65,66).

Molly also expressed concern about what she would do if her depression lasted more than a few days. Molly stated she didn't think her plan would work for more than a few days. The Consultant used active listening as Molly expressed her concerns and asked Molly what she thought she might need to do to make her plan work for more than a few days (70). The Consultant assured Molly she has the answers to her own questions and focused his teaching on how she could use the skills she has learned to deal with depression and future child-management issues (67,68). The Consultant worked with Molly on coming up with solutions to her concerns using the skills she already has.

To continue his teaching on addressing future-oriented situations (63), the Consultant asked Molly to think about several situations and how she could use her skills to address them. These situations included what she would do if Macy did not come home for two days and Molly did not know where she was; what she would do if she caught Micah burning some trash next to the house; and what she would do if she entered a depressive state and her relatives couldn't watch the children.

*These questions are designed to allow the Consultant to teach generalization and self-reflection, and assess what more Molly needs to understand to effectively handle future situations using the skills she has acquired (61,62,63,67).*

**Day 44:** During his visit with the family, the Consultant observed Micah going out the front door wearing only shorts in 40-degree weather. When Molly sees this, she calls Micah back in and tells him to put on a shirt and shoes before he leaves. Micah begins to argue and Molly instantly stops him by telling him that if he does not put on his shirt and shoes, he will not go outside. Micah immediately goes and puts on his shirt and shoes. When this is explored with Molly, she reports that most of the time she doesn't need to actually levy any consequences when using "corrective teaching" because the idea that she will use them keeps her children in line. When asked why this works, Molly says that she does follow through with consequences when she needs to and the children know she means business. So when she tells them to do something or else, they listen. Molly is again praised for **her ability** (70) to see **how** (62) her use of "corrective teaching" **affects how** her children behave (61).

Molly then asked the Consultant what she should do about Alex wanting to join a boys club in town; she is not sure she can trust him to stay where he is supposed to be. The Consultant explored how Molly has successfully handled monitoring situations like this in the past and assured her that she had the answers to fix this one, too (68,69). Molly was unable to think of how she could address her concerns in this situation so the Consultant left this as an assignment and encouraged her to remember how she had gotten the chil-

dren to come home by their curfew. Molly also was unsure about how she would arrange for Alex to get to and from the meetings (64,65,66). The Consultant again assured Molly that he had confidence in her ability (70) to manage her children. He taught her to generalize skills by posing a "what if" question back to Molly (61). The Consultant asked, "What if you needed Alex to get to and from the meetings so you could have afternoons free? What way have you found that works to access support resources and monitor the children when you are depressed?" The Consultant assured Molly that she has the ability to find a solution using her knowledge and skills (69).

Without providing the answer, the Consultant was able to get Molly to verbalize that she could get her neighbor to provide a ride and could talk to the staff at the boys club to make sure Alex is being supervised. The Consultant praised Molly's generalization and self-reflection (61,62).

*The Consultant is again assessing and teaching Molly how to generalize the skills she has acquired to problem situations (61,63). The Consultant also has assessed the need to increase his teaching of generalization to further enhance Molly's skills and assure long-term maintenance (63).*

**Day 47:** On the next visit with the family, the Consultant takes time to talk to the children to assess how they see things in the family. All three said their mother was nicer and they were getting along better (62).

*The Consultant explored this further to assess the children's abilities to self-reflect and generalize.*

Macy was able to talk about how telling her mom where she was going and calling if she went someplace else kept her mother from nagging (62). She also said she knew that if she drank and got caught, she would be in trouble at home and probably get grounded for a week, as well as possibly be taken out of the house. The Consultant chose to use the issue of drinking to see how well Macy could address future situations (61,63). He asked Macy what she would do if a really cute guy was at a friend's house and wanted her to drink. Macy said she would say "No," but added that if she was spending the night at her friend's house, she would be tempted to drink. Macy's answers were shared with Molly so she could monitor situations in which Macy may be tempted to drink and check on her more often.

Alex and Micah had difficulty expressing self-reflection but both could say that if they don't do what their mother says, they get in trouble. They also were able to demonstrate this understanding in two situations (61). In the first one, Micah told Alex to get some candy from the kitchen. Alex refused because their mother had told them it was for later and he didn't want to get in trouble. In the other situation, Alex goaded Micah into getting into some of Molly's old clothes and Micah said they had to ask first. Both boys were praised for being able to obey their mother's rules in these different situations (61,68).

Later in the visit, Molly said she had called the boys club and had enrolled Alex in the program (61). Molly said she called the club and asked about its policy on when boys can come and go. She was told that the club has an open-door policy but does not permit boys to walk into certain programs whenever they want. If Alex is involved in one of these organized programs, he must stay once he arrives. The club also can provide Molly with information about the times for these programs and how long they last. The club also told Molly that school buses will drop boys off at the club and the club has a van that takes some kids home (71). Molly expressed pride in her own efforts to solve this problem. The Consultant praised Molly because she does know how to fix problems that might require a different type of monitoring (61,67,68, 69,70,71).

*On **Day 49**, Molly is answering her own questions and has demonstrated on three occasions how she can generalize her skills to different situations and answer future-oriented questions. Molly also is verbalizing more self-reflection about the importance of monitoring the children in order to prevent them from getting into more trouble.*

*The Consultant begins to assess if he can move into Phase VI in his intervention. Molly is able to generalize the skills she has acquired to various situations, can self-*

*reflect on how her behaviors affect her children's behaviors, and has plans set up for future circumstances that may arise. The skills Molly has acquired remain functionally sound and the children continue to be safe and cared for in Molly's home. She is using the skills independently without any prompts or guidance from the Consultant. The Consultant decides to move to Phase VI and do a final evaluation and assessment to determine if Molly's abilities to manage her children's behaviors and her depression are likely to be maintained without the Consultant present. The Consultant spent five hours with the family in Phase V.*

# Phase VI

Phase VI is the Phase to begin assessing victory. Victory is where you determine that the problems that brought you into the home are now being addressed effectively by the family. Victory is when the family has achieved competency in using skills to fix its problems. It is incredibly exciting to watch a family that was struggling and in crisis become confident and effective. This is noted by measurable changes in the frequency or intensity of the referral problems between the beginning of services and Phase VI .

When you first began working with the family, you started with one BAS and have, through your intervention, taught the family several skills. That took dedication and time on your part and the family's part to accomplish. Now you want to make sure that the family can retain the skills they developed by taking time to evaluate and determine that the family "has it." The Boys Town Family

Preservation program is competency based and Phase VI is where that is most evident. By dedicating a Phase to the final evaluation and assessment of the family's competencies, abilities, and confidence, you're attempting to ensure that things will not fall apart once you leave. This is the final check to ensure that the family's skills will keep the family together.

At this point the Consultant has successfully empowered the family members to see success and feel competent to handle situations on their own.

Let's examine the focus, assignments, intensity, and requirements necessary to end services.

## Focus

Your primary purpose in Phase VI is to evaluate the intervention with a family to determine if the criteria for ending services has been met. Is the family confident in its ability to maintain the changes in the home? Is the family using the skills correctly and consistently? At this time, family members should be successfully generalizing skills to different situations, understanding their roles in creating the changes within the home, and addressing future-oriented situations. In Phase V you focused your teaching on these areas. In Phase VI you do not praise family members when they use skills in situations that have specifically been taught, and only occasionally praise the family's use of generalization and self-reflection. By the end of Phase VI, even praising generalization and self-reflection should decrease. By decreasing praise, you continue to fade the family members from looking to you for support to looking to the skills they developed. This reliance on their use of skills will foster a sense of skill reciprocity.

Phase VI assesses any reciprocity that is occurring between family members. Reciprocity is an interchange of rewards. It is the feeling of self-satisfaction members have in the use of their skills. For example, a child might report reciprocity in using the skill of "sharing" because when he shares, his big brother will play with him more. The big brother might report reciprocity in his use of anger control skills he learned because now he is not so mean to his brother and his mother yells at him less frequently. Reciprocity helps maintain skills as all parties feel they are getting something from their efforts. Focus remains on ensuring that the family maintains the skills necessary to stay intact, and feels confident and self-assured that it will stay that way.

Let's summarize the focus of Phase VI:

### Evaluate
- family's confidence-72
- generalization-73
- self-reflection-74
- goal attainment-75
- competency in using skills-76
- reciprocity-77

## Assignments

As mentioned earlier, Phase VI is the final check on the family's abilities and skill usage. Assignments are designed to maintain the family's capacity to generalize and self-reflect on its skills. However, because independence is the goal of Phase VI, assignments might not be given. By now the family has the necessary competency to use skills and the confidence to use them. Therefore, any assignments that are given should demonstrate this confidence by being general and related to the family's ability to solve problems. An example of a general-ly stated assignment is asking family members who have learned skills to deal with aggression and conflicts why their home seems so much quieter and calmer in recent weeks.

You should be very cautious during Phase VI about how much praise you give the family. You don't want family members to perform for you or be dependent on you in order for them to recognize that they are doing well. You want family members to sense reciprocity from their skill usage which will provide its own rewards and satisfaction to the family. They should be feeling so competent and independent in their abilities that they know longer find it necessary to look to you for approval, praise, or support.

Let's say a family is feeling very successful, and during one of your visits a problem arises. Do not praise the skill the family members use to fix the problem. You can simply acknowledge the fact that the family did fix the problem or choose to ignore the family's efforts altogether. If the problem is continuing, leave and tell the family members to let you know how things go the rest of the day or how they dealt with the problem. You want the family members to fix their own problems and derive their feelings of accomplishment from what they have done independently. The more you can get the family members to focus on why they feel successful and the part they played in that success, the more confidence they will have in their ability to maintain this success in the long run.

To summarize assignments in Phase VI:

- focus on family's abilities
- focus on family's goals
- don't give assignments every visit
- assignments should be general

## Intensity

Intensity continues to fade from Phase V levels, the time spent with the family continues to decrease, and the length of time between visits increases. This fading promotes the family's capabilities by demonstrating that you don't need to be there. Your increased absence conveys to family members that they are competent and confident enough to succeed without your assistance. Family members may even be feeling so confident that they might wonder why you are still in the home. Visits generally are very brief, lasting from 15 to 30 minutes, just long enough for you to assess the family's success and maintenance of social concept skills.

To summarize intensity in Phase VI:

- visits are less frequent
- less time is spent with the family
- visits last from 15 to 30 minutes

## Ending Services

Because the Boys Town Phases Model is competency-based, services are ended when the family competently meets certain criteria. These criteria are:

- The family and referring agency feel the child is no longer in danger of being removed from the home.
- You are comfortable with the family's level of skill acquisition.
- The referral behaviors have been addressed by the family.
- The family is feeling success from its new-found skills.
- The family is confident in using the skills.

- Family members understand how the skills work and what roles they had in achieving goals.
- The family is making statements expressing independence.
- The family can access necessary resources independently.

Individual family members may state that there are still some problems but that the referral problems are under control. Now family members have the skills needed to address these problems, and know how to fix their problems themselves and to obtain community resources if needed.

## Example: Phase VI

*The Consultant begins to assess if Molly and her children are using the skills competently, correctly, and consistently enough to keep their family together and maintain the gains they accomplished during services (76).*

**Day 51:** Molly reports that she had sent Macy to school with a stomachache today, and she asked the school nurse to call her if Macy's pain got worse. The nurse did call and suggested that Molly take Macy to the doctor. Molly said she canceled her haircut appointment and took Macy to the doctor's office (76). Molly was irritated to find out that Macy just had a flu virus and the doctor couldn't do anything about it. Molly self-reflected that she was glad she took Macy to the doctor (74), though, because now she could try to keep the boys away from Macy so they wouldn't get sick, too. The

Consultant only listened to Molly's story, and did not provide any praise as Molly had independently used her skills of "monitoring" and "prioritizing" to meet her children's needs (72,73). Molly also was spontaneously reporting reciprocity for having taken Macy to the doctor (77).

**Day 54 and 58:** Molly is demonstrating during visits that she is consistently monitoring her children and meeting their basic needs (76). Molly continues to report that she is comfortable with the current situation in her home, and that while problems still exist, she feels she can fix them (72). Molly and the children are reporting positive things about each other and are expressing confidence in their abilities to keep things going so they can live together (72).

Molly and the children have demonstrated within their capabilities the ability to generalize, self-reflect, and address future-oriented situations. Only once during Phase VI did Molly ask the Consultant for help; that happened when she was having trouble getting her psychiatrist to rearrange an appointment time for her. The Consultant left Molly with the assignment of telling him how she worked through this problem with the psychiatrist. The family is not reporting problems (75) during the Consultant's visits and conversation usually is focused on their activities or friends. The family has made several statements about when the Consultant was leaving (72).

The Consultant assesses that the family members are confident in using the skills they've acquired (both with their current issues and ones that may arise in the future), that they understand how the skills work and their roles in achieving goals (75), and that they are making statements expressing independence. Molly and the children have made comments indicating they are experiencing reciprocity in using the skills (77). This indicates to the Consultant that Molly and her family have successfully completed the program and that he can end services. The Consultant spent 1.5 hours with the family in Phase VI.

## Summary

The Phases Model of intervention is a framework that provides Consultants with both a structure for treatment and the freedom to individualize that treatment to the families they are serving. (See the Phases Summary Guide at the end of the chapter as a quick reference to the main elements of the Phases framework.) As we are all aware, no two families are alike and a model that suggests such a thing would be doomed to failure. The Boys Town Model of intervention is designed to adapt to the individual needs of the families we serve. Due to the intense amount of assessment that occurs throughout treatment, individualized treatment is the end product.

At times families have special needs, such as limitations on their mental capabilities. It may be difficult for these developmentally disabled family members to demonstrate generalized use of the skills. In other families, one family member may excel in learning and maintaining new skills; others may demonstrate an extreme independence at the beginning of services. In each of these scenarios, the Model can be adapted to a particular family's capabilities and limitations. Each family's pace, style, and needs can be accommodated while implementing Phases. Similarly, a Consultant's style also will mesh easily within the framework of Phases.

As described in this chapter, specific outcomes must be seen before a Consultant moves on to the next Phase. These outcomes help the Consultant understand the differences and similarities between each Phase. The Model is flexible and fluid in that most Consultants flow from one Phase to the next. It is not a rigid, abrupt step. Many times the family will benefit from small aspects of the next Phase or a previous Phase. You may even find that you need to go back to a Phase. This might occur if you are in Phase II and find that you haven't identified and increased the correct BAS. You can go back to Phase I to identify and increase another BAS. However, you need to remember that there are specific behaviors and indicators tied to each Phase. In each Phase, the structure of the Model allows for the freedom to be creative and individualize. Nonetheless, the majority of issues need to be accomplished in a definite order for progress to be successful and effective.

The Phases Model was founded on behavioral principles. We have tried to simplify and articulate how these principles work within the Model. However, we realize one of the shortcomings of this manual is that we assume the reader has a foundational knowledge of Social Learning Theory. If you have a strong understanding of how behavior is learned through operant and classical conditioning, many of the Phase components will make greater sense to you. If you are having difficulty understanding some aspects of the Model and why Phases are used as a framework, you may benefit from reviewing behavioral theory. One source we recommend for review is Keith Miller's workbook, *Principles of Everyday Behavior Analysis*, 2nd ed. (1980).

Because the Phases framework works on building a family's strengths and assists the Consultant in gauging progress by certain skill-acquisition indicators, it does not rely on time as a measure for success. Being competency-based and not time-based, the Phases Model can provide a framework for working with families in a less intensive intervention program. In fact, Boys Town has adapted the Phases Mosel as a guide for providing family-centered services in longer-term (six months to two years) and less intensive (one to eight hours per week) programs that help families learn skills to improve functioning. Regardless of the intensity of the program, identifying the family's strengths, building skills, and measuring outcomes with specific criteria can be accomplished using the Phases Model.

Supervisors have discussed how this program Model affects their work, with some stating that it is indispensable to supervision (Lenerz, Peterson, Ferguson, Authier, & Daly, 1995). In both weekly consultation and annual reviews, it is used as a tool for monitoring Consultant performance. Supervisors and Consultants concur that it sets up clear, concrete, and specific expectations for performance evaluations. They both value the fact that feedback can be given in a way that is objective and based on established criteria, rather than being influenced by personal or political factors.

In addition to this objectivity in the evaluation process, supervisors note that having this specific program Model provides a valuable structure for training new Consultants, as well as guiding experienced Consultants in their treatment of families. The Phases structure can be used to help assess whether treatment is appropriate, to help a Consultant stay focused on a family's treatment agenda, and to delineate appropriate outcomes that are expected for a family. In determining whether a family meets the criteria to progress in treatment, a supervisor's observations can be used to supplement those of a Consultant, lending reliability to the process. Moreover, all of these supervisory duties can be accomplished with consistency across all Consultants, reducing the extent to which individual personalities and characteristics contribute to service outcomes.

At the administrative level, the Phases Model also has proven beneficial. It has been shown to be an effective way of familiarizing referring agencies with the program, which in turn has helped referring agencies choose clients who would most benefit from the program. Administrators have commented that the Model has clearly delineated the roles, responsibilities, and expectations of Consultants and supervisors.

Here at Boys Town, we believe in the effectiveness of our structured Model of intervention and hope. We are confident that after reading this book, you do too.

# Phases Summary Guide

## I

Identify strengths
Increase a strength
Begin establishing relationship
Begin assessment
Identify family agenda and goals
Identify situation endangering child
High intensity

## II

Identify one social concept
Build on strength to teach skills in social concept area
Continue assessment
High intensity
Consistently praise family's use of skills in first social concept area
Occasionally praise strengths in other social concept areas

## III

Identify and teach to a second social concept area
Build on strengths to teach skills in second social concept area
Continue assessment
Occasionally praise family's use of first social concept skills
Evaluate progress toward goals, meeting agenda, reducing risk to children
High intensity

## IV

Promote conceptual understanding of why skills work
No new concept or skills introduced (new behaviors can be taught to make a skill more effective)
Occasionally praise learned skills
Promote use of generalization and self-reflection
Encourage family to use skills to fullest extent possible
Decrease intensity
Evaluate goal attainment

## V

No new concepts, skills, or behaviors taught
Teach generalization, self-reflection, and independence
Prepare for future-oriented situations
Use conceptual terms
Build family's confidence
Family finds ways to meet own resource needs
Evaluate family's competency in using skills
Low intensity

## VI

Evaluate family's understanding of concepts
Evaluate family's ability to generalize to handle future situations
Explore for reciprocity
No teaching to concepts, skills, or behaviors
Promote family independence
Very low intensity

## General Phase Guidelines for Intervention Techniques

Active Listening - All phases
Exploration - All phases
Effective Praise - All phases

Metaphors - All phases
Circular Refocusing - All phases (except I)
Reframing - All phases
Role-Play - All phases (except I & VI)
Confrontation - All phases (except I & VI)
Mediation - All phases (except VI)

Crisis Intervention - All phases (except VI)
Ignoring - All phases
Prompts - All phases (except I & VI)
Modeling - All phases (except VI)
Assignments - All phases
Criticism by Suggestion - All phases (except I & VI)

# References

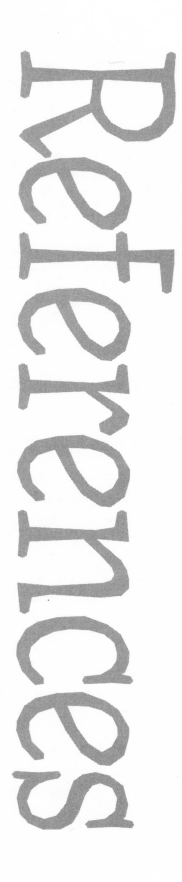

Alexander, J., & Parsons, B. (1982). **Functional family therapy.** Monterey, CA: Brooks/Cole Publishing Company.

Baldwin, J.D., & Baldwin, J.I. (1986). **Behavior principles in everyday life** (2nd ed.). Englewood Cliffs, NJ: Prentice-Hall.

Bandura, A. (1977). **A social learning theory.** New Jersey: Prentice Hall.

Barker, P. (1985). **Using metaphors in psychotherapy.** New York: Brunner/Mazel.

Barth, R.P. (1990). Theories guiding home-based intensive family preservation services. In J.K. Whittaker, J. Kinney, E.M. Tracy, & C. Booth (Eds.), **Reading high-risk families: Intensive family preservation in human services** (pp. 89- 112). New York: Aldine de Gruyter.

Berg, I.K. (1991). F**amily based services: A solution-focused approach.** Milwaukee, WI: Brief Family Therapy Center Press.

Berg, I.K. (1994). **Family based services: A solution focused approach.** New York: W.W. Norton & Co., Inc.

Black, S. (1992). In praise of judicious praise. **The Executive Educator**, October, 24-27.

Brockopp, G.W. (1973). Crisis intervention: Theory, process and practice. In D. Lester & G.W. Brockopp (Eds.), **Crisis intervention: Counseling by telephone.** Springfield, IL: Thomas.

Brophy, J.E. (1981). Teacher praise: A functional analysis. **Review of Educational Research, 51**(1), 5-32.

Burke, R.V., & Herron, R.W. (1992). **Common sense parenting: A practical approach from Boys Town.** Boys Town, NE: Father Flanagan's Boys' Home.

Caplan, G. (1964). **Principles of preventive psychiatry.** New York: Basic Books.

Center for Dispute Settlement (1988). **Parent/adolescent mediation training manual.** Washington, DC: Author.

Cohen, S., & Willis, T.A. (1985). Stress, social support and the buffering hypothesis. **Psychological Bulletin, 98**(2), 310-357.

Cowger, C.D. (1994). Assessing client strengths: Clinical assessment for client empowerment. **Social Work, 39**(3), 262-268.

Dawson, P., Robinson, J., & Johnson, C. (1982). Informal social support as an intervention. **Zero to Three, 3**(2), 1-4.

Dowd, T., & Tierney, J. (1992). **Teaching social skills to youth: A curriculum for child-care providers.** Boys Town, NE: Boys Town Press.

Falcone, A., & Rosenthal, T. (1982). **Delivery of rural mental health services.** Cleveland, OH: Synapse.

Father Flanagan's Boys' Home (1990). **Boys Town Family Home Program consultation manual.** Boys Town, NE: Author.

Father Flanagan's Boys' Home (1991). **Boys Town Family Home Program training manual** (3rd ed.). Boys Town, NE: Author.

Feldman, L.B. (1992). **Integrating individual and family therapy.** New York: Brunner/Mazel.

Finkelhor, D. (1986). **A sourcebook on child sexual abuse.** Beverly Hills, CA: Sage.

Fleischman, M.J., Horne, A.M., & Arthur, J.L. (1983). **Troubled families: A treatment program.** Champaign, IL: Research Press Company.

Fuoco, F.J., & Christian, W.P. (1986). **Behavior analysis and therapy in residential program.** New York: Van Nostrand Reinhold.

Garrett, A. (1942). **Interviewing: Its principles and methods.** New York: Family Service Association of America.

Gibbs, J.T., & Huang, L.N. (1990). **Children of color: Psychological interventions with minority youth.** San Francisco: Jossey-Bass Publishers.

Goldstein, H. (1990). Strength or pathology: Ethical and rhetorical contrasts in approaches to practice. **Families in Society, 71**(5), 267-275.

Goldstein, J., Freud, A., & Solnit, A. (1973). **Beyond the best interest of the child.** New York: Free Press.

Gordon, D. (1978). **Therapeutic metaphors.** Cupertino, CA: META Publications.

Greenspan, S.I. (1987). Special issue, Infants in multirisk families: Case studies in prevention intervention. **Clincial Infants Reports, 3.**

Hallock, S. (1989). Making metaphors in therapeutic process. **Journal of Reality Therapy, 9**(1), 25-29.

Hartman, A., & Laird, J. (1983). **Family centered social work practice.** New York: Free Press/Macmillan.

Hausman, W., & Rioch, D. (1967). Military psychiatry: A prototype of social and preventive psychiatry in the United States. **Archive of General Psychiatry, 16**(6), 727-739.

Hepworth, D.H., & Larsen, J.A. (1990). **Direct social work practice: Theory and skills** (3rd ed.). Belmont, CA: Wadsworth Publishing Company.

Hudgins, J.L. (1992). The strengths of black families revisited. **Urban League Review, 15**(2), 9-20.

Ivey, A., & Authier, J. (1971). **Micro counseling: Innovations in interviewing, counseling psychotherapy and psychoeducation.** Springfield, IL: Charles C. Thomas.

Johnson, L.C. (1983). Networking: A means of maximizing resources. **Human Services in the Rural Environment, 8**(2), 27-31.

Jooste, E.T., & Cleaver, G. (1992). Metaphors and metaphoric objects. **Journal of Phenomenological Psychology, 23**(2), 136- 148.

Kadushin, A. (1983). **The social work interview.** New York: Columbia University Press.

Kagan, R., & Schlosberg, S. (1989). **Families in perpetual crisis.** New York: W.W. Norton & Co., Inc.

Kamii, C. (1984). Viewpoint: Obedience is not enough. **Young Children, 39**(4), 11-14.

Kempe, C.H., Silverman, F.N., Steele, B.F., Droegemueller, W., & Silver, H.K., (1962). The battered child syndrome. **Journal of the American Medical Association, 181**, 105-113.

Kinney, J., Haapala, D., & Booth, C. (1991). **Keeping families together: The Homebuilders model.** New York: Aldine de Gruyter.

Lazarus, A.A. (1993). Tailoring the therapeutic relationship or being an authentic chameleon. **Psychotherapy, 30**(3), 404-407.

Lenerz, K., Peterson, J.L., Ferguson, C.C., Authier, K. & Daly, D. (1995). **Use of a structured service delivery model in family preservation.** Research paper submitted for publication, Father Flanagan's Boys' Home.

Littlejohn-Blake, S.M., & Darling, C.A. (1993). Understanding strengths of African American families. **Journal of Black Studies, 23**(4), 460-471.

Longres, J.F. (1991). Toward a status model of ethnic sensitive practice. **Journal of Multicultural Social Work,** 1, 41-55.

Martin, G., & Pear, J. (1988). **Behavior modification: What it is and how to do it.** New Jersey: Prentice Hall.

Maslow, A.H. (1954). **Motivation and personality.** New York: Harper and Brothers.

McGowan, B.G. (1990). Family-based services and public policy: Context and implications. In J.K. Whittaker, J. Kinney, E.M. Tracy, & C. Booth (Eds.), **Reaching high-risk families: Intensive family preservation in human services** (pp. 65-87). New York: Aldine de Gruyter.

Meyer, W. (1979). Informational value of evaluative behavior: Influences of praise and blame on perceptions of ability. **Journal of Educational Psychology, 71**(2), 259-268.

Miller, L.K. (1980). **Principles of everyday behavior analysis** (2nd ed.). Belmont, CA: Wadsworth Publishing Company.

Morgan, L.J., Fisher, M., Anderson, G., & Kinney, J. (1990). **The Homebuilders model and major counseling theories: A comparative analysis.** Unpublished work. Presented in a reader at a social worker and family preservation seminar at the University of Washington in Seattle.

Nelson, K.E., Saunders, E.J., & Landsman, M.J. (1993). Chronic child neglect in perspective. **Social Work, 38**(6), 661-671.

O'Leary, K.D., & O'Leary, S. (1977). **Classroom management: The successful use of behavior modification.** New York: Pergamon Press.

Patterson, G.R. (1971). **Applications of social learning to family life.** Champaign, IL: Research Press.

Patterson, G.R. (1982). **Coercive family process.** Eugene, OR: Castalia.

Phillips, E.L., Phillips, E.A., Fixsen, D.L., & Wolf, M.M. (1974). **The teaching family handbook** (rev.ed.) Lawrence, KS: University of Kansas, Bureau of Child Research.

Polansky, N.A., Chalmers, M.A., Buttenwieser, E., & Williams, D.P. (1987). **Damaged parents.** Chicago: University of Chicago Press.

Rodwell, M.K. (1987). Naturalistic inquiry: An alternative model for social work assessment. **Social Service Review, 61**(2), 231-246.

Saleeby, D. (1992). **The strengths perspective in social work practice: Power in the people.** White Plains, NY: Longman.

Sarason, I.G., & Ganzer, V.J. (1973). Modeling and group discussion in the rehabilitation of juvenile delinquents. **Journal of Counseling Psychology, 20**(5), 442-449.

Sullivan, W.P. (1989). Community support programs in rural areas: Developing programs without walls. **Human Services in the Rural Environment, 12**(4), 19-24.

Schwenk, T.L., & Bittle, S.P. (1979). Applicability of crisis intervention in family practice. **The Journal of Family Practice, 8**(6), 1151-1158.

Teare, J. (1994). **Project summary: Evaluation of parent-adolescent mediation.** Unpublished research study, Father Flanagan's Boys' Home.

**The world almanac and book of facts** (1994). Mahwah, NJ: Funk and Wagnells Corp.

Timbers, G.D. (1975). Achievement place for girls: Token reinforcement, social reinforcement and instructional procedures in a family style treatment setting for "pre-delinquent" girls. **Dissertation Abstracts International, 35**(9B), 4636.

Tracy, E.M., & Whittaker, J.K. (1990). The social network map: Assessing social support in clinical practice. **Families in Society: The Journal of Contemporary Human Services**, October, 461-470.

Truax, C., & Carkhuff, K. (1967). **Toward effective counseling and psychotherapy: Training and practice.** Chicago: Aldine.

Trute, B., & Hauch, C. (1988). Building on family strength: A study of families with positive adjustment to the birth of a developmentally disabled child. **Journal of Marital and Family Therapy, 14**(2), 185-193.

University of Utah Graduate School of Social Work (1989). **Action for child protection.** National CPS competency-based training project. Presented at the First National Advisory Committee Meeting.

Watzlawick, P., Weakland, J., & Fisch, R. (1974). **Change: Principles of problem formulation and problem resolution.** New York: W.W. Norton.

Zigler, E., & Black, K.B. (1989). America's family support movement: Strengths and limitations. **American Journal of Orthopsychiatry, 59**(1), 6-19.

# Bibliography

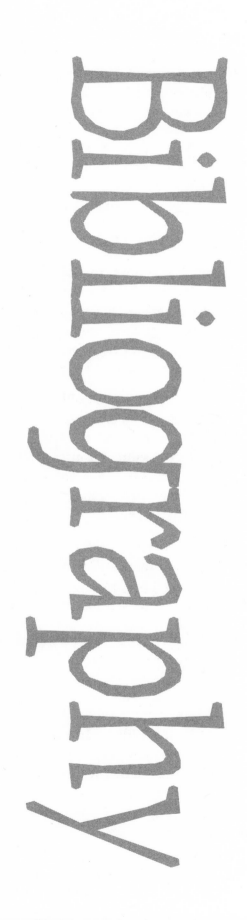

Bolton Jr., F.G., Morris, L.A., & MacEachron, A.E. (1989). **Males at risk: The other side of child sexual abuse.** Newbury Park, CA: Sage.

Brassard, M.R., Germain, R., & Hart, S.N. (Eds.)(1987). **The psychological maltreatment of children and youth.** New York: Pergamon Press.

Dowd, T., & Tierney, J. (1992). **Teaching social skills to youth: A curriculum for child-care providers.** Boys Town, NE: Boys Town Press.

Finkelhor, D. (1979). **Sexually victimized children.** New York: Free Press.

Gabarino, J., Brookhouser, P., & Authier, K. (1987). **Special children, special risks: The maltreatment of children with disabilities.** New York: Aldine de Gruyter.

Helfer, R.E., & Kempe, R.S. (1987). **The battered child** (4th ed.) Chicago: University of Chicago Press.

Laird, J., & Hartman, A. (Eds.) (1985). **A handbook of child welfare: Context, knowledge and practice.** New York: Free Press.

Miller, L.K. (1980). **Principles of everyday behavior analysis.** Pacific Grove, CA: Brooks/Cole Publishing Company.

Minuchin, S. (1974). **Families and family therapy.** Cambridge, MA: Harvard University Press.

U.S. Department of Health and Human Services, National Center on Child Abuse and Neglect (1992). **A coordinated response to child abuse and neglect: A basic manual** (The user manual series). Single copies are available free through the Clearinghouse on Child Abuse and Neglect Information, PO Box 1182, Washington, DC, 20013-1182.

U.S. Department of Health and Human Services, National Center on Child Abuse and Neglect (1993). **Child neglect: A guide for intervention** (The user manual series). (Contract No. HHS-105-89-1730.) Washington, DC: Westover Consultants.

U.S. Department of Health and Human Services, National Center on Child Abuse and Neglect (1993). **Child sexual abuse: Intervention and treatment issues** (The user manual series). (Subcontract No. S105-89-1730.) Washington, DC: Westover Consultants.

Whittaker, J.K., Kinney, J., Tracy, E.M., & Booth, C.M. (1990). **Reaching high risk families: Intensive family preservation in human services.** New York: Aldine de Gruyter.

# Index